Intermetropolitan Migration in Canada:

Changing Determinants Over Three Decades

R. Paul Shaw

Published by NC Press Ltd.
in cooperation with Statistics Canada
and the Canadian Government Publishing Centre,
Supply and Services Canada.

© Minister of Supply and Services Canada — 1985
Catalogue number: 89-504-E

Canadian Cataloguing in Publication Data
Shaw, R. Paul.
   Intermetropolitan Migration in Canada
Also published in French under title:
Migration intermétropolitaines au Canada
Co-published by: Statistics Canada.
Bibliography: p.
Includes index.
ISBN 0-920053-72-6 (bound). — ISBN 0-920053-70-X (pbk.)
1. Residential mobility - Canada.   2. Migration,
Internal - Canada.   3. Labor mobility - Canada.
I. Statistics Canada.   II. Title.
HB1989.S48 1985   304.8'0971   C85-099428-4

We would like to thank the Ontario Arts Council and the Canada Council for their assistance in the production of this book.

New Canada Publications, a division of NC Press Limited,
Box 4010 Station A, Toronto, Ontario M5H 1H8

Printed and bound in Canada

Table of Contents

Appendices

List of Tables

List of Tables

List of Figures

List of Figures

Appendix Tables

Appendix Figures

Author's Preface

This book is an extension of my work on migration which began with
Migration Theory and Fact in 1975. At that time, I observed that "traditional" market forces appear to diminish as influences on migration as
societies become increasingly wealthy. Traditional market forces include
factors such as wages, cost of living variables, or situations of economic
stress involving unemployment or poverty. The idea that such factors
may be diminishing in their effect on migration follows from two broad
premises. First, as societies become wealthier over time, their members
tend to be motivated less and less by monetary considerations alone.
My experience in less developed countries suggests that amenities and
leisure activities, for example, are far less significant in decisions to migrate
than they are in countries of North America or Western Europe. Second,
wealthier societies tend to install more "safety nets" to protect citizens
from some of the consequences of economic stress. Unemployment insurance, for example, helps cushion the financial consequences of
unemployment to the extent that it may reduce pressure on people to
leave places that are economically depressed. If these two premises are
correct, an implication for government is that traditional tools of manpower policy for influencing the distribution of labour between places
such as higher wages, job-related training, or relocation grants, may have
less impact on potential migrants.

Students of migration have only begun to explore such ideas.
Those who dominate the analysis of migration in North America, most
of them economists, continue to emphasize monetary aspects of traditional labour market forces. Sociologists and demographers have confronted non-market factors more directly, but their findings are much

more tentative as a result of weaker theoretical underpinnings and an associated lack of rigorous empirical testing. By focusing on changing determinants over three decades in a country which is wealthy by world standards and which has greatly expanded its social security and fiscal programs, I have attempted to undertake more than just another search for determinants of migration. Canada is a society in which traditional economic factors can reasonably be expected to have declined sharply as influences on migration over time. My hope is that this study will help to promote clearer understanding of why this may be so, and generate fuller debate on its desirability in the future.

In the course of preparing this book, I have received invaluable assistance and advice from several friends and colleagues. For critical commentary, I wish to express my gratitude to Larry S. Bourne (University of Toronto), Gary S. Fields (Cornell University), Larry H. Long (U.S. Bureau of Census), Craig McKie (Statistics Canada), Paul Reed (Statistics Canada), James W. Simmons (University of Toronto), Leroy O. Stone (University of Western Ontario and Statistics Canada), and John Vanderkamp (University of Guelph). In particular, thanks are due to Leroy Stone and John Vanderkamp for pointing out errors of interpretation and to Paul Reed for insisting that my assumptions concerning economic and statistical modelling be more accessible.

I am also indebted to Jo-Anne Belliveau and John Turner for generous assistance involving computer processing; to Marie-Claire Couture and Jane Godby for helpful editing and preparation of graphics; to Sue Deane and Audrey Sirois for their wizardry on the word processor; and to Judy Buehler for overseeing publishing arrangements. All of these people are on staff at Statistics Canada.

The views expressed in this book are those of the author and do not reflect the official position of Statistics Canada.

R. Paul Shaw
Ottawa

Chapter 1

In Search of Fundamentals

Introduction

Migration exerts a potent force on the growth and change of Census Metropolitan Areas in Canada. A CMA – in Statistics Canada terminology – is a continuous built-up area having a population of 100,000 or more and serving as a main labour market. The main labour market area corresponds to a commuting field where a significant number of people are able to travel daily to work in the main built-up area. CMA's alone accounted for almost 70% of Canada's total population growth between 1951-81. The number of CMA's in Canada has grown from 17 according to the 1961 Census to 24 according to the 1981 Census. These are ranked by size in Figure 1.1, and are identified by geographical location in Figure 1.2.

Between 1976-81, CMA's served as points of origin or destination for more than 2.5 million migrants. Given that Canada is a small open economy with a combined CMA population of only 13.5 million in 1981, the arrival or departure of over 2 million people represents a major socio-economic phenomenon. Furthermore, falling rates of natural increase (births minus deaths), have accentuated the importance of migration to the extent that it is currently the major vehicle through which Canada's national locus of urban growth is changing over a relatively short period of time.

The historical impact of migration on individual CMA's is conveyed in Figure 1.3. Growth rates have been calculated for 22 CMA's on the basis of 1971 Census boundaries. Oshawa CMA and Trois-Rivières CMA are not included in Figure 1.3 as these populations have, as yet,

Figure 1.1: Population in Census Metropolitan Areas, 1981

Distribution of the Population, 1981

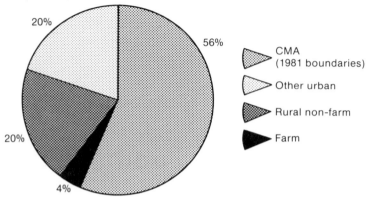

Census Metropolitan Areas by Population Size, 1981

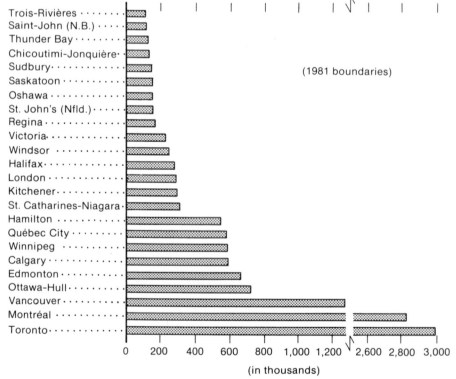

(in thousands)

Source: Derived from 1981 Census of Canada, Statistics Canada.

Figure 1.2: Geographical Location of Census Metropolitan Areas

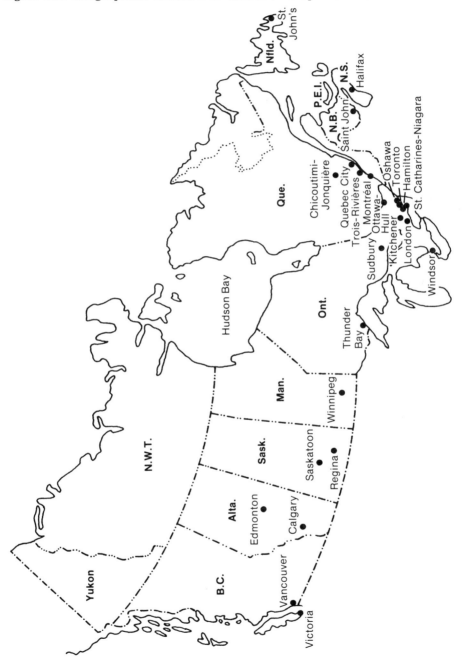

Figure 1.3: Population Growth Rates for Twenty-Two Census Metropolitan
Areas in Canada, 1951-81 and 1976-81

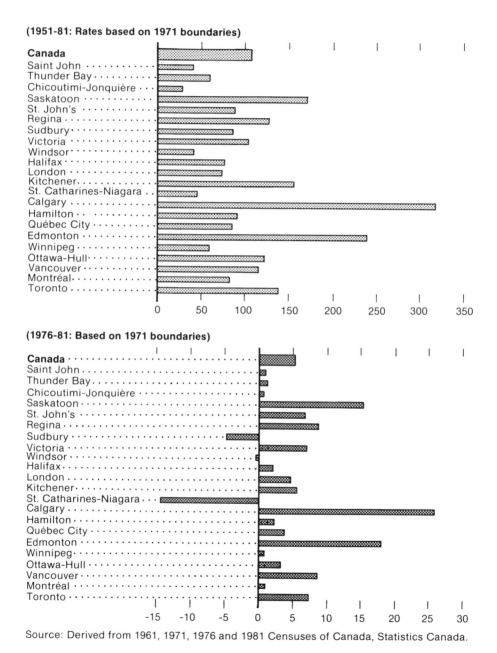

Source: Derived from 1961, 1971, 1976 and 1981 Censuses of Canada, Statistics Canada.

to be adjusted according to 1971 Census boundaries. Boundary considerations are, of course, extremely important when comparing intercensal growth rates.[1] Figure 1.3 shows that Calgary and Edmonton have grown at rates of 4-5% per year over the last 30 years! Migration is clearly the major contributor in their case since rates of natural increase during the period were no more than 2% per year. Saskatoon and Kitchener also stand out as big gainers, followed by Toronto, Regina, Ottawa-Hull, Vancouver and Victoria. Each of these CMA's experienced population growth in excess of 100% between 1951-81.

In contrast, slow growth CMA's include Chicoutimi-Jonquière, St. Catharines-Niagara, Saint John, Thunder Bay, Windsor and Winnipeg – all of which experienced growth rates below Canada's national average. Indeed, during the most recent census period (1976-81), Figure 1.3 reveals that three CMA's experienced negative rates of growth (St. Catharines-Niagara, Sudbury and Windsor), whereas five others barely registered positive rates of growth (Saint John, Thunder Bay, Chicoutimi-Jonquière, Winnipeg and Montréal). For these CMA's, net migration was negligible or negative. Bear in mind that these growth rates – calculated on 1971 Census boundaries – differ from those calculated on 1981 Census boundaries. For some CMA's 1981 Census boundaries have grown as new territory and population has been annexed by political mandate.

Such wide differentials in growth rates between CMA's have been working continuously to shift the locus of urban activity westward as well as away from some of Canada's largest cities (eg., Montréal, Winnipeg). Data presented in the Appendix to Chapter 1 reveal that only nine CMA's increased their share in Canada's metropolitan population between 1951-81. In order of size, these are Toronto, Vancouver, Ottawa-Hull, Edmonton, Calgary, Kitchener, Regina, Saskatoon and Sudbury. Combined, their share in Canada's total metropolitan population grew from 43% in 1951 to 52% in 1981. Of the remaining CMA's, Hamilton, St. John's and Victoria retained relatively constant shares, whereas the balance took on a notably smaller share.

Table 1.1 indicates just how variable migration can be to and from CMA's. Since migration is not one homogeneous entity, its origins or destinations have been identified in Table 1.1 as other CMA's, non-metropolitan areas, or immigration of the foreign born. Observe that when numbers of net migrants are small or even negative for some CMA's, migration activity into or out of the CMA may be relatively

TABLE 1.1: A Comparison of Migration To and From Census Metropolitan Areas, 1966-71 and 1976-81

CMA's	Migra-tion period	Other CMA's			Non-metropolitan areas			Immi-gration	Total net internal plus immi-gration
		In	Out	Net	In	Out	Net		
Calgary	1966 - 71	36,110	26,026	10,085	42,300	26,620	15,680	24,040	49,805
	1976 - 81	88,735	33,710	55,025	69,175	58,640	10,535	30,440	96,000
Chicoutimi - Jonquière	1966 - 71	3,615	8,505	−4,890	6,920	7,215	−295	1,340	−3,845
	1976 - 81	3,335	6,430	−3,095	6,245	5,960	285	445	−2,365
Edmonton	1966 - 71	28,430	31,900	−3,470	52,020	34,165	17,885	21,510	35,895
	1976 - 81	63,085	35,760	27,325	72,390	65,930	6,460	27,735	61,520
Halifax	1966 - 71	10,755	15,785	−5,030	21,580	20,530	1,320	6,105	1,205
	1976 - 81	15,125	19,510	−4,385	24,455	24,720	−265	3,865	−785
Hamilton	1966 - 71	25,870	21,205	4,665	19,885	18,190	1,695	26,530	32,890
	1976 - 81	31,975	29,660	2,315	18,370	23,810	−4,810	10,730	8,235
Kitchener - Waterloo	1966 - 71	15,210	10,880	4,330	17,680	14,390	3,290	15,125	22,745
	1976 - 81	17,525	18,885	−1,330	18,675	18,730	−55	6,850	5,465
London	1966 - 71	21,565	17,060	4,505	21,000	18,010	2,990	15,055	22,550
	1976 - 81	20,340	23,525	−3,185	23,755	22,380	1,375	5,860	4,050
Montréal	1966 - 71	44,925	78,875	−33,950	115,465	88,780	26,685	115,345	108,080
	1976 - 81	41,925	120,115	−78,190	97,420	124,830	−27,410	64,495	−41,105
Ottawa-Hull	1966 - 71	41,480	30,060	11,420	44,080	27,580	16,500	27,605	55,525
	1976 - 81	58,380	66,530	−8,150	41,030	40,505	525	18,740	11,115
Québec City	1966 - 71	15,265	17,145	−1,880	36,885	16,510	20,375	5,930	24,425
	1976 - 81	15,035	23,095	−8,060	32,430	25,755	6,675	4,425	3,040
Regina	1966 - 71	7,000	16,005	−9,005	18,465	11,590	6,875	3,080	950
	1976 - 81	10,630	11,755	−1,125	17,325	14,430	2,895	3,255	5,025
St. Catharines - Niagara	1966 - 71	12,330	14,700	−2,370	10,915	10,145	770	10,825	9,225
	1976 - 81	14,520	17,400	−2,880	10,015	12,290	−2,275	4,560	−595
St. John's	1966 - 71	2,730	6,595	−3,865	11,705	6,390	5,315	1,965	3,415
	1976 - 81	4,575	7,395	−2,820	9,640	9,820	−180	1,360	−1,640
Saint John	1966 - 71	3,220	3,775	−555	6,630	6,670	−40	1,400	805
	1976 - 81	4,405	5,020	−975	7,475	9,180	−1,705	1,095	−1,585
Saskatoon	1966 - 71	6,650	15,010	−8,360	20,590	13,060	7,530	3,370	2,540
	1976 - 81	12,110	11,180	930	23,005	16,180	6,825	3,765	11,520
Sudbury	1966 - 71	7,810	8,755	−965	15,015	10,375	4,640	4,410	8,085
	1976 - 81	4,070	10,990	−6,926	8,215	13,975	−5,760	850	−11,830
Thunder Bay	1966 - 71	4,605	5,650	−1,585	6,555	4,815	1,740	2,955	−370
	1976 - 81	4,685	7,260	−2,565	7,715	6,000	1,715	1,545	695
Toronto	1966 - 71	95,330	84,770	10,770	90,200	120,885	−30,685	262,280	242,280
	1976 - 81	127,435	109,095	18,340	96,350	123,660	−27,310	152,890	143,920
Vancouver	1966 - 71	69,220	28,625	40,595	62,335	56,475	5,860	71,670	118,125
	1976 - 81	78,575	40,245	38,330	65,320	85,365	−20,045	61,250	79,535
Victoria	1966 - 71	19,760	11,280	8,480	15,890	11,700	4,190	8,570	21,240
	1976 - 81	25,080	16,185	8,895	20,115	20,415	−300	6,560	15,155
Windsor	1966 - 71	9,895	10,390	−495	8,705	9,140	−435	13,250	12,320
	1976 - 81	7,060	14,250	−7,190	7,565	12,630	−5,065	5,780	−6,475
Winnipeg	1966 - 71	19,830	28,070	−18,260	38,760	29,380	9,380	23,780	14,920
	1976 - 81	22,005	42,295	−20,290	35,210	37,500	−2,290	19,135	−3,445

large. In the case of Montréal, for example, net migration from other CMA's was minus 78,000 between 1976-81; from non-metropolitan areas it was minus 27,000. Yet during the same period, migration to or from other CMA's totalled 162,000 whereas migration to or from non-metropolitan areas totalled 222,000. Observe also that immigration of the foreign born often raises negative net internal rates of migration. Again, in the case of Montréal, net migration from internal sources was minus 105,000; when we add effects of immigration, however, overall net migration was minus 41,000. Finally, observe that between 1966-71 and 1976-81, that net migration to most CMA's underwent a decline. This applies particularly to Montréal, Sudbury, Windsor and Winnipeg. This trend can be attributed to increased attractiveness of non-metropolitan areas in recent times, shifts in intermetropolitan migration westward, and several socio-economic influences to be examined in this study.

When migration to a Census Metropolitan Area increases or declines over time, its impact on the level and structure of economic activity can be severe.[2] A loss of income earning households, for example, can affect local government revenues and expenditures (through the tax base), as well as consumer demand for goods such as real estate and rental housing. If children or older people are heavily represented among new arrivals, the demand for specific services such as schooling or hospital facilities can be affected. Moreover, if urban communities experience a consistent loss of population through emigration, they may become susceptible to a heavy drain on their social and economic vitality. This follows from the almost universal finding that migration is selective of younger, more educated, more dynamic elements of the population.[3]

Of course, the importance of migration to individual CMA's should not be thought of in quantitative terms alone. Quality considerations play an extremely important role as well. To appreciate this point we need only acknowledge that some CMA's are more capable of attracting and retaining migrants with higher levels of human capital than are others. Figure 1.4 illustrates this with respect to the migration of university educated males between 17 of Canada's largest CMA's over the 1976-81 period. Compare the situation of Toronto and Winnipeg. With respect to in-migration of the "highly educated", Toronto emerges as a disproportionate gainer with an index of 1.33. This index derives from a comparison of in-migration rates for Toronto and all CMA's combined. It thus standardizes for differences in population size between CMA's as well as the migration experience of all CMA's taken together.[4] In contrast, Winnipeg is located on the other end of the "continuum" with an index of .54. Relative to Winnipeg then, Toronto benefits

Figure 1.4: Disproportionate In- and Out-Migration of the University Educated Among Census Metropolitan Areas, 1976-81

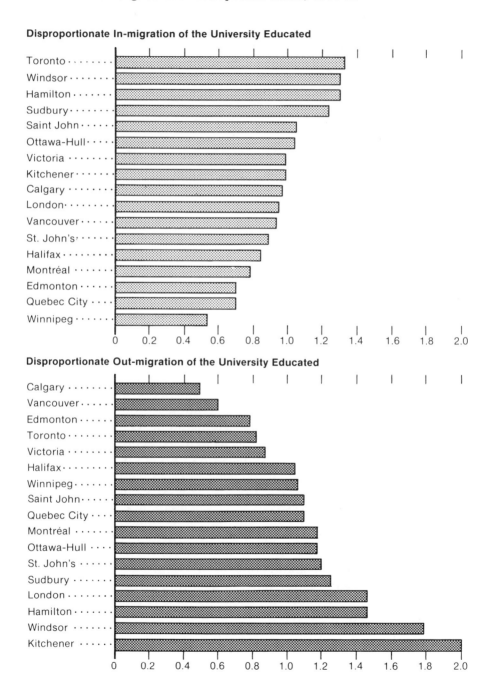

disproportionately from the in-migration of more educated migrants by a factor of $1.33/.54 = 2.46$. Since Toronto also loses fewer male university educated migrants relative to Winnipeg (right side of Figure 1.4), it is evident that it both attracts and holds onto educated migrants more than most other CMA's.

In view of the scenario above, it is hardly surprising that migration in Canada is viewed as an extremely complex process. Planners and policy-makers have expressed a great deal of interest in monitoring, if not controlling, the vicissitudes of migration on the development of towns, cities or entire regions.[5] Some policy-makers have questioned whether migration might better serve as a tool for interurban or interregional equalization policy. Specifically, the reallocation of human capital from one metropolitan area to another (eg., more educated people) has been viewed as a possible means of reducing inequalities in the distribution of income and wealth.[6] In addition, the geographic mobility of labour between urban centres has been viewed as a possible adjustment mechanism that might help to "clear out" excess labour supply (urban unemployment) or labour demand (urban job vacancies).

Others have questioned whether improved access to information might bolster social as well as private returns to interurban mobility. Access to information is clearly important when an unemployed person in one city considers a distant city where his particular skills may earn a higher rate of return. It is also important when households aspire to a different "public goods package" by "purchasing" a different urban community (police, fire, sanitation and other government facilities). Moreover, it is likely to bear on the decision-making process of important population subgroups who seek places offering specialized educational facilities, health advantages or retirement benefits. In such cases, the "search process" may be confounded by unforeseen distortions in, say, urban labour or housing markets. When this happens, and should households fail to relocate successfully, then return or repeat migration may be the only viable solution. This can impose heavy costs on the individuals involved and on society collectively.

Still others have questioned whether government policies which have had unintended, if not negative, effects on migration might have been anticipated in advance. For example, the implementation of language Bill 101 in the province of Québec, and related speculation concerning separatist policy, seems to be a case in point. The vice-president of Québec's largest employer's organization (Le conseil du patronat) claimed "The social, cultural and particularly economic costs are too great –

especially in the case of anglophones and those who speak other languages – to remain indifferent to some 200,000 departures recorded in the last five years. . . (the departure of so many people). . . represents a major loss in tax revenues and therefore an additional fiscal burden that remaining taxpayers must share together".[7] Regarding the future, the Secretary of State (Québec) released results of a recent survey by the Centre de recherches sur l'opinion publique (Montréal) which found that one of every five adult English-Quebeckers expects to leave the province during the next five years, mainly because of language-related job difficulties.

All this is to say that the force of migration on the well-being of cities and regions in Canada has prompted a great many questions about its causes, consequences and possible avenues for policy intervention. Accordingly, it seems appropriate to begin a study of intermetropolitan migration in Canada by asking, "What do we know about its determinants?". After all, anticipating the consequences of an event seldom facilitates good policy or long-range planning. Effective policy intervention requires an understanding of causes. And in this respect, there is no question that we know far too little about the determinants of urbanward migration in Canada. Most research of the last two decades has simply described spatial movements of populations between central city and fringe areas, whereas other studies, seeking to analyze rates of in- or out-migration, have typically been hampered by limited data on migration as well as its social and economic correlates. (Pioneering work in this respect has been undertaken by Leroy Stone: 1967, 1969, 1978, 1979.)

Possibly, the most glaring gap in our understanding, stems from the fact that past studies of in-migration to CMA's (or out-migration), have been conducted without knowledge of the characteristics of the sending region (or destination region).[8] Thus, urban planners and policymakers have not been able to decipher the "why's" of migration in terms of the *joint effects* of both the "pushes" and "pulls" involved. Rather, causes of migration to, from or between metropolitan areas have typically been imputed or inferred on the basis of studies of interprovincial or interregional migration.

This study hopes to take our understanding of metropolitan migration in Canada further. It focuses solely on the determinants of intermetropolitan migration. Other important issues concerning the consequences of migration on individual CMA's or the more recent "turnaround" of migration flows from metropolitan to non-metropolitan areas, are being taken up in related studies designed to complement this inquiry.[9]

Objectives and Methodology

Two objectives guide the theoretical and empirical work of this study. Our first objective is to construct a model of intermetropolitan migration which has both explanatory and predictive utility. Assuming that migrants do not drift around aimlessly but make conscious decisions about where to settle, we intend to develop a perspective on why migrants go where they do. We also intend to discuss differences between CMA's which we believe are relevant to the migrant's decision about where to locate. To test our model, we intend to examine variations in migration flows between CMA's over four time periods spanning three decades. We believe that this process is conducive to deciphering the behaviour of the "average" or "typical" migrant in terms of his/her response to "objectively" measured differences between CMA's.

Rather than decipher migration behaviour from scanty data on subjective perceptions of individual migrants, this study is based on secondary data (place-to-place migration from census sources), objective measures of broad "structural" differences between CMA's (e.g., wages, climate) and multivariate statistical techniques. Guiding premises in our work are that (i) individuals are rational, (ii) that they seek to maximize their monetary and non-monetary well-being, (iii) that objectively measured differences between CMA's convey information that is relevant to decision-making, and (iv) that - subject to information constraints – individuals will perceive and evaluate the desirability of "competing" places on this basis. These premises are incorporated in a broadly conceived cost/returns model in Chapter 3. It is on the basis of these premises that when objectively measured differences between CMA's are correlated with migration to or from them, that subjective motives concerning the desirability of these characteristics (and places) are imputed to migrants.

It would not be correct to say that our approach will identify "true" causes of migration or that it can be aligned with a fully developed theory about migration decision-making per se. Nor would it be correct to say that we aim merely to identify correlates of migration in the process of evaluating speculative hypotheses. More appropriately, this study seeks to identify plausible determinants of migration. These will be aligned with a reasonable explanatory framework about how people judge the attractiveness of different places. Depending on the amount of information available or sought out, we suggest that many determinants evaluated in this study will operate directly on the migrant's utility calculus whereas others will operate indirectly. Some determinants will operate directly in the sense that migrants will actually perceive "structural" or objectively measured characteristics of faraway places (employment growth, climate), and will adjust their migration decisions accordingly. Other determinants are likely to operate indirectly, for example, as general indicators of potential economic growth or development (capital investment). Then again, some determinants may enter the migration decisions of, say, highly informed individuals whose behaviour, in turn, may influence the migration decisions of less informed individuals – via a demonstration effect.

Why study determinants of intermetropolitan migration per se? Though migration flows between CMA's represent only one source of migration to and from metropolitan Canada, they contain several important advantages from an analytical standpoint. First, the migration process can be analyzed within an identifiable system of origin and destination cities. This means that socio-economic characteristics of origin as well as destination CMA's can be taken into account when evaluating why people go where they do. Previous understanding of metropolitan migration in Canada has been limited largely by an analysis of "pull" factors only (correlates of in-migration) or "push" factors (correlates of out-migration).

Second, CMA's are much more homogeneous as labour or housing markets than, say, provinces. This is important when measuring socio-economic characteristics to which migrants are thought to respond. For example, the response of a migrant to unemployment or wage levels can be evaluated much more rigorously when such influences are measured specific to a CMA than across an entire region. This point has been effectively illustrated in two U.S. studies.[10] The implication for our analysis is that several determinants of migration in Canada can be evaluated more rigorously in an intermetropolitan context than in an interprovincial or interregional context.[11]

Third, inter-CMA migration matrices can be constructed to produce a large number of migration flows for statistical analysis. By pooling migration data from different census time periods, we can augment the size of our "sample" so as to carry out statistical testing with greater confidence.

To place the magnitude of intermetropolitan migration in perspective, Table 1.2 provides an overview of the "migratory status" of the Canadian population. In row A, movers are distinguished from migrants in the sense that the former change residence but do not cross municipal boundaries. In contrast, migrants do both. Between 1976-81 approximately 5 million Canadians migrated, representing 22.7% of Canada's population aged five years or more. Of these, approximately 3.4 million, or 66.5%, moved within the same province, 1.1 million crossed provincial lines, 556,000 originated from outside Canada (recent immigrants). Migration to, from or between CMA's accounted for just over one-half of all migration between 1976-81. Of these, approximately 670,000 were intermetropolitan migrants, 712,000 moved from non-metropolitan Canada to CMA's, 773,000 moved in the opposite direction, and 436,000 originated from abroad. Again, we emphasize that our interest in intermetropolitan migration has less to do with its absolute size than with the advantages it construes from the standpoint of deciphering determinants of migration.

The second objective of this study is to evaluate several hypotheses concerning the changing nature of migration determinants in a society which is evolving over time. Is the decision to migrate in Canada dominated by economic or work-related factors to the same extent "today" as it was in the past? Are levels of living in Canada such that increasing numbers of migrants are changing cities as an "exploratory" activity, as a "consumption" activity, or in response to quality of life considerations (eg., better climate, or amenities)? If economic motives or influences are beginning to wane in the decision to migrate, what might this imply for government policy designed to influence the pace or direction of migration? While conclusive answers to such questions would undoubtedly require analysis of *all* types of migration, our focus on intermetropolitan migration contains the advantage that changing determinants can be examined in a relatively controlled context over a relatively long period of time.

To reflect on the questions raised above as well as our modelling objectives, 29 hypotheses have been formulated for evaluation in this study. Eight of these are relevant to an important ongoing debate concerning the efficiency of migration in Canada and its effects on interregional inequality. As a group, these eight hypotheses are referred to as a 'core hypothesis'. This hypothesis merits special comment; it serves as a frame of reference which runs throughout the entire contents of this book.

TABLE 1.2: Migration Status of the Population of Canada, 1966-71 and 1976-81

	Five-year period covered by the census			
	1966-71	1976-81	1966-71	1976-81
	(1)	(2)	(3)	(4)
	000's	000's	%	%
A. Total population aged 5 years and over	19,717	22,280	100.0	100.0
Movers[1]	9,236	10,605	47.4	47.6
Migrants[2]	4,720	5,068	23.9	22.7
B. Migrants from:				
Same province	2,766	3,370	58.6	66.5
Different province	850	1,142	18.0	22.5
Outside Canada	826	556	17.5	11.0
Residence not stated	278	NA	5.9	NA
C. Migrants moving to, from or between				
Census Metropolitan Areas (CMA's)	2,415	2,591	100.0	100.0
Moving between CMA's	502	670	20.8	25.9
Moving from non-metropolitan				
Canada to CMA's	684	712	28.3	27.5
Moving from abroad to CMA's	666	436	27.6	16.8
Moving from CMA's to non-metropolitan				
Canada	563	773	23.3	29.8

[1] Movers are those who occupied a different dwelling of residence from the one they occupied five years earlier.
[2] Migrants are those who crossed a municipal boundary when moving (see Appendix 2 to Chapter 1).
NA No account . . . In the 1981 Census, the category "residence not stated" for place of previous residence does not exist. Values were imputed to the other categories for non-response cases.
Source: 1971 and 1981 Censuses of Canada, Statistics Canada.

Our 'Core Hypothesis'

We hypothesize that the influence of "traditional" market variables on metropolitan migration in Canada has diminished over time.[12] This may be due to a crowding out process whereby (i) higher standards of living and the pursuit of leisure may have dampened the response of migrants to labour market forces, (ii) growth of social security programs may have cushioned the effects of, say, unemployment and thus motivation to migrate for work, and (iii) fiscal policies may have exerted unintended effects on migration. Were this hypothesis to be confirmed, it would imply that traditional tools of manpower policy for influencing migration between metropolitan labour markets, such as job creation, skill enhancement, or wages, would be less effective currently than they might have been in the past.

The rationale underlying our 'core hypothesis' can be *crudely* illustrated with respect to three hypothetical societies in Figure 1.5. At one end of the continuum, Figure 1.5 depicts an extremely poor society in which government revenues are assumed to be miniscule, manpower planning is assumed to be weak, and government programs bearing on welfare of workers are assumed to be limited if not negligible (eg., minimum wage laws, unemployment insurance). In this case, poverty conditions are assumed to be such that the marginal utility of an extra dollar of income is so high that wages and job opportunities dominate all other factors in the migration decision. In our hypothetical middle-income society, we continue to assume – for convenience – that the influence of government on the labour market remains marginal or insignificant. In this case, however, higher levels of production, standards of living and labour saving technology are postulated to promote the substitution of labour for leisure to the extent that higher incomes and job considerations are now in competition with other variables in the migration decision. These would include desirable climate, desired schooling, etc. Finally, in the rich societal context (eg., Canada), we assume that higher standards of living are interacting with a plethora of government policies and social security programs to the extent that the influence of "traditional" labour market variables has further diminished in the migrant's utility calculus. For example, programs to redistribute national tax revenues within a society (ie., equalization payments), might combine with generous unemployment insurance payments to benefit region 'A' over 'B' to the extent that the "pull" of otherwise attractive incomes at 'B' on potential migrants at 'A' might be cancelled out.

As crude as our interpretation of Figure 1.5 may be it is not without parallels in the real world. Data assembled in Table 1.3, for example, convey that the proportion of migrants moving for income or job-related reasons drops quite substantially as we move from "relatively poor" to "middle-income" to "relatively rich" countries. In addition, there is some indication that income or job-related reasons may be less prevalent in the migration decisions of Canadians than Americans. Admittedly, these impressions are based on surveys which differ greatly in terms of

Figure 1.5: A Crude Classification of Factors Influencing Migration at Various
Levels of Economic Development

Relative Level of Economic Development	DETERMINANTS OF MIGRATION		
Poor country	Labour market mechanism		
Middle- income country	Labour market mechanism	Social amenities	
Rich country	Labour market mechanism	Social amenities	Social security

TABLE 1.3: Survey Results on the Prominence of Job and Income-Related Considerations in Decisions to Migrate, Selected Countries at Various Levels of Development

Level of development	Per cent giving job or income-related reasons	Sources
A. Relatively rich countries		
Canada, 1982, migration to:		
British Columbia	26	Special survey by
Alberta	50	Statistics Canada (1982)
Canada, 1972:		
Migrants who left rural communities	46	Monu (1982)
Canada, 1964 - 75:		
Young adults who left Nova Scotia:		
All	29	
Males	37	Ralston (1981)
United States, 1974 - 76	49	Long & Hansen (1979)
Representative samples:		
1963	58	Lansing & Mueller (1967)
1966	50	Bureau of Labor Statistics
1945 - 46	63	Current Population Survey
England, 1953 - 63:		
Migrants moving more than 100 miles	57	Stillwell (1978)
France, 1950:		
Migrants to Paris	50	Fielding (1966)
Interprovincial migrants	60	
B. Middle-income countries		
Chile, 1960:		
Migrants to Greater Santiago	60	Elizaga (1966)
Mexico, 1965:		
Migrants to Monterey	70	Browning et al. (1968)
Peru, 1956:		
Migrants to Lima	61	Mar (1961)
Venezuela, 1961:		
Migrants to Guidad Guyana	43	MacDonald et al. (1969)
C. Relatively poor countries		
Indonesia, 1951:		
Migrants to Djakarta	74	Heeren (1955)
Ghana, 1965:		
Migrants to urban areas	82	Caldwell (1970)

questionnaire content and methodology. They also ignore differences in age structures between countries which will bear on the proportion of migrants interested in labour force versus, say, retirement reasons for migrating. Yet, the declining importance of job and income-related factors seems indisputable. The extent to which higher standards of living and social security factors may be responsible is, of course, a question to be taken up here.

Turning to Canada, if the effect of labour market variables on migration has diminished over time, and if changing social security or fiscal policies are partly responsible, then the data assembled for this study should offer a revealing test. By organizing our intermetropolitan migration data according to pre-1971 and post-1971 periods, we can evaluate the effects of distinct policy and economic developments that took effect after 1971. These include (i) the 1971 revision of the Unemployment Insurance Act, (ii) increased generosity of federal transfers to the Atlantic provinces, (iii) effects of the post-1973 oil price increases on fiscal capacity of the western provinces, including the establishment of the Alberta Heritage Fund, and (iv) restructuring of Canada's tax system and its likely effects on home ownership. Details on these post-1971 developments will be provided later.

Study Organization

To set the stage for our analytical work, Chapter 2 asks what we know about place-to-place migration in Canada based on the analysis of interprovincial and interregional migration. Acknowledging that no study has evaluated socio-economic determinants of intermetropolitan migration in Canada, findings on interprovincial migration are assessed as a backdrop to the formulation of our own theoretical and empirical work.

Chapter 3 elaborates our theoretical model of migration, hypotheses and variables. Its design and interpretation borrows from findings distilled in Chapter 2. Major questions or points of interest are expressed, formally, as hypotheses.

Chapter 4 focuses specifically on the changing importance of "traditional" market variables versus fiscal variables over time. It makes use of four data sets on intermetropolitan migration flows covering 1956-61, 1966-71, 1971-76 and 1976-81. For each of these migration periods, 17 Census Metropolitan Areas (CMA's) are included in the analysis. They correspond to the 17 CMA's first identified by the 1961 Census with populations in excess of 100,000. By 1981, seven more urban centres had qualified as CMA's, raising the total number to 24. The more recent CMA's have not been included in our sample for two reasons. First, data on socio-economic or explanatory variables have not always been available for the new CMA's. Also, data on the new CMA's are at times, suspect, in the sense that they have not been systematically collected and published over long periods of time. Second, analysis of an identical group of CMA's fits nicely with the idea of examining the behaviour of a cohort, undergoing change, as Canadian society evolves over time. Our maximum sample size is thus $(17 \times 16) \times 4$ periods = 1,088 intermetropolitan migration flows.

Chapter 5 re-evaluates the findings of Chapter 4 when migration flows are disaggregated into eastern versus western flows, and when migrants are disaggregated into three educational subgroups. In the latter case, migrants are also disaggregated to correspond more closely to individuals in the labour force. Our concern here is to ascertain the degree of geographical or socio-economic heterogeneity in migration flows (ie., aggregation bias).

Chapter 6 is organized into two parts; the first part provides a general summary of findings; the second part relates these findings to research and policy issues.

Finally, information of a more detailed or technical nature such as data on migration rates, definitions of explanatory variables, data sources, etc., has been relegated to appendices. Students of migration are advised to pay particular attention to the Appendix to Chapter 4. This Appendix provides details on the "functional form" of the empirical model evaluated in this study. Choice of an appropriate functional form involves several methodological decisions which are all too often neglected or underplayed in studies of migration. The result is usually a loss of important information or errors of estimation.

Major Findings

The most distinctive finding of this study is that our 'core hypothesis' has received confirmation in two ways. On the one hand, our empirical results convey that the influence of several economic variables on intermetropolitan migration such as wages, employment opportunities and business activity, has shrunk over time. This is evident when these determinants are evaluated for migration previous to 1971 and after 1971. For example, our conception of a relatively full "traditional" economic model "explains" approximately 56% of the variance in migration in the pre-1971 period versus only 31% in the post-1971 period (see Table 4.4). This finding is consistent with one dimension of our 'core hypothesis' that improvements in productivity, labour-saving technology, and higher standards of living may be currently prompting the pursuit of non-work activities to the extent that, say, earnings differentials figure less in the migrant's utility calculus.

On the other hand, our empirical results convey that public sector variables such as federal equalization payments and unemployment insurance are more relevant to explaining intermetropolitan migration in Canada after 1971. When such variables are added to our "traditional" economic model, they raise the explanatory power of the model considerably for the post-1971 period but not for the pre-1971 period. Furthermore, when our migration data are disaggregated into geographical regions (east versus west), fiscal variables make a far more significant showing as determinants of migration from the east – where public sector interventions have been most concentrated – than in the west. This finding is consistent with another dimension of our 'core hypothesis' that more generous social security-type provisions (particularly after 1971) may be cushioning the effects of, say, unemployment on earnings. That is, they may be reducing the motivation to migrate for income or job reasons alone. If so, some social security or fiscal policies aimed at improving various aspects of social or economic welfare in Canada may be having unanticipated, if not undesirable, side-effects on migration.

Conclusions concerning our 'core hypothesis' are not likely to be undermined by the impact of changes in Canada's demographic or spatial structure over time. Nor do they imply that migration per se is on the decline. Rather, the determinants of intermetropolitan migration are changing as Canadian society evolves over time, as individual preferences and tastes change, and as some variables partially displace the relevance of others. An implication of these findings is that traditional tools of manpower policy for influencing migration between metropolitan labour markets, such as job creation, skill enhancement, or wages, are likely to be less effective currently than they might have been in the past.

Our results also confirm several hypotheses concerning the effects of individual variables on migration. For example:

1) Distance between Census Metropolitan Areas (CMA's) has declined over time as a deterrent to migration. This is probably due to declining costs of transport and telecommunications. Declining transport costs are relevant to reduced "fixed costs" of relocation whereas declining telecommunications costs are relevant to reduced "psychic costs" of moving away from, say, friends and relatives.

2) Non-commonality of language between CMA's has increased in importance as a deterrent of migration. More specifically, migration from predominantly English-speaking CMA's to the predominantly French-speaking CMA's of Montréal and Québec City has declined in more recent times. We suggest that the "nationalist" and language policies (eg., Bill 101), pursued by the provincial government of Québec are partially responsible.

3) CMA's with a higher incidence of more educated persons (eg., some university training or a university degree), are more likely to "send out" migrants than are CMA's with a lower incidence of such persons. This finding sits well with the predictions of 'human capital theory' since more educated persons are thought to have greater access to information concerning opportunities in distant labour markets, (as well as to job transfers and higher rates of remuneration).

4) A higher incidence of violent crime at a CMA is not likely to deter migrants from going to that CMA.

5) Harsh winter climate – as measured by cumulative snowfall - seems to affect the location decisions of migrants. All else held constant, migrants are more likely to go to, say, Vancouver or Victoria for reasons of climate and are less likely to leave these CMA's for other CMA's for reasons of climate.

6) If a CMA experiences a high rate of immigration of foreign born persons, it is also likely to attract more migrants from other CMA's. This finding provides *tentative* support for the idea that immigrants may stimulate labour market opportunities at a CMA through their consumption, investments and entrepreneurial talent. This interpretation is directly opposed to the idea that foreign immigrants merely deplete scarce jobs, and are thus likely to deter the in-migration of "native" job-seekers.

Another major finding of this inquiry is that our attempt to isolate major determinants of metropolitan migration has encountered a good measure of success. We have evaluated several models which exhibit a considerable degree of consistency in their ability to account for variations in *aggregate* intermetropolitan migration flows. Significant explanatory variables in our model include wages, growth of industrial employment, residential construction activity (as a business cycle indicator), opportunities for female employment, rates of immigration, generosity of unemployment insurance, federal equalization grants, distance between CMA's, commonality of language/culture between CMA's and levels of education (ie., educational selectivity).

We have focused initially on the determinants of *aggregate* migration because most available data on migration and its determinants have been collected and disseminated in aggregate form (ie., not disaggregated by subregion or by migrant characteristics). Thus, when planners or policy-makers attempt to predict migration flows among specific places, they are usually in need of empirical models that will decipher the behaviour of the "average" or "typical" migrant in terms of "structural" differences between places of origin and destination. This is not to say, however, that we have assumed that intermetropolitan migrants are entirely homogeneous in terms of their needs or their response to opportunities at different locations. This would be tantamount to assuming that one theoretical/empirical model might work equally well for all migrants; that requirements for disaggregated data need not be rigorous; and that aggregate empirical models might be used as a reliable policy guide for influencing the behaviour of specific target groups.

To reflect on the homogeneity question, we have also evaluated our models – in "building block" fashion – when intermetropolitan migration flows have been disaggregated by region and by educational attainment of the migrants themselves. Disaggregations by region produce notable changes in the significance of individual explanatory variables. As noted above, the fiscal variables in our model perform quite differently for the eastern versus western region. We also found that commonality of language between CMA's is more important to explaining migration from eastern than western Canada.

The most striking impression concerning our disaggregation of migrants by educational attainment is that results are remarkably similar across educational subgroups. One has to look hard, for example, to show that distance seems to be more of a deterrent to migration among the more highly educated, or that non-commonality of language between CMA's is less of a deterrent among the more highly educated. Furthermore, we find that when our models are calibrated on migration rates pertaining to the "general population" versus those pertaining to the "population of labour force ages", results are highly similar. This implies that a "structural analysis" of the migratory behaviour of both the general population and those of labour force ages is equally well suited to unravelling major determinants of migration in Canada.

Finally, our results promise to be of use to planners and researchers if only because this is the first study to systematically evaluate the determinants of intermetropolitan migration in Canada. In this context, it is reasonable to say that many of our empirical estimates offer an advantage over previous studies of migration in Canada. This stems from the fact that our migration data and most of our explanatory variables pertain to Census Metropolitan Areas which, as units of analysis, are far more homogeneous than, say, provinces or entire regions. Homogeneity in this sense allows a far more rigorous test of the relationship between migration and variables such as distance, wage rates, employment growth and unemployment. Measurement of these variables gains in precision for CMA's over, say, provinces. Our point then, is that many of the empirical coefficients reported in this study should serve as a more reliable guide to the "true" significance of determinants of long-distance migration in Canada than has been available in the past.

Footnotes

1. Between 1956-81, Census Metropolitan Areas (CMA's) have undergone changes in their geographical boundaries. In most cases, this happens when growing fringe areas are incorporated into the CMA. In other cases, boundary changes have been initiated by political mandate at the provincial or local government level. The effect of such changes on the comparability of CMA data over time is problematic. Thus the population estimates in Figure 1.1 and the Appendix Tables to Chapter 1 are adjusted to conform to 1971 Census boundaries. Additional concerns about boundary changes, as they affect migration analysis, are taken up in the Appendix to Chapter 4 in the section "Changing CMA Boundaries".

2. See Bourne (1982), Gertler and Crowley (1977), Lithwick (1970), Simmons (1977), Weller (1982).

3. See Shaw (1975: Chapter 2).

4. These indices have been derived by dividing two ratios constructed from 1976-81 data on intermetropolitan migration among Canada's 17 largest CMA's (those listed in Figure 1.4). Our methodology can be illustrated with respect to Toronto.

    First, we calculate Toronto's rate of in-migration of university educated male migrants. The numerator in this rate is the absolute number of university educated male migrants aged 15 years and over who moved to Toronto from 16 of Canada's largest CMA's between 1976-81. The denominator is the absolute number of males aged 15 and over who were residing in Toronto in 1976. The resulting rate is 12.29 per hundred. This rate is then divided by a corresponding rate, for all 17 CMA's combined, of 12.16. This produces ratio 'A' = 12.29/12.16 = 1.01. We have thus standardized in-migration of university educated males to Toronto relative to Canada's 17 largest CMA's combined.

    Second, Toronto's rate of aggregate in-migration for the general population (all ages) is calculated. The numerator in this rate is the absolute number of all migrants who moved to Toronto from 16 of Canada's largest CMA's between 1976-81. The resulting rate is 8.2 per hundred. This rate is divided by a corresponding rate for all 17 CMA's combined which equals 10.8. This produces ratio 'B' = 8.2/10.8 = .76.

    Relative to the experience of all CMA's it is clear that Toronto does "better" with respect to the in-migration of university educated migrants (Ratio A = 1.01) than it does with respect to the general population (Ratio B = .76). This performance is expressed as an index by dividing ratio 'A' by 'B' = 1.01/.76 = +1.33.

5. See Courchene (1981), Economic Council of Canada (1982), Norrie et al. (1982), Polèse (1981), Winer and Gauthier (1982) and Vanderkamp (1982).

6. This follows from the premise that human capital is far more mobile as a factor of production than, say, fixed capital (eg., a factory), and that its contribution to gross national product is large (ie., 60-70% in North America).

7. Excerpt from an address by Ghislain Dufour to the Canada-Israel Chamber of Commerce.

8. A recent study by Simmons (1980) is an exception insofar as he examines the impact of a number of geographical factors on migration between urban-centred regions. His analysis takes two forms. To evaluate the impact of socio-economic factors on migration he analyzes rates of in-migration and out-migration to 124 urban-centred regions. In this case, origin and destination characteristics are not simultaneously evaluated (see his Tables 2 and 3). In contrast, to evaluate the impact of geographical variables (or barriers) on migration he analyzes migration flows among a sample of 124 urban-centred regions. This part of his analysis represents an unusual and unique contribution (see his Tables 5 and 6).

9. One study, tentatively titled "Population Turnaround in Canada: Explaining Changing Settlement Patterns", is in the planning stages by the Research and Analysis Division of Statistics Canada.

    With respect to the metropolitan – non-metropolitan "turnaround", the share of Canada's total population in non-metropolitan areas actually increased from a "low" of 44.9% in 1971 to 45.6% by 1981 (see Appendix Table A.1.1). In doing so, it consumed 51.2% of Canada's population growth between 1971-81 compared with only 31.6% between 1951-61 and 22.4% between 1961-71. This "turnaround" – visible in the United States as well as in Canada - is provoking a good deal of thought on its possible causes. One thing is clear, however. The idea that it implies rejection of "big, impersonal cities" or a "back to the land ethic", and thus the future demise of metropolitan Canada must be treated with skepticism. Evidence is accumulating that the "turnaround" is more likely a function of (i) lower tax rates on residential and commercial land on the metropolitan fringe, (ii) decentralization of business activity away from the urban core made possible by improved telecommunications, and (iii) improved commuter networks between non-metropolitan places of residence and metropolitan places of work.

10. The studies are cited, and an example is elaborated, in the Appendix to Chapter 4 "More on Aggregation Bias".

11. This is not to say, however, that analysis of inter-CMA migration flows is entirely superior to analysis of interprovincial or interregional migration probabilities. While some variables gain in precision for CMA's, it is also true that other variables are likely to be more "natural", or available for provinces (or entire regions). For example, the provision of public goods and the setting of tax rates comes, in part, under provincial jurisdiction; the data on unemployment insurance (used in this study) are more readily available for regional or provincial aggregates than CMA's; this is also the case for most federal transfers. Second, from a policy viewpoint the province is more likely (if any level of government is) to be able to influence migration patterns than the CMA. Third, by concentrating on CMA-migration, a number of important components of population growth for the CMA's themselves tend to be ignored. It is conceivable, in principle, that different CMA's rely on different sources of population growth (from other CMA's, from non-CMA cities, from rural areas and from immigration) to a greater or lesser extent. This could affect the migration pattern among CMA's.

12. A version of this hypothesis was first presented in the author's **Migration Theory and Fact** (p.134) as follows; "Generally, as a society progresses along a development continuum . . . the importance of the economic factor (eg., situations of economic stress, wage and employment differentials, etc.), diminishes as an influence on migration". In a review symposium in **Demography**, Larry Long (1977, p.557-62) commented on the above as follows: "This conclusion is prophetic, for much discussion of the "causes" of migration in the last few years has concerned the theme that migration in the U.S. has become more strongly influenced by various amenities like climate and recreation. Shaw drew this conclusion before there was widespread publicity given to the "resurgence" of population growth in non-metropolitan areas, and in this instance he has identified a theme that is likely to dominate many analyses of internal migration in developed countries for years to come."

Chapter 2
Place-to-Place Migration in Canada: What We Know

Introduction

Much of our knowledge about the determinants of place-to-place migration derives from an ambitious econometric literature which has sought to establish the relative importance of social and economic variables.[1] Many such studies have examined migration between metropolitan areas or regions in the United States. Far fewer have examined migration between provinces or regions in Canada. To date, no study has systematically evaluated the determinants of intermetropolitan migration in Canada.

One way of approximating the determinants of intermetropolitan migration in Canada would be to review the empirical literature on the United States. If Canadian society was structured exactly like American society, this would probably suffice. In contrast, we might limit our review to studies of interprovincial migration in Canada. If interprovincial migrants behaved exactly like intermetropolitan migrants then this would probably suffice. Obviously, neither assumption is likely to be tenable. This implies that studies of place-to-place migration in both contexts merit review.

Our aim in this chapter is to focus solely on the literature on interprovincial migration in Canada. From a theoretical standpoint, this will introduce important methodological issues which are common to studies of migration in Canada and most other developed countries. From a practical viewpoint, it will introduce the major determinants of long-distance migration in Canada. Insights gleaned from the literature on Canada will then be supplemented with findings on intermetropolitan migration in the United States when we formulate our theoretical/ empirical model in Chapter 3.

If Courchene's (1970, p.574) claim that "Migration is an economic event, this much is clear", has an element of truth, a review of the econometric literature would seem to be an appropriate point of departure. One advantage of econometric inquiry is that researchers have pursued their study of migration with theoretical rigor to the extent that useful models have been developed. By and large, the same does not apply to the other social sciences. In addition, economists have systematically deduced hypotheses which have received wide evaluation. This has resulted in a wealth of quantitative estimates of elasticities on the *relative* importance of social and economic variables in interregional migration flows. Recent econometric studies also contain the advantage that more attention has been devoted to non-monetary variables. Fortunately, economists have not remained entirely blind to the narrow focus or academic bias of earlier work.

The balance of this chapter is organized as follows; it introduces the costs/returns investment model as the now popular interpretation of migration among economists; it summarizes results of early tests of the human investment model using data on interprovincial migration in Canada in and around 1951-66; it presents results of more recent tests which have utilized far larger data sets; and it offers a general assessment of the relative importance of social and economic variables in interregional migration in Canada.

Our review draws on a variety of studies that are extremely dense in terms of theory, empirical measurement and statistical estimation. It should be borne in mind that any attempt to provide a non-technical summary in a short space runs the risk of dealing with some points superficially.

Appropriate Theory

Most economic studies interpret place-to-place migration in one of two ways. One has its origin in Hicks' (1932) *The Theory of Wages,* the other in Sjaastad's (1962) seminal article "The Costs and Returns of Human Migration".

Hicks' dictum that migration is a response to wage differentials gave rise to the so-called "macro-adjustment model" of migration. Basic to this model is the idea that labour is a factor of production, and that all factors (labour and capital) seek out opportunities where their rate of return (appropriately defined) is greatest. Labour is expected to move from regions of low relative labour demand to areas of high relative demand if the move results in higher wages. It will continue to do so until the demand and supply of labour, and thus wage rates, are in equilibrium between the two areas. If there were no costs to relocation, the model would focus simply on differential returns to various jobs as a sufficient condition to determine whether or not labour moves.

The macro-adjustment model focuses on wage rates per se under the assumption that labour markets perform as markets where prices or average wage rates adjust upward or downward to situations of excess demand or supply. If they adjust very quickly to disequilibrium, a "market clearing mechanism" is said to exist in a flexible or "flex-price" market. It follows that if labour markets were flex-price, then a condition of surplus labour would bid wage rates down to the extent that employers would hire all labour to the point that involuntary unemployment would not exist.

Disenchantment with the macro-adjustment model began with criticism of the assumption that labour can be freely "traded", much like durable goods in a flex-price market. In reality, flex-price markets arise only when (i) the object of exchange is fairly homogeneous, (ii) information flows indicating excess demand and supply conditions are rapid and effective, and (iii) there is little or no attachment between buyer and seller. Needless to say, such criteria seldom apply to labour markets in North America. Rather, labour markets today are more likely to be "fix-price" markets where the object being exchanged is heterogeneous; where non-price aspects of competition are important; where information about the various terms of exchange that will clear markets is highly incomplete; and where contracts may be drawn up to fix a fair price (wage) between buyer and seller. In short, the macro-adjustment model assumes flexibility when, in reality, labour markets have become increasingly rigid, if not segmented.

As we shall see, doubts about the utility of the macro-adjustment model have been borne out by empirical studies. Specifically, wage and unemployment variables have not performed as expected, and the "symmetry" assumption which restricts origin and destination characteristics to be of equal significance is under fire. (The nature of the "symmetry" assumption is taken up in the Appendix to Chapter 4.) In addition, the model has little relevance for other important migratory groups including those moving for educational reasons, climate, retirement or as job transfers. Moreover, it is difficult to adapt the model to the migration decision of households which might be motivated to migrate if a member is unemployed yet might also resist migration for a job or higher earnings if a wage earning spouse is present. This is of no small importance because household units, not individuals, dominate migratory flows. These and other shortcomings suggest that the focus of the macro-adjustment model is too narrow.

Sjaastad's human capital investment model interprets migration in quite a different way. Instead of focusing on labour as an "aggregate" or homogeneous entity, it allows for heterogeneity and pays greater attention to non-monetary considerations. The economic returns to migration consist of the net discounted present value of expected future lifetime earnings that individuals can expect to gain from migration. The economic costs consist of the present value of foregone earnings plus any money and non-money costs directly associated with migration. References to non-monetary costs can be expanded quite easily to include social or psychic costs and returns (eg., climate, culture). For example, the model acknowledges that social costs to migration are likely to increase with age as people develop broader or deeper community ties over time.

Another appealing feature of the human capital model is that it emphasizes expected *future* lifetime earnings. As young persons have a longer time to capitalize on their migration investment than older persons, this concept provides an economic rationale for the prevalence of more young men and women among migrants. In addition, the idea of "expected returns" acknowledges the possibility that wage differentials may be adjusted by potential migrants should they expect to incur unemployment while searching for a job at a new destination. Finally, the human capital investment framework is at ease with the greater prevalence of migration among households with more educated members or with multiple income earners since it can balance costs and returns of migration for the household as a whole.

Many empirical studies claim support for the human capital model of migration. Upon closer inspection, however, we find that several of its more "intricate" tenets have not been subjected to rigorous evaluation. For example, support for the human capital model rarely, if ever,

derives from rigorous tests of the Sjaastad model per se. Researchers usually replace "future lifetime earnings" with actual wage or income differentials, and they almost always discard the discount rate under the assumption that it is constant across all regions. This means that confirmation
of, say, wage and distance effects on migration is, at best, supportive
of a broadly conceived costs/returns framework rather than the *expected
future earnings hypothesis*.

How "expected lifetime earnings" might actually be measured
represents another problem. Many migrants change occupation or industry as well as their place of work. To assume that they know future
earnings potential in the new occupation or industry seems far-fetched.
Adequate tests of the expected returns assumption would require no less
than panel data which are in extremely short supply. While some studies
have moved in this direction, results have been mixed. One such study,
reviewed in the Appendix to Chapter 2, claims to find little support for
the income expectations hypothesis (see also, Leffler and Lindsay:1979).

Finally, critics of the human capital model profess that assumptions concerning "purposive rational behaviour" have not been sufficiently
thought out. Do potential migrants continuously go about assessing opportunities among "competing" locations in order to decide to invest in
migration or not? DaVanzo (1981) argues that economists recognize that
real people do not behave this way. It is just that the outcome of their
behaviour often accords with predictions of such a model. If this is so,
how do we deal with survey findings which show that potential migrants
are not sufficiently informed to calculate a great many costs and returns
to migration (Lurie and Rayack:1966, Glantz:1973, Shaw:1974b,
Gustavus and Brown:1977). To answer that migrants behave only "as
if" they consciously weigh pecuniary and non-pecuniary returns is clearly
not sufficient. Rather, it is more realistic to say that some people probably do make very intricate calculations (eg., those considering a job
transfer), that some make relatively informed calculations (eg., those
who search for and secure a job before migrating), whereas others make
extremely crude calculations (eg., poorly educated, unemployed workers
who migrate in search of a job). Put differently, the "as if" clause is pro-
gressively giving way to more concrete ideas about sources and costs
of information, decision-making risks, and more realistic assumptions
about "rational expectations".[2] It is these considerations which constitute
the hard technical nut, yet to be cracked, in efforts to model individual
choices.

Irrespective of the criticisms offered above, the human capital model has served as a launching pad for rich and varied thought on the determinants of migration. It is sufficiently superior to its "competitors" that it now dominates the way that migration is interpreted. Social scientists might well part company with the model if costs and returns are represented strictly à la Sjaastad (1962), but they would be less justified in doing so were the model more broadly conceived to permit empirical "filling out".

Early Studies

The early econometric studies reviewed here were published in and around the 1970's. Significant contributions include Courchene (1970), Laber and Chase (1971), McInnis (1969;1971), and Vanderkamp (1970;1971). These studies employ multiple regression techniques to evaluate aspects of the costs/returns framework.[3] They utilize data from the 1961 Census of Canada, or time-series family transfer accounts to evaluate determinants of interregional or interprovincial migration within a network of identifiable origins and destinations. They are important to this inquiry because they permit a consensus on some broad correlates of place-to-place migration.

We begin with findings which derive from highly aggregative studies. As expected, each study confirms that wage or income levels have a significant effect on migration (hereafter 'M_{ij}' which is defined as the number of migrants originating from place 'i' destined for place 'j' divided by the origin population of 'i').[4] This implies, that persons, on average, move from low-income to high-income areas toward maximizing their returns to employment, and equalizing wage rates between regions. However, credit goes to Courchene (1970) and Vanderkamp (1971) for showing that model specifications which restrict origin and destination characteristics to be of equal significance obscure "true" wage effects (ie., the symmetry assumption).[5] They show that wage levels at destination 'j' are, on average, more strongly correlated with M_{ij} (a positive effect) than are origin wage levels (a negative effect). For an explanation, we borrow from Vanderkamp (1971) who suggests that high income in a sender region can play a dual role; as income foregone due to migration (a hypothesized negative effect on migration), and as a source of financing movement (a hypothesized positive effect). The overall influence of origin income on migration, therefore, becomes mixed and uncertain. Indeed, Vanderkamp's finding that income in the origin region exerts a weakly positive effect leads him to speculate that better sources of financing may improve the allocative efficiency of migration.

All studies of interregional migration in Canada corroborate that distance has a stronger negative effect (ie., explains a larger share of the variance in the regressions), than could possibly be accounted for by transport costs alone. Vanderkamp (1971) suggests that physical measures of distance between regions subsume (a) the income costs connected with moving, (b) the psychic costs of moving, (c) the difference in psychic incomes associated with sender and receiving regions, and (d) the uncertainty about income prospects due to lack of information. Under component (a) we might include income lost due to unemployment while moving; under (b) we might include the cost of adjusting to new surroundings, search for a new home, etc. Vanderkamp also suggests that components (a) and (b) probably contain sizeable fixed costs and, possibly, declining marginal costs with increasing distance. Thus, he provides a rationale for estimating the effects of distance nonlinearly (ie., log transformation), because the slope between migration and distance may become less negative with greater distance.

Courchene (1970) explicitly evaluates the impact of unemployment levels on M_{ij}. Courchene's evaluation using census data reveals that unemployment exhibits the expected negative effect at places of destination but at levels below statistical significance. As for origin effects, unemployment is largely positive (as expected) and some of the coefficients are significant. On the basis of both coefficient size and levels of significance (student 't' values), Courchene concludes that migration from 'i' to 'j' is affected more by unemployment at origin than destination – just the opposite of what holds for income.

Let us now consider the relevance of wage and distance effects when migration flows are disaggregated by socio-economic characteristics. Disaggregations were performed by Courchene (1971) and McInnis (1971). A later study by Marr et al. (1978) is also relevant here as it takes up a controversial finding reported by McInnis.

Both Courchene and McInnis report that earnings differentials are significant to the migratory behaviour of all age groups but that they exert stronger effects on younger than older migrants. This lends support to the lifetime earnings premise of the human capital model that younger migrants have a longer time to capitalize on their expected returns. It also marries well with the idea that social costs to migration are likely to be greater among older persons. In addition, Courchene evaluates the relative influence of origin versus destination wage levels on each age group and confirms that destination wages "out-perform" origin wages in all cases.

Courchene and McInnis also find that higher earnings differentials have a larger effect on more educated migrants than among those with, say, elementary education. This agrees with the human capital interpretation, as education tends to increase the benefits as well as decrease the costs of moving. But does more education really reduce costs of moving? Both McInnis and Courchene predict "yes", but McInnis' results go against expectation. He finds that the deterrent effect of distance increases, not decreases, with higher levels of education. He also reports that distance has more of a deterrent effect among professionals than, say, craftsmen, labourers or farmers.

According to the human capital model, we would expect the labour market for the more highly educated to be more national in scope. We would also expect those with higher education to have access to better information concerning job opportunities. If so, then costs of information search should be lower, chances of making errors of judgment should be less, and time unemployed between moves should be reduced (especially among job transfers). Others, such as Greenwood (1975) and Schwartz (1976), suggest that higher education also reduces the importance of cultural and family ties (ie., the psychic cost of distance). In addition, if the more highly educated are also wealthier then relocation costs of migration may be perceived as less important. In short, there are many reasons for expecting that the effect of distance on M_{ij} should be less, the higher the level of education. The later study by Marr et al. (1978) is relevant here as they use 1966-71 data to address the controversial results reported by McInnis. Their results not only corroborate those reported by Courchene but agree with several studies on migration in the United States. There would appear to be a consensus then that the education/distance tradeoff has been confirmed.

In addition to the above, Courchene's (1970) study reports that levels of education at origin exert a significant positive effect on M_{ij}; that rates of M_{ij} are lower from the province of Québec; that federal transfers to provinces (eg., equalization payments) tend to dampen out-migration; and that unemployment insurance transfers to provinces 'i' also exert a negative effect on out-migration. With respect to unemployment levels, Courchene submits that an increase in unemployment in province 'i' will tend to "push" people out, but as unemployment insurance benefits increase (as a result of greater unemployment), this will tend to inhibit interprovincial migration. Courchene's results on federal transfers to the provinces are particularly relevant to current debates on the "equity-efficiency" tradeoff. This will be taken up later.

Finally, both Vanderkamp and Courchene ask whether the response of migrants to variables such as income and distance has changed over time. Vanderkamp's results, using time-series data, show that the coefficients on income and distance do, indeed, vary over time and that the payoff to migration is less favourable when the labour market is slack (times of high unemployment) than when it is near full employment. This implies that migrants respond (correctly) less to existing opportunities when there is a general slack in the labour market. Courchene reports essentially the same thing. Migrants appear to have been more responsive to income differences over time and the deterrent effect of distance appears to have declined over time. The finding on distance certainly makes sense if we think of its "barrier effects" being reduced with improved transport systems, cheaper airfares, improved telecommunications etc.

Later Studies

More recent work on the determinants of migration in Canada has been dominated by three studies. These include Grant and Vanderkamp's (1976) study of interprovincial and interlocality migration between 1965-71 using data derived from tax records combined with unemployment insurance records; Robinson and Tomes' (1982) study of lifetime interprovincial migration using individual data from the 1966-71 Census; and Winer and Gauthier's (1983) study of interprovincial migration between 1951-78 using family allowance and tax filer data.

Each of the aforementioned studies make use of relatively large or specialized data sets to evaluate place-to-place migration at various levels of disaggregation. In general, they provide further confirmation on the importance of distance and income considerations in migration; that wage levels at destination "outperform" those at origin; that French ethnicity or residence in Québec is negatively related to M_{ij}; and that higher levels of education at places of origin are positively correlated to M_{ij}. (We continue to define M_{ij} as previously.)

In the case of unemployment, results continue to be mixed. Grant and Vanderkamp (1976) submit that unemployment variables make a poor showing in their regressions. Winer and Gauthier conclude that unemployment performs as expected in some cases, not at all in others, and with mixed effects in still others. Their results – some of which derive from "Courchene-type equations" – give the *overall* impression that unemployment at origin exerts significant positive effects on M_{ij} whereas unemployment at destination is far more ambiguous. Similar conclusions can be drawn from Marr et al. (1978). Unemployment in the origin area exhibits the expected sign for six of seven educational subgroups and is statistically significant for three. In contrast, unemployment at places of destination does not exhibit the expected effects. If we combine these results with survey findings that the unemployed are more likely to uproot than the employed, then measures of unemployment at origin might be retained as potentially more useful while discarding unemployment at destination.[6]

Turning to individual studies, Grant and Vanderkamp (1976) raise two important methodological questions concerning the choice of an appropriate income variable. First, they ask "Does additional information about income components add anything to the explanation of migration behaviour?" To address this question they define three types of income: wage income, self-employment income, and other income (which includes pension, rental and investment income). On the basis of their regressions they conclude that wage income coefficients are indeed largest and most significant. In contrast, the other income variables are not very important.

Second, Grant and Vanderkamp ask what kind of income variable represents the theoretical notion of "expected incomes" most appropriately? Do potential migrants base their income expectations on differences between the *average* incomes of place 'i' versus 'j'? Or do potential migrants calculate their expected incomes in terms of, say, the income experience of a recent cohort of previous migrants? If the answer to the latter question is "yes", then this would imply that potential migrants have sufficient information to calculate the income experience of previous migrants. It would also imply that they have sufficient foresight to anticipate what is going to happen in their own case. Moreover, it would mean that potential migrants base their income expectations on the "short-run" income experience of past migrants which (i) may well consist of a small group with large "random" income components and/or (ii) might have significant "transitory" elements (eg., unusually low incomes due to unusually high unemployment, or unusually high incomes to an economic boom).

The analysis conducted by Grant and Vanderkamp shows quite clearly that migrants respond to "average" income differentials. That is, the "failure" of migrants to respond to income measures that might contain "transitory" or "random" elements suggests that migrants are more concerned with maximizing lifetime returns as conveyed by real average income differentials between places. This constitutes a measure of support for the human capital model. Yet, it is important to note that in another and more recent study, Grant and Vanderkamp (1980) report weak support, at best, for the human capital model. Since their results derive from a rather specific set of research questions, they are summarized in the Appendix to Chapter 2.

Turning to the study by Robinson and Tomes (1982), the authors ask whether individual migrants behave in ways that are consistent with aggregate studies which usually assume that populations are homogeneous. To address this question, they examine the probability of moving or staying in terms of a great many individual characteristics. They are particularly interested in the effects of self-selection on monetary returns to migration. They borrow from Greenwood (1975, p.402) who states the problem thus; "The fact that individual A migrates, while otherwise comparable B does not, suggests that an important difference does exist between individuals. . . Individual A may be more motivated to invest in human capital formation, not only in migration, but in other forms as well. If such were the case, the earnings of the remaining cohort from which the migrant is drawn may provide a lower boundary for the earnings the migrant would have received in the absence of migration".[7]

While the results of Robinson and Tomes (1982) must be interpreted with caution, they lend themselves to the following broad conclusions. First, their evidence is consistent with the hypothesis that self-selection works to place the more dynamic elements of the population into the "mover" group. Specifically, they show that people who actually move out of province 'i' earn more at their new province of residence than "average" stayers at place 'i' would have earned had they also moved to province 'j'. In addition, Robinson and Tomes impute the wage differentials faced by each potential migrant and show that larger wage differentials are associated with greater probabilities of moving. They claim that this finding constitutes impressive evidence in favour of the human capital model. (See, however, evidence to the contrary in the Appendix to Chapter 2.)

Second, they find that the probability of moving is positively associated with more years of formal schooling (except in the case of Québec). The probability of moving is also positively related to the possession of a university degree (including Québec). Further disaggregation of education variables, however, does not improve our understanding of migration (eg., apprenticeship or vocational training).

Third, they find that contrary to anglophones, schooling attainment among francophones is negatively related to emigration from Québec. The overall effect of French language on migration from Québec remains negative even when monetary returns to migration are controlled. While the authors conclude that language (or French ethnicity) influences migration through channels other than wage or income earning effects they submit that this finding is difficult to rationalize in terms of the usual hypothesis concerning education and migration. In addition, they suggest that such effects are working to produce a bilingual society in Québec (French, and French/English bilinguals), versus a unilingual society in English Canada.

Fourth, they report that mobility diminishes with greater age, residence in small towns or rural farm areas, and family size. Large family size is interpreted by the authors as implying greater costs of moving.[8]

The Equity:
Efficiency Debate

The study by Winer and Gauthier (1983), prepared for the Economic Council of Canada, ambitiously sets out to evaluate the impact of fiscal as well as "private" market variables on interprovincial migration. In common with the present study, it addresses the so-called "equity: efficiency debate". Accordingly, we shall discuss Winer and Gauthier's findings in somewhat greater depth. First, however, let us elaborate on the nature of the issues involved.

The so-called equity:efficiency debate has been on and off for some time now. It has received added impetus with the renegotiation of Canada's fiscal arrangements and the publication of a major "consensus" document by the Economic Council of Canada entitled *Financing*

Confederation (1982). Much of the current debate rests on a key assumption that migration is responsive to fiscal differences.

On the equity side, the Canadian government has long embraced the policy of transferring funds via equalization payments to poorer provinces toward achieving "horizontal fiscal balance". One aim is to ensure that individuals of given economic circumstances receive the same kinds of essential public services, while incurring the same tax burden, whether they live in a relatively wealthy, heavily populated province or a poorer, sparsely populated province. The debate, with respect to migration, stems from criticism that equalization programs subtract from the allocative efficiency of the Canadian economy.[9]

It has been argued, perhaps most forcefully by Courchene, that efficiency costs arise when equalization payments induce people to remain in, or move to, poorer provinces of the country where their marginal product is lower than it would be in the wealthier provinces. Courchene feels that equalization and associated transfer payments are partially to blame for persistently lower returns to employment in the Atlantic provinces than in the country as a whole. Why? Because the market forces that would naturally work to induce migration from low- to high-income regions (and thus equalize earned incomes across the country) are alleged to have been short-circuited by a fiscal structure that, via the equalization program, subsidizes residence in regionally depressed areas. This has been coined the "transfer-dependency hypothesis" (Courchene:1981, Winer and Gauthier:1983).

Juxtaposed to Courchene's view is the position taken by Boadway and Flatters (1982) which forms a theoretical backbone of the Economic Council's *Financing Confederation.* They maintain that Courchene has a point but that even greater efficiency costs will arise if governments fail to pursue complete equalization of fiscal capacity. Emphasis is on "complete" because the important differences in fiscal capacities today stem from provincially controlled natural resource revenues which result in the provision of public goods (schools, parks) at lower-income tax rates. Alberta serves as a case in point. Its fiscal capacity has been enhanced greatly since 1973 when its vast oil resources enjoyed higher rates of return following the oil price-hikes by OPEC. Boadway and Flatters argue that unless this type of fiscal inequity is balanced through equalization payments, unrestricted migration will respond to differences in fiscal capacity (as well as to differences in personal incomes) to the extent that inefficiency will ensue.

To clarify what Boadway and Flatters have in mind, consider the example in *Financing Confederation* (1982, p.29), where an Alberta resident with a market income of $10,000 receives a net increase in fiscal benefits of $1,000, while his identical counterpart, with respect to market income, in Ontario does not. If labour mobility is perfectly responsive to real income differentials among regions, then Ontario residents, seeing the new fiscal benefits in Alberta, will begin to move there, depressing wages in Alberta and raising them in Ontario (Norrie et al. 1982). This may take place to the point that the influx of migrants into Alberta may drive down its average wage rate below the wage rates in other provinces. Why? Because migrants, at the margin, may take lower productivity jobs in Alberta than they presently occupy, since increased public services and/or reduced tax rates will offset the decline of gross pay available to them. Were this to happen, unabated, then Alberta might ultimately attract too large a population relative to its employment opportunities – due to its fiscal attractiveness. To prevent this from happening, Boadway and Flatters suggest aggressive pursuit of "horizontal fiscal balance" to prevent inefficient "rent-seeking" as against efficient "wage-seeking" migration between regions.

In the process of evaluating the crucial assumption that migrants respond to differential fiscal capacity, Winer and Gauthier observe that historical patterns of interprovincial migration changed after 1971. The west has been attracting far more migrants than previously, Ontario has diminished in importance as a destination, and a turnaround is evident in migration to the Atlantic provinces. The authors question whether these new patterns and reversals can be attributed to (1) the effects of mushrooming "natural resource rents" on fiscal capacity in the west (eg., oil revenues in Alberta following upon the 1973 price hikes by OPEC), and (2) more aggressive federal equalization and unemployment insurance transfer payments in the east? Or, does the evidence suggest that individuals are overwhelmingly concerned with job prospects when choosing between labour markets, meaning that the expectation of fiscal benefits is not significant in migration decisions?

The evaluation performed by Winer and Gauthier is conducted in two parts. The first part pertains to a re-evaluation of Courchene's (1971) results on the impact of unemployment insurance and government transfers on "out-migration". In the second part of their study, the authors focus on an additional variable "national resource rents" (NRR). Greater differences in NRR between provinces are hypothesized to influence migration by providing more social services and benefits without adding to the individual's tax burden. As noted previously, this variable is expected to be relevant to westward migration, particularly after 1973. The authors use tax filer data for the period 1966-77, which allows them to combine information on NRR with market variables and other fiscal variables, to evaluate a "fuller" empirical model. Our review is limited to the second part which the authors offer as a more comprehensive evaluation.

Results presented by Winer and Gauthier are displayed across 12 tables covering four income groups and four regional aggregates. While difficult to summarize and not conclusive, they convey the following broad impressions. First, the higher the level of unemployment insurance generosity at province 'i' or 'j', the less people will leave 'i' and the more people will move to 'j'. This applies more to "low-income" than "high-income" individuals. It is also more applicable to migrants originating from the Atlantic provinces.

Second, the greater the differential in natural resource rents (NRR) between province 'j' and 'i' (ie., NRR_j/NRR_j), the greater the rate of migration from 'i' to 'j'. This is generally applicable to both low- and high-income individuals. However, it is more relevant to low- and high-income migrants destined for Alberta and British Columbia.

Third, levels of federal purchases in province 'i' or 'j' do not have a clear effect on M_{ij}.

Fourth, levels of federal transfers to persons have a positive effect, rather than the expected negative effect at origin on the migration of poorer persons. In contrast, it has the expected negative effect on high-income individuals. As in other studies, the authors speculate that such transfers may be used by the poor to finance a move.

Fifth, the larger the difference in unconditional government transfers to province 'j' versus 'i' (ie., equalization payments), the larger migration between province 'i' and 'j' by low-income people (as expected). Among high-income level people, however, the effects of such grants are less discernable.

Sixth, fiscal structure seems to be more relevant to explaining gross out-migration from the Atlantic provinces (versus gross in-migration), and gross in-migration to Alberta and British Columbia (versus gross out-migration). This, the authors suggest, may be the result of the presence of return migrants on gross in-migration from Alberta and British Columbia. The presence of return migrants is likely to obscure their results because, unlike new migrants, they are returning home to a known entity and thus may not be motivated by perceived differences in net fiscal benefits across provinces. (See Appendix to Chapter 4, "Aggregation Bias".)

Winer and Gauthier also consider several "market" variables and their regressions provide a wealth of information on the stability of estimated coefficients across income groups and regions. One pattern worthy of note is the tendency for the coefficient on distance to grow in both size and statistical significance with higher income status. Another pattern of note, particularly in the Atlantic region is for the poorest groups to be less responsive to wage effects than the "middle-income" groups. Add to this the finding – acknowledged by the authors – that the very poor and richest groups are least responsive to "natural resource rents" and we find that those conforming most to expectation are the middle-income groups. This implies that it is the very poor who are not benefiting by migration due, possibly, to high costs involved in relocation, insufficient human capital to take advantage of alternative opportunities, and lack of information on alternative opportunities. In contrast, the rich may not be as responsive to wage and fiscal effects in view of their attained wealth or the possibility that they may be in higher-income occupations that are in some way "tied" to their place of residence (eg., managers who own their own companies, doctors or lawyers with established offices, clientele etc.). If this were true it might help explain McInnis' previously reviewed finding that the coefficient on distance increases with education – assuming that the rich dominate the higher educational groups.

With respect to the current efficiency:equity debate, Winer and Gauthier conclude that (1) fiscal benefits, fuelled by natural resource rents, do increase the odds of migrating to the west, especially for low income individuals, and (2) that equalization payments reduce these same odds. Thus, while confirming Courchene's earlier findings, they imply that negative effects of equalization and transfer payments to the Canadian east have been overstated, that existing programs are helping to prevent westward rent-seeking, and that complete horizontal fiscal balance is probably justified to further prevent inefficient rent-seeking. A more recent study by Mills et al. (1983) implies much the same thing.

Closer examination of the studies above, however, suggests that too much is being made of too little evidence. Vanderkamp (1984) observes that Winer and Gauthier come to a (perhaps qualified) conclusion regarding their hypotheses when the "score" is close to even in the sense that the number of significantly wrong signs in a dozen or more regressions is close to the number of significantly right signs. With regards to one of their "strongest" findings that fiscal capacity – as represented by NRR – has had an impact on migration to Alberta and British Columbia the "score" is only five to four. Likewise in the study by Mills et al. (1983) fiscal capacity is of the expected sign and statistical significance for only three of seven regions. Moreover, evidence supporting their hypotheses pertains to out-migration from relatively resource rich provinces. Out-migration from regions in Canada thought to be sending rent-seeking migrants westward does not appear to be significantly affected by variables measuring fiscal surplus.

In addition, it is important to question whether NRR is influencing migration through its fiscal effects (ie., "free" benefits without taxes), or through its effects on income and employment. In regressions performed by Winer and Gauthier (1983, Tables 2.3 and 2.4) without NRR, employment growth variables at place of destination perform consistently well for the Atlantic region, and exhibit the expected sign in 13 of 18 regressions in Table 2.3. Once NRR is added in Tables 4.2 and 4.3, however, employment variables do not perform as well in the Atlantic region and coefficients on the income variables drop to an extent for all migrants taken together. This implies that NRR may be intercorrelated with employment and income. Might migrants be pursuing job opportunities and higher incomes in the west which have been fuelled by NRR? If so, this would imply economic efficiency. Unfortunately, additional regressions provided by the authors do not help the reader to resolve the degree of intercorrelation between NRR, employment growth and incomes. This question will be evaluated in our empirical work.

Relative Importance of Variables

An advantage of the studies reviewed above is that the measurement and representation of dependent and independent variables follows a set of relatively standardized procedures. If each study was identical in sample quality, level of data aggregation, and types of explanatory variables, it would be possible to rank the relative importance of their findings on the determinants of migration using rigorous criteria. For example, we might ask the following. Which explanatory variable(s) consistently exhibits the expected sign as dictated by theory? Second, is the variable(s) consistently statistically significant at acceptable levels (eg., .01 level)?[10] Third, does the variable(s) demonstrate a reasonably stable elasticity in aggregate studies – in disaggregated studies? Fourth, if a variable(s) demonstrates the expected sign at statistically significant levels, does it continue to do so when data are examined for different geographical units (eg., regions versus provinces) or for different socio-economic subgroups (eg., educational subgroups)? Fifth, if two or more explanatory variables meet the criteria above, which accounts for the largest share of the variation in migration rates. (eg., contribution to R^2)?

Of course, the studies reviewed throughout this chapter do differ considerably in methodology and model specification. This means that judgments concerning relative importance of social and economic variables cannot pretend to be rigorous. At best, the variables listed below satisfy, in a general way, most of the criteria noted above.

Distance: Of all variables evaluated in studies of interprovincial migration in Canada, only "distance" between provinces of origin and destination performs well in terms of all the criteria above. Measures of distance consistently exhibit expected negative effects and they do so at levels of statistical significance which are superior to all other variables considered. In addition, regression coefficients on distance exhibit relatively stable elasticities (ie., approximately -1.0 to -1.3 in aggregate studies). Distance variables also appear to make a relatively large, if not the largest contribution to R^2.

Language/Ethnicity: Variables representing differences in language or French/English ethnicity between provinces of origin and destination consistently exhibit a statistically significant negative effect on interprovincial migration. They capture the fact that rates of migration to and from Québec to all other provinces are generally lower than migration among provinces of English language/culture. Most studies represent the French/English dichotomy as a "dummy" variable where migration flows to and from Québec are assigned a "1" versus "0" for all others. While it is difficult to establish the contribution of this influence to R^2, it is clearly far less important than distance.

Measures of Self-selection: Micro or panel data tell us that migration from places declines with age and family size, and increases with level of education. Because variations in age or family size tend to be small across provinces, self-selection considerations in aggregate studies are usually represented by education alone. In general, the evidence suggests that the higher the proportion of, say, university graduates in a provincial population, the higher the level of out-migration is likely to be (as expected).

Income or Wage Differentials: In terms of consistency of expected sign and levels of statistical significance, income effects would appear to take fourth place after distance, language/ethnicity and educational self-selection. In terms of contribution to R^2, income effects would appear to be second only to distance. An important qualification, however, is that it is the level of income at places of destination that almost always exhibit expected positive effects at highly significant levels. Several studies report elasticities ranging 2.0 to 3.5 on destination income. In contrast, regression coefficients on income at places of origin are usually much smaller. Often they border on being statistically insignificant and in some cases they do not even exhibit the expected negative sign.

Fiscal Variables: "Federal Government Equalization Payments to Provinces" and "Unemployment Transfer Payments to Persons" often exhibit the expected negative effect on out-migration from provinces, at statistically significant levels. This variable would appear to be significant in aggregate studies because it exhibits a strong negative effect on migration from the Atlantic provinces to other provinces. In contrast, "Natural Resource Rents" (eg., from oil in Alberta) often exhibits the expected positive effect on in-migration to provinces in aggregate studies because it exhibits a strong pull on migration to Alberta and British Columbia. Overall, elasticities or contributions to R^2 are difficult to gauge as both variables perform differently in terms of expected sign and significance. That is, performance depends on how provinces or migrants are grouped (eg., by regions, by levels of income). Measured thus, fiscal variables should be construed as "promising variables" which merit further evaluation.

Unemployment: Unemployment measures, at both province of origin and destination, perform poorly in terms of consistency of expected sign, statistical significance, and stability of regression coefficients. When they are evaluated as independent influences on migration, researchers invariably spend considerable effort trying to reconcile the unexpected findings with theory. If unemployment variables are to be included at all, origin unemployment, not destination unemployment would seem to be the relevant variable.

Population Scalars: Some studies, while normalizing migration (M_{ij}) by the origin population (P_i), have included population of the destination province (P_j) as an explanatory variable. As such, P_j is included to represent the size or "visibility" of distant labour markets. Sometimes P_j exhibits a positive sign (as expected) at statistically significant levels. When it does so, it usually boosts the R^2 value. The problem with variables such as P_j, however, is that they are often intercorrelated with other explanatory variables such as incomes. Thus, their inclusion in a migration function runs the risk of biasing the estimation of other coefficients that have clear theoretical interpretations.[11] If P_j is to be retained for its possible "scalar" or informational effects, a system of simultaneous equations will have to be estimated to eliminate interactive effects with other explanatory variables.

Finally, it is reasonable to assume that measures of distance, wage differentials, language/ethnicity, educational selectivity and fiscal structure would combine to account for a reasonable share of the statistical variation in place-to-place migration rates in Canada. In this context, an $R^2 = .50$ might be thought of as "respectable". However, levels of R^2 should not be used as an indicator of success alone. They should be judged in conjunction with (i) the correspondence between empirical results and theoretical expectation, (ii) levels of significance for each explanatory variable, and (iii) tests assuring that residuals are normally distributed.

Some of the studies reviewed above claim extremely high levels of "explanatory" success. Winer and Gauthier (1983), for example, seldom report R^2 values of less than .80, and frequently report R^2 values in excess of .90. Again, however, it is important to judge such findings in terms of the overall theoretical and statistical significance of the independent variables involved. Results in Winer and Gauthier's Table 4.10 serve as a good example. Their equation 'X' for the "PNT group" contains 12 independent variables and is performed on only 63 observations. It reveals four statistically significant variables at the .01 level, and produces an $R^2 = .786$. The same equation for the "All Group", performed again on 67 observations has only one significant variable. Yet, it retains an $R^2 = .740$. The message for students of migration and policy-makers attempting to interpret the significance of such results is: Beware!

Conclusion

Our interest in metropolitan migration cannot afford to ignore the many methodological directives, theoretical insights and empirical findings which have been spawned by past econometric inquiry. Our review of the literature has taught us that simple model specifications of a decade or so ago are no longer tenable. It is important to be cognizant of such problems as "aggregation bias" or assumptions inherent in symmetrical models. (See the Appendix to Chapter 4 for elaboration.) We have also come to appreciate that strict adherence to the macro-labour adjustment model or the human capital investment model is no longer defensible. Contentious findings have placed too many essential assumptions into question. (See the Appendix to Chapter 2 for elaboration on the human capital model.) And, we have come to suspect that the days of confident policy prescription are a long way off. Students of migration may be inching toward consensus on some determinants of migration, but they must also concede that today's "consensus" is riddled with qualification.

Emphasis, of course, has been on economic models and statistical evaluation. The reason is simply that statistical models are required to evaluate the *relative* importance of determinants of place-to-place migration, and economists have dominated this line of inquiry. Surprisingly little modelling work of this nature has been undertaken in other social sciences because non-pecuniary variables including cultural values and ideological motivations are so difficult to quantify.

Returning full-swing to Courchene's claim that "migration is an economic event", there can be no doubt that economic variables are important. How important? It is difficult to say. In a relatively rich country such as Canada, there are many indications that economic pressures on individuals have let up by virtue of higher levels of individual earnings and in the presence of national security programs (eg., welfare, unemployment insurance). Such information should be borne strongly in mind when drawing inferences from models which purport to "explain" large shares of the variance in migration rates in terms of economic variables alone (ie., R^2 of .80 to .90). Coefficients on several economic variables may be highly significant but the jump from a "significant coefficient" to a workable policy intervention may be light-years apart. We shall have more to say about such issues as we reflect on our own empirical results in Chapter 6.

Footnotes

1. The term "econometric literature" is used loosely to encompass studies which perform evaluations of models containing economic variables and employing regression-type statistical analysis.

2. The theory of rational expectations as it involves time, information and uncertainty in decision-making is reviewed in Kantor (1979), Nelson and Winter (1983).

3. Econometric analysis of place-to-place migration requires that migrants be identified according to their place of past residence as well as their place of current residence. The Census of Canada provides "five-year" migration data for all persons who moved during a five-year period preceding the day of census. Other sources of migration data include federal taxation files, unemployment insurance data, and family allowance transfer data collected by the Department of National Health and Welfare. These sources allow researchers to construct one-year migration flow matrices between provinces of known origin and destination. The one-year matrices are often pooled over several years to produce large data sets. Accordingly, the dependent variable in most econometric studies is a five-year or a one-year rate of place-to-place migration. (See Chapter 4 for elaboration.)

    Having identified flows between each origin 'i' and destination 'j', place-to-place migration studies then require information on socio-economic characteristics of each place 'i' and 'j' (ie., independent or explanatory variables). The objective is to account for variation in the size of migration flows between places 'i' and 'j' in terms of differences in characteristics between place 'i' and 'j' (eg., wage rates), or, the distance separating them. When selecting information on origin and destination variables, appropriate attention must be paid to relevant time frames. For example, if migration from 'i' to 'j' over a five-year period is expected to be influenced by, say, wage rates at 'i' or 'j', it would not be appropriate to measure wage levels at the end or even at the middle of the migration period. Why? Because wage levels at the end of the period are likely to have been influenced by migration itself. Accordingly, the line of causality will be obscured. Usually researchers dealing with one- or five-year migration data measure origin and destination characteristics at the beginning of the migration period. In econometric jargon, this helps to minimize "simultaneous equation bias" (see the Appendix to Chapter 4).

4. This definition of M_{ij} is used in most studies reviewed in this chapter. In our own empirical work, however, we modify this definition of M_{ij} (see the Appendix to Chapter 4, p. 183-5).

5. In regression equations the symmetry assumption is in play if variables are evaluated in ratio format; wage 'j' divided by wage 'i', or log (wage 'j' divided by wage 'i'); see Appendix to Chapter 4.

6. See Lansing and Mueller (1967), Yezer and Thurston (1976).

7. The relevance of this problem for modelling migration can be stated thus. Suppose that individuals who become "movers" are "self-selected" in the sense that they are higher-income earners or more dynamic economic agents in the population. If this were the case, it would not be appropriate to evaluate their economic incentives to migrate in terms of the *average* incomes of all people at their places of residence versus the average incomes of all people at alternative or competing places. Moreover, it would not be appropriate to evaluate their *returns* to migration by comparing their income after they move with the average income of unlike individuals who stay behind (ie., possibly less dynamic people). This would tend to overstate

their income gains from migration. Rather, meaningful evaluation of the influence of income on the migration decision of the "self-selected" would require comparison of (1) an estimate of their *actual* income *previous* to their move, (or what they would earn were they not to move), specific to levels of education, work experience, etc., versus (2) an estimate of the actual income accruing to migrants with the same characteristics who now reside at alternative or competing destinations. In effect this is the comparison that Robinson and Tomes set out to make. And in doing so, they provide a more rigorous test of the response of a "typical" migrant to expected income differentials.

8. Farber (1983) makes the point that family size may be a good proxy for "risk aversion".

9. As if in support of "horizontal fiscal balance", Polèse (1981) makes yet another significant point concerning unrestricted migration. He maintains that migrants embody not only labour but also other sources of growth such as capital, education and "advances in knowledge", not to mention their possible effects on scale economies. He also suspects that migrants embody these sources for growth at a proportionately higher level than the population of in-migration regions. If so, then over a given period, in-migrants will raise the per capita income of that region and increase the disparity gap relative to the sending region (if that region has a lower per capita income). With this in mind, Polèse submits that state transfer payment schemes, which may in fact discourage people from moving, may not be as detrimental to regional economic disparities as "Courchene-type arguments" maintain.

10. Decision rules concerning statistical significance and their interpretation in cross-sectional migration studies are elaborated in Chapter 4, footnote 2.

11. When I submit that P_j may bias the estimation of other coefficients (ie., a downward bias), I am thinking about the strong positive correlation between wage rates and city size which has been observed in several countries. However, the point could be made that by excluding P_j, coefficients on, say, wages might be biased in the other direction. That is, they might appear more important than they truly are. Vanderkamp (1977), for example, has argued that the P_j variable may represent a kind of labour turnover concept. In a personal communication, he further maintains "P_j could play a legitimate behavioural role; for example, consider the choice faced by a potential migrant in London (Ontario), between Windsor and Toronto, which are roughly equi-distant destinations. Would not the size of the Toronto labour market make that a more attractive destination than Windsor, all other things equal? The argument for including P_j may be stronger in the context of CMA-migration since the size variable refers more specifically to a labour market. The only way to judge the importance of P_j (and any possible bias effects) is to include it in the empirical model. . . ." I am inclined to agree with this interpretation but with the caveat that if P_j is to be included in a migration model then (a) its intended role should be specified much more clearly than it usually is, and (b) its interactive effects with other explanatory variables should be eliminated by estimating a system of simultaneous equations.

Chapter 3
Theory, Hypotheses and Variables

Introduction

The performance of economic variables in studies of migration leaves little doubt that a viable model of intermetropolitan migration should be constructed on a solid economic foundation. In keeping with our review of 'Appropriate Theory' in Chapter 2, we plan to treat migration as a form of individual optimizing behaviour within a *broadly conceived* cost/benefit framework. Guiding premises in the application of this framework are that man is rational; that he/she seeks to maximize his/her pecuniary and non-pecuniary well-being; that objectively measured differences between places convey information that is relevant to migration decision-making; and that – subject to information constraints – individuals will perceive and evaluate the desirability of "competing" places on this basis.

Within the cost/benefit framework, rationale will be provided and hypotheses will be formulated about the influence on migration of:

1) labour market conditions – wages, jobs, unemployment,

2) the business cycle – residential building,

3) fiscal sector variables – unemployment insurance transfer payments, government equalization payments, government revenues from natural resources,

4) additional economic considerations – housing costs, home ownership, dual income-earning households, impact of immigrants on consumption and production,

5) fixed and psychic costs of relocation, and information – distance between places, shared language,

6) social or amenity considerations – crime, climate,

7) selectivity considerations – age and educational attainment.

Since we intend to consider a large number of variables, it will be helpful to communicate the following about our "research strategy". First, our approach to selecting explanatory variables is more eclectic than would be possible were we to employ a tighter analytical framework. Some of our hypotheses, therefore, are framed in a looser, exploratory fashion, somewhat in the tradition of earlier studies of migration. This approach will allow us to test or retest the relevance of selected variables that otherwise might be excluded from consideration on the grounds that (i) they fall outside the domain of a more narrowly focused model, or (ii) they have been shown to be insignificant in other migration contexts. Such testing and retesting is important because this is the first study of the determinants of intermetropolitan migration in Canada and empirical precedents have yet to be clearly established.

Second, when we test hypotheses in later chapters we will proceed in "building block" fashion. Under clearly stated assumptions, explanatory variables will be added to a basic economic model to produce more complete or complex models. In the process, some explanatory variables will be eliminated from consideration. We do not intend, therefore, to test all of the hypotheses formulated in this chapter by estimating only *one* empirical function. Such a procedure would run the risk of hopelessly confounding the effects of possibly interrelated variables.

Third, details concerning the functional form of our empirical model or the exact nature of our migration measure will not be taken up until Chapter 4, and particularly in the Appendix to Chapter 4. These are methodological issues. They should not be confused with the task at hand which is to sketch out a generalized cost/benefit model. And on this note, permit me to forewarn that while migration models today

may appear similar to those of "days gone by", theoretical underpinnings have changed a great deal. Migration theory has become increasingly reflective, if not wiser. Accordingly, we attempt to elaborate rather
fully the rationale behind our model and selection of variables.

A Generalized Cost/Benefit Framework

From the potential migrant's standpoint, *voluntary* migration can be construed as a form of optimizing behaviour. Potential migrants will attempt
to optimize their overall quality of life (Q) in terms of expected economic,
social, political and environmental conditions. Limiting our discussion
to voluntary moves by *civilians* among a set of *unrestricted* destinations
'j', this optimizing behaviour can be represented formally as follows;

1) $0 < P(M_{ij}) \leq 1.0$, if and only if,

2) $IU_j(t) - IU_i(t) > 0$, with,

3) $IU_j = \int_{t=0}^{n} Q_j(t)e^{-rt} \, dt - C,$

4) $IU_i = \int_{t=0}^{n} Q_i(t)e^{-rt} \, dt,$

where; $P(M_{ij})_t =$ probability of migrating from place 'i' to 'j' at time 't';
IU_j, IU_i = the individual's discounted utility streams at place 'j' and 'i';
Q_j, Q_i = overall quality of life that exists or is expected at 'i' or 'j'; r
= discount factor reflecting the degree of consumption time preference
for the typical individual (eg., household head); C = initial fixed cost
of migration relocation.

Equations (1) and (2) tell us that the probability of migrating from
place 'i' to 'j' will be greater than '0' if and only if the overall utility to

residing at place 'j' (IU_j) exceeds that to remaining in 'i' (IU_i). Equations (3) and (4) provide *general* information on how IU is measured. Equation (3) tells us that the expected utility to residing at place 'j' (IU_j) depends on some composite measure of the "quality of life" (Q) at place 'j', minus the initial fixed cost of migration and relocation (C). Equation (4) tells us what the expected utility to remaining at place 'i' would be were the potential migrant to remain. Subtracting equation (3), which includes costs of migration, from equation (4) tells us whether the net outcome of leaving place 'i' or 'j' would exceed zero. If so, individuals at place 'i' are predicted to be favourably disposed to migrating.

Note that equations (3) and (4) introduce a time factor by which Q_j and Q_i are summed over years 'n' and then discounted by an appropriate rate of interest 'r'. This means that the model explicitly recognizes that potential migrants are likely to take a long-run view of the benefits to moving to place 'j' versus staying at 'i'. Were this not so, some might never migrate.[1]

Equations (1) through (4) represent a generalized cost/benefit framework in the sense that potential migrants are expected to assess differences in the quality of life (Q_j versus Q_i) in terms of a *broad* composite of several interdependent socio-economic components. A comprehensive measure of Q would take into consideration (i) levels of income, growth of employment, or prospects for economic growth stemming from the availability of natural resources, technology, etc., (ii) general living conditions such as the cost of living, climate and crime rates, and (iii) conditions bearing on individual opportunities including availability of schooling for children, opportunities for females in the labour market, racial discrimination, etc. A comprehensive measure of the cost component (C) would take into consideration monetary costs of moving (eg., airfare and transportation of household effects), as well as psychic costs (eg., pertaining to the move itself and readjustment to new locations).

The framework above represents no more than a starting point. First, it requires filling out in terms of specific variables thought to figure in the migrant's utility calculus. Selection of appropriate variables should be dictated by theory or by empirical precedent such as has been established in our review of the literature in Chapter 2.

Second the framework above does not tell us which variables are likely to be more important than others in the migrant's utility calculus. Traditional economic variables such as wages and job opportunities will certainly play an important role. But to proceed on the assumption that migration is only an economic event would be to ignore a provocative literature claiming that non-economic or quality-of-life variables are the prime movers.[2]

Third, the model above does not tell us how migratory individuals will be if $IU_j > IU_i$. We are informed only that the motivation or propensity to migrate will exceed '0'. One implication is that some people may be more stationary or inert than others in the face of *identical* opportunities. We are referring here to the propensity of migration to be "selective" of younger, more dynamic elements of the population. Implications of a changing age structure for the determinants of migration are also relevant here (eg., growth of retirement migration).

Fourth, the model implied above does not address several micro-aspects of the decision-making process. Are opportunities $X_i. . . X_n$ perceived and evaluated in exact terms or in a lagged or distorted way? Are they perceived in multiplicative or additive fashion involving an acceptable "threshold" combination of, say, incomes plus jobs plus housing, plus environment, etc. Some studies of migration choose not to specify explicit decision-making functions, though it would seem desirable to evaluate alternative forms whenever possible.[3]

Finally, the model implied above pays little attention to the possibility that tastes may have changed over time (eg., marginal utility of income). The same applies to the influence of "non-traditional" variables in the decision to migrate. When such influences derive from, say, public policy intervention they may compete with more traditional variables in the migrant's utility calculus (eg., differential wage rates). Recall from Chapter 1 that the major hypothesis running throughout this study is that the influence of traditional labour market variables on migration is undergoing change. On the one hand, improvements in productivity, labour-saving technology, and higher standards of living may be prompting the pursuit of leisure activities to the extent that earnings differentials per se figure less in the migrant's utility calculus. In addition, segmented labour markets, firm-specific training, unions, and professional licensing may be dampening the responsiveness of potential migrants to perceived earnings differentials.[4] On the other hand, fiscal or social security programs may be cushioning the effects of, say, unemployment on earnings, thereby reducing pressure on individuals to migrate for income reasons alone. Such developments may not only diminish the influence of labour market variables per se on migration, they may subtract from the range of options open to policy-makers to influence migration.

With the above in mind, let us begin to fill out our generalized cost/benefit model with an appropriate labour market component.

Representing the Labour Market

Labour market studies of migration often reduce the model implied by equations (1) through (4) to the extent that it focuses *exclusively* on monetized economic components of Q. For example, Sjaastad's (1962) human investment theory expressed the present value (PV) of net expected benefits to migration $(IU_j - IU_i)$, simply in terms of differential wages (W) and costs of relocation (C), as follows:

$$5) \quad PV = \int_{t=0}^{n} W_j(t)e^{-rt} - C_{ij} \quad - \int_{t=0}^{n} W_i(t)e^{-rt} ,$$

whereas, Laber and Chase (1971) operationalized (5) in their study of interprovincial migration as;

$$6) \quad PV = (W_j - W_i)/r - C_{ij},$$

where; in empirical testing, the discount factor 'r' typically drops out under the assumption that it is relatively constant across regions; and where C_{ij} is almost always represented by distance in miles between places.

Models in the spirit of (5) and (6) were originally formulated without regard to other labour market variables such as growth of jobs or employment. Rationale for *not* considering employment or unemployment stems from the assumption that markets are perfectly competitive (including perfect information). Wage rates were assumed to adjust upward to reflect a shortage of labour growth (or job vacancies) or downward to reflect an oversupply of labour (involuntary unemployment). Thus, differences between labour markets in the present discounted value of lifetime earnings (PV), were considered to be the prime determinants of labour force mobility.

We now know that labour markets *do not* perform according to the assumptions above. Countless examples of imperfections exist. These involve limited or incorrect information, rigidities in wage rates, or institutional and occupational barriers to certain jobs (eg., professional licensing, union barriers).[5] Many of these imperfections have been taken up in the context of "dual" or "segmented labour market" theory.[6] While such theories have not, as yet, received conclusive proof, they are valuable for their realistic description of many facets of the labour market which depart from simplifying assumptions of classical economics. In short, they imply rejection of the assumption that the labour market resembles a bourse; that it functions as a place where buyers and sellers meet to transact their business and where all vacancies in the economy are continually open to all workers on the same terms and conditions (see Chapter 2, "Appropriate Theory").[7]

The relevant point for the development of our model then, is that unemployment and job vacancies are likely to exist side-by-side with high wage rates to the extent that they will exert independent effects on the migrant's utility calculus.[8] Thus, we provide at least one rationale for considering income opportunities in conjunction with employment opportunities (including risk of unemployment). This point will be taken up again in the process of expanding on our employment variables.

Income Opportunities/Wage Variants

To evaluate the influence of income per se on intermetropolitan migration we have constructed four alternative wage variants (W). Each differs in terms of information that has been entered in multiplicative fashion. Only one will be retained after preliminary testing (ie., to be undertaken in Chapter 4).

Wage measures are preferable over, say, median family income for three reasons. First, wages should be more sensitive to short-run economic conditions since variations in average hours are accounted for, and non-wage income is excluded. Second, as demonstrated by Grant and Vanderkamp (1976), coefficients on wage income are likely to be larger and more significant than on other income components such as self-employment or other income (see Chapter 2). Third, use of median family income data from, say, census sources would require interpolation over long periods of time (eg., between 1971 and 1981).

Our first wage variant (W1) contains no adjustment for, say, cost of living differentials between places or the possibility of unemployment upon arrival at a new destination. It assumes that differentials in average actual wage levels (W) adequately portray the present value of expected net earnings gains to migration;

7) $W1_j = \overline{W}_j$

(if: $W1_j - C > W1_i$, then $P(M_{ij}) > 0$.

Our second wage variant (W2) assumes that migrants adjust the average or nominal wage at place 'i' and 'j' by expected cost of living differentials (CPI), to arrive at real earnings differentials. Whether migrants, in fact, consider real income is the subject of ongoing debate in several studies of migration in the United States.[9]

8) $W2_j = \overline{W}_j/CPI$

if: $W2_j - C_{ij} > W2_i$, then $P(M_{ij}) > 0$.

Our third wage variant (W3) adjusts W2 for the probability of being unemployed (U) while either at place 'i' or upon arrival at place 'j'. Thus, nominal wages are further adjusted to derive an "expected wage";

9) $W3_j = (1 - U) (\overline{W}_j)/CPI$

(if: $W3_j - C_{ij} > W3_i$, then $P(M_{ij}) > 0$.

This version is used by Laber and Chase (1970). In combination with C_{ij}, it accounted for some 50-60% of interregional migration in Canada. It builds on the important work of Michael Todaro, where wages – adjusted for the probability of unemployment – have been shown to outperform simpler wage models in several less developed countries.[10] To some extent, wage variants adjusted for unemployment have also been shown to be superior to simpler wage models in developed countries.[11]

Our final wage variant (W4) adjusts W3 for the likelihood that (i) unemployed persons receive unemployment insurance compensation (UI), and (ii) that UI benefits differ between places. Availability of unemployment insurance may alter the performance of wage differentials in the sense that a "public" influence is imposed on the "private" operation of the labour market. Say, for example, that $W_j = W_i$ but that unemployment at place 'j' is 0% whereas it is 50% at place 'i'. Equation (9) would lead us to believe that individuals would be strongly motivated to migrate to 'j' given that $[W_j > W_i (1 - .50)]$. In a world of unemployment insurance, however, the impact of 50% unemployment on earnings will be substantially buffered through unemployment insurance payments;

10) $W4_j = [(1 - U) (\overline{W} \cdot T') / CPI]_j - [U(UI^* \cdot T'') / CPI]_j$

if: $W4_j - C_{ij} > W4_i$, then $P(M_{ij}) > 0$

where; T' = average total weeks worked per year; T'' = average total weeks that UI benefits may be collected; UI^* = average weekly payment of UI benefits. This type of wage variant is discussed at length in Winer and Gauthier's (1983) study of interprovincial migration though it is not evaluated in their empirical work.[12]

Which is the preferred wage variant? If potential migrants are sufficiently informed to perform intricate calculations and if they do so in multiplicative fashion, then a more complex wage variant such as W3 or W4 may be appropriate.[13] If, on the other hand, potential migrants know little of cost of living differentials (eg., insufficient information), if they are ill-informed about their chances of unemployment at alternative labour markets, or if they do not adjust incomes in the fashion indicated by equations (8) through (10), then wage variant W1 might well suffice. Our preference is for a simpler wage variant such as W1 if only because equations such as (8) and (10) may involve unrealistic assumptions concerning the availability of required information.

The discussion above lends itself to four testable hypotheses:

Hypothesis 1:
The greater the differential between city 'j' and 'i' in earnings ($WAGE_j > WAGE_i$), the greater the probability of migrating from 'i' to 'j' (M_{ij}) will be.

Hypothesis 2:
Asymmetry will be evident in the impact of origin and destination earnings (WAGE) on M_{ij} for reasons given in Chapter 2.

Core Hypothesis 3:
Earnings considerations (WAGE) will exert a smaller impact on M_{ij} "today" than in the past.

Hypothesis 4:
Simple wage variants (WAGE1 vs WAGE4) are likely to represent the present value of expected net earnings benefits to migration as well as more complex multiplicative variants.

In our empirical work, WAGE is represented as the average "industrial" weekly wage and salary of Census Metropolitan Areas (CMA's), at the beginning of the migration period under study. WAGE is based on an industrial composite of enterprises with 20 or more employees. Definitional details on WAGE and all variables in equations (8) and (9) are presented in Appendix 1 to Chapter 3. *This appendix provides measurement and source details on all empirical variables in this study.*

Job Opportunities

If Hypothesis 4 were confirmed, this would not necessarily imply that potential migrants ignore the probability of unemployment or the availability of unemployment insurance. It might only convey that they do not perform intricate adjustments to their earnings expectations in multiplicative fashion. Possibly, migrants are "risk averse", implying that an increase in job probability (or reduced unemployment probability), may weigh more heavily than an equivalent increase in wage rates.

If we consult the literature on intermetropolitan migration in the United States, we find that some authors maintain that employment variables exert a stronger influence on migration than do wages or incomes.[14] As Fields (1976, p.413) puts it, "This suggests. . . that it may be the availability of jobs, more than the incomes paid once in those jobs, which is the primary determinant of labour force migration". The idea that migrants may be risk averse represents yet another rationale for considering employment opportunities in conjunction with wage differentials in deterministic models of migration.

On the other side of the coin, however, many researchers report that measures of unemployment perform poorly in aggregate studies of migration (see Chapter 2). This pertains particularly to the effects of unemployment at places of origin. An oft-quoted conclusion by Greenwood (1975, p.411) sums up the dilemma thus; "One of the most perplexing problems confronting migration scholars is the lack of significance of local unemployment rates in explaining migration".

Why the poor performance of unemployment? First, it is important to recognize that average unemployment rates are comprised of many different individuals who experience unemployment for different lengths of time throughout the year. A 10% unemployment rate at place 'j', for example, does not necessarily imply that 10% of the labour force is hard pressed for work all of the time (ie., a chronic subgroup). Rather, unemployment is much like a "pool" fed by a large turnover of workers each year. For example, when unemployment in Canada averaged 11% in 1982, almost 30% of the labour force experienced *some* unemployment. Of these, a large majority spent less than three months without jobs. Such unemployment may not motivate migration directly, particularly among families with dual job-holders. A recent survey of unemployment in the United States, for example, revealed that 48% of all households with an unemployed husband contained an employed wife.[15] A recent survey of unemployment in Canada revealed that male family heads accounted for only 18% of the unemployed in families, whereas wives of the male head and dependent children or relatives accounted for 27% and 36%, respectively (Shaw:1985).

Second, average unemployment rates may be a highly imperfect index of the tightness or looseness of alternative labour markets. Local unemployment rates, for example, tend to be erratic over time (due to temporary layoffs) and may understate numbers of workers searching for jobs (so-called "discouraged workers" who are not included in official unemployment rates). Moreover, as Fields (1976) maintains, migrants are likely to be more concerned about turnover in the labour market; thus, they are likely to be more attentive of the rate at which hiring for new jobs is taking place.

Third, the unemployed have been described as workers who ordinarily might not consider migration as one of their options. This description derives from important survey work by Lansing and Mueller (1967). They speculate that the relatively low level of educational attainment of the unemployed suggests that such individuals might be less aware of, or responsive to, alternative employment opportunities elsewhere.[16]

In addition to the above, recall that unemployment insurance is expected to buffer the effect that unemployment will exert on individual earnings. As Courchene (1970) observes, a high unemployment rate at place 'i' may suggest that the unemployed should be feeling pressure to "move out", but the availability of unemployment insurance is likely to act, simultaneously, as a retainer.

The discussion above leads to the following hypotheses:

Hypothesis 5:
The greater the differential between city 'j' and 'i', in the growth of new employment ($JOBS_j > JOBS_i$), the greater the probability of migration from 'i' to 'j' will be (M_{ij}).

Core Hypothesis 6:
Job considerations will exert a smaller effect on M_{ij} "today" than in the past.

Hypothesis 7:
High unemployment at city 'j' will deter in-migration and high unemployment at city 'i' will promote out-migration. The effects of unemployment at origin 'i', however, are likely to be obscured to the extent it will influence M_{ij} less than unemployment at destination 'j'.

In representing the effects of job opportunities (JOBS) on migration, we would have preferred using measures of "new hires", "layoffs" and "quits" as employed by Gary Fields (1979). However, for Canada, such data are not in adequate supply. Accordingly, employment opportunities are represented here by the growth of new jobs in industry. Our data derive from the same source as our measure of industrial wages and salaries. Not included in the employment growth data are new jobs in businesses hiring less than 20 employees, jobs in the health sector, in agriculture, in fisheries or in religious institutions. JOBS measures employment growth in establishments with 20 or more employees per thousand CMA labour force employed in establishments of 20 or more employees. JOBS is measured at the beginning of the migration period under study. See Appendix 1 to Chapter 3, for definitional details and data sources.

Unemployment (UNEMP) measures the number of unemployed males and females per thousand labour force of CMA's. UNEMP is measured at the beginning of the migration period under study. Appendix 1 to Chapter 3 provides definitional details and source details.

The Business Cycle

When Vanderkamp (1970) evaluated a simple wage/distance model using time-series data on interprovincial migration in Canada, he observed that the model worked better for some years than others. He attributed the difference to economic slack or a downturn in the business cycle.[17]

Information on business cycles may be relevant to the labour market component of our model for different reasons in different contexts. For example, were we to use time-series data in the absence of employment variables (as in Vanderkamp's study), information on business cycles might usefully reflect growth or decline in job opportunities. In contrast, if cross-section data are used for one period of time, again in the absence of employment variables, then information on business cycles may usefully reflect regional differences in growth or decline of job opportunities. For example, Chang (1976) reports that each region in Canada experienced the same number of major building cycles between 1951-70, but that the timing and the turning points of the cycles were quite different across regions. Finally, depending on how business cycles are measured, there are grounds for arguing that "business cycles" might usefully reflect jobs and related opportunities that are not "picked up" by usual measures of employment growth. Since we include both wage and job variables in our model, it is this last aspect of the business cycle that interests us most here.

Among the best indicators of the business cycle are new orders for durables, changes in inventory and housing starts. Our concern is with housing starts or the residential building cycle. Unlike the short-term business cycle, swings in residential construction cycles are at times violent, fluctuating anywhere from -9.0% to 21% over a three-year period (Chang:1976). Short-run fluctuations in residential construction are principally determined by the availability of credit, the builder's expected profit and government policies – especially monetary policy and those of federal housing authorities such as Canada Mortgage and Housing. And since tight money policy is usually in effect when business is expanding, while relatively easy money policy is usually in effect in periods of business recession, the mortgage loans and hence residential construction tend to be counter-cyclical to the business cycle.

How might differentials in residential building construction between places exert effects on migration that would not be "picked up" by variables measuring job opportunities associated with the general business cycle? Consider the situation of construction workers. Workers in construction comprise between 5-10% of Canada's labour force. In the absence of a continuous employer-employee relationship, except for key employees of larger firms, there is little opportunity for construction workers to build up seniority or job security. Instead (apart from unemployment insurance compensation), they must carry the full risks of discontinuous income alone or in conjunction with their own union local (Jenness:1975). Thus, construction workers fall into the category we have labelled "the secondary labour market" (see footnote 7 to this chapter). In response to differentials or swings in residential construction *per se*, they are quite mobile geographically. Jenness (1975) reports that more than half sampled from CMC registration had moved between labour markets in their last three jobs; 20% to 30% had moved between provinces.

In addition to the above, differences in residential construction tend to promote employment opportunities in economic subsectors that are often excluded in the derivation of standard employment growth indices. For example, the measure of employment growth used in this study is based on an industrial composite from statistics on companies employing 20 or more employees. Growth of residential construction, however, creates employment and income opportunities for smaller scale self-employed contractors, independent real estate agents, and a multitude of small-scale suppliers (roofers, plumbers, electricians, etc.).

Finally, greater residential construction activity at a place may be attractive to potential migrants in its own right. Not only does it convey that a place is undergoing expansion rather than decline, but the fact that builders anticipate profits suggests that the capital value of current housing stock is on the rise.

To my knowledge, the first study to systematically evaluate the effects of building activity on migration was undertaken by the author in the development of a large-scale urban simulation model in Canada.[18] Building construction, as measured by dwelling starts per thousand population *at the beginning* of the migration period, emerged as a highly significant variable in "explaining" rates of net internal migration and net migration of the foreign born to Census Metropolitan Areas. Subsequent work on migration flows in Canada as well as in several other countries confirms that building activity, as represented by dwelling starts, is a useful variable for accounting for variations in place-to-place migration flows.[19] Furthermore it is reasonable to assume that measures of residential construction will be relatively independent of migration over the short-run, because its short-run behaviour is likely to be influenced more by the availability of mortgage funds, interest rates, housing grants, vacancies, changes in the volume of construction activity, incomes and relative prices *prior* to the time of migration than at actual time of migration (Evans:1969, Chang:1976, Wilkinson et al.: 1976). This, of course, is important from the standpoint of minimizing "simultaneous equation bias" between residential construction and M_{ij} (see Appendix to Chapter 4).

The discussion above lends itself to the following hypotheses:

Hypothesis 8:
The greater the difference between city 'j' and 'i' in building cycles as represented by residential dwelling starts ($DS_j > DS_i$), the greater the probability of migration from 'i' to 'j' (M_{ij}).

Core Hypothesis 9:
DS will exert a smaller effect on M_{ij} "today" than in the past.

Our measure of building construction (DS) is represented as the number of residential dwelling starts per thousand Census Metropolitan Area's population, at the beginning of the migration period under study. See Appendix 1 to Chapter 3 for definitional details and data sources.

Fiscal Variables

Thus far, we have hypothesized that a number of "traditional" labour market variables (eg., wages, jobs), will exert a smaller impact on intermetropolitan migration "today" than in the past. Yet, confirmation of hypotheses concerning these variables would not necessarily imply confirmation of our more generally construed 'core hypothesis' (as described in Chapter 1). Rather, declining relevance of more traditional variables in recent times might only mean that individuals have undergone a change in "tastes". Income, for example, might matter less "now" because of diminishing marginal utility of money or because public goods are now preferred relative to private goods. Furthermore, if recent times were characterized by slowed economic growth and slack labour markets, and if these aspects of the business cycle *were not* controlled in empirical modelling, then smaller impacts of wage and job variables "today" might be no more than a transitional phenomenon due to adverse cyclical conditions.

An implication for the development of our model then, is that Hypotheses 3, 6 and 9 must be evaluated in conjunction with variables which lend themselves to a more precise 'core hypothesis' interpretation.

This follows from the assumption that a causal chain is operating in which (a) a number of "non-traditional" variables have been inspired by recent public policies aiming to enhance social security, (b) these variables are at least partly responsible for "crowding out" or tempering the influence of more "traditional" labour market variables on migration, and (c) potential migrants have reacted to these influences by adopting attitudinal changes to more traditional variables. If "non-traditional" variables can be shown to account for more of recent migration patterns, and if their growing impact goes hand-in-hand with diminishing effects of more traditional variables, then it would seem reasonable to maintain that a cause and effect relationship is in play.

The kinds of non-traditional variables that we have in mind include unemployment insurance and federal equalization grants, as well as recent policies affecting personal income taxes and national resource revenues. For the most part, these variables form the fiscal component of our model.

Unemployment Insurance

Since the 1971 revisions to the Unemployment Insurance Act, generosity of unemployment insurance (UI) in Canada has come to vary widely across provinces (see Figure 3.1). Following Courchene (1970), we propose that these differentials are influencing the response of the "average" unemployed worker to "pushes" and "pulls" in the labour market. This may be happening to the extent that were migration policies to attempt to reduce unemployment at place 'i' by boosting wages and job opportunities at 'j', they might be less effective in mobilizing unemployed workers "today" than in the past.

The idea that UI influences the response of workers to labour market opportunities follows from the theory of consumer choice between goods and leisure. If UI alters a worker's "income possibility frontier" or "budget constraint", it may alter his allocation of time between work and non-work activity. If it is sufficiently generous, it might also be leisure-inducing, it may raise the duration of unemployment spells by reducing pressure on job-search, and it may increase the "reservation wage" necessary to lure unemployed workers back into the labour market. (This point is elaborated more formally in Appendix 2 to Chapter 3.)

Figure 3.1: Total Federal Unemployment Insurance Transfer Payments to Persons in Provinces Per Thousand Dollars of Total Provincial Wage and Salary Income

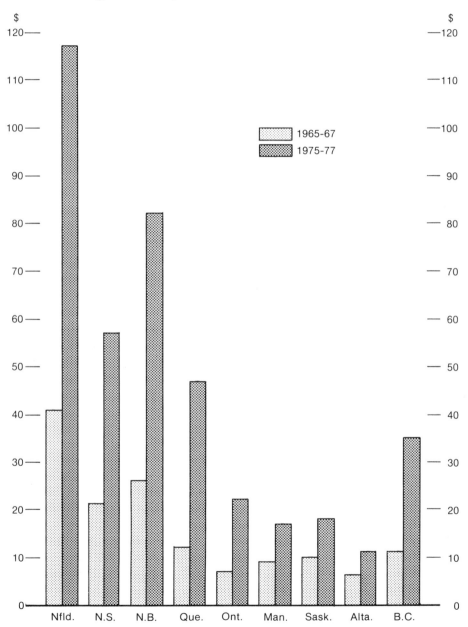

Fortin and Newton, (1982) review several studies to conclude that the 1971 revision to the Unemployment Insurance Act raised the official unemployment rate by an amount ranging from .7 to 2.0 percentage points. In contrast, they point out that changes in unemployment insurance in the United States, where benefits are appreciably less, have increased the aggregate unemployment rate by no more than .25 percentage points. Regional differentials in the effects of the 1971 UI revisions are also evident. Maki (1979), for example reports increases in unemployment rates of .2 percentage points in Ontario to 1.6 percentage points in the Atlantic provinces. British Columbia, Québec and the Prairie provinces fall in between at .8 to 1.1 percentage points. Finally, a study by Beach and Kaliski, (1983) reports that amendments to Canada's unemployment insurance program in 1979 – which slightly reduced UI generosity – had the effect of reducing the duration of unemployment among prime age males.[20]

Turning to the effects of unemployment insurance on labour mobility per se, our review of the Canadian literature (Chapter 2), conveys that UI affects migration, particularly from the Atlantic provinces. Evidence for the United States, however, does not lend itself to clear conclusions about the effects of UI. One of the few studies to examine the relationship has been conducted by Fields (1979) on intermetropolitan migration. He reports that a variable measuring the *amount* of UI benefits exhibits a statistically significant positive effect at destination, as hypothesized. It does not, however, exhibit the expected negative effect at origin. An additional variable measuring the availability of UI exhibits a statistically significant negative effect at origin, as expected, but assumes a statistically significant unexpected effect at place of destination. In view of these findings, Fields concludes that the amount or availability of UI may have some effect on migration but that the results raise as many questions as answers.[21]

Our view is that unemployment insurance considerations are likely to be more important to place-to-place migration in Canada than in the U.S. because the level and duration of Canadian UI is far greater. After the 1971 revision to Canada's Unemployment Insurance Act, the after-tax wage-replacement ratio increased from approximately 66% to 90% for individuals earning the average industrial wage or less. Fortin et al. (1982) constructed "indices" to show that the "wage subsidy for unstable unemployment" in Canada ranges from 72% to 302% in 1981, with an observed average of 180%. By comparison, in the United States, even when federally extended benefits are taken into account, the authors calculate that the approximate range for the subsidy is 42% to 146%, with a median of about 63%.

Now, given that the effects of unemployment insurance, (UI), on migration may not be adequately represented by wage variable W4 (see Hypothesis 5), we shall consider its independent effects as follows:

Hypothesis 10:
The greater the difference between 'i' and 'j' in the generosity and ease of obtaining unemployment insurance benefits ($UI_j > UI_i$), the less the probability of migrating from 'i' to 'j' will be (M_{ij}).

Hypothesis 11:
Asymmetry will be evident in the effect of origin and destination UI on M_{ij} as availability of unemployment insurance at origin 'i' may also facilitate M_{ij} by providing financing for relocation.

Core Hypothesis 12:
UI benefits will serve to dampen M_{ij} more after the generous 1971 revisions to Canada's Unemployment Insurance Act.

Generosity and availability of UI are represented by two measures. Generosity is represented as the average weekly UI benefit to wage ratio (UIGEN). This measure is identical to that used by Fields (1979) and Winer and Gauthier (1983). Availability is represented as the probability of receiving UI if unemployed (UIPROB). This measure parallels that used by Fields (1979). Complete definitional details and data sources are provided in Appendix 1 to Chapter 3.

Equalization and Related Payments to Provinces

The equity:efficiency debate reviewed in Chapters 1 and 2 places considerable emphasis on the possible effects of fiscal transfers on migration. Recall that Courchene (1970), and more recently Winer and Gauthier (1983), report evidence consistent with the argument that (1) fiscal transfers retard emigration from the Atlantic provinces, and (2) this may reduce the efficient allocation of workers to their place of best competitive advantage.

If we think of equalization and related transfers as including welfare payments, then we can also point to several studies on migration in the United States which conclude that "welfare and assistance payments" exert expected effects on both in- and out-migration. Of course, there are qualifications galore. Cebula (1979) reviews the literature to show that such variables are more likely to be relevant to the migration of blacks than whites, to the poor than the relatively wealthy.

Unlike unemployment insurance payments, federal equalization and related transfers in Canada go to relatively disadvantaged provinces, not persons (see Figure 3.2). Thus, governments of resource poor provinces are likely to allocate the transferred funds in ways that will enhance public utilities (eg., highways, schools), without placing an extra tax burden on their "resource poor" population. A potential problem with evaluating the effects of equalization payments etc., on migration is that assumptions of independence between such transfers and growth of employment and wages come into question. At the very least, equalization and related payments will create jobs in government as well as in a variety of contracting and service jobs to do with the functioning of public utilities. If such transfers create jobs that are as equally productive to Canada as elsewhere, then arguments about federal transfers reducing economic efficiency would lose ground.

With the above in mind, we formulate our hypotheses as follows;

Hypothesis 13:
The greater the difference between city 'j' and 'i', in access to federal government equalization and related transfers to provinces (GRANT$_j$ > GRANT$_i$), the greater the probability of migration from 'i' to 'j' will be (M$_{ij}$).

Core Hypothesis 14:
GRANT will have more of an effect on M$_{ij}$ after 1971, in view of increased allocations to eastern Canada.

Federal government equalization and related transfers to provinces (GRANT), are represented empirically as "general purpose transfers" or "unconditional grants", divided by the population of each province, at the beginning of the migration period under study. Values for GRANT have been assigned to cities according to the province they fall in. GRANT includes statutory subsidies, shares of federal income taxes on corporate undistributed income, shares of federal estate taxes, equalization payments

Figure 3.2: General Purpose Transfers: From the Federal to Provincial Governments Per Capita, 1971 Dollars

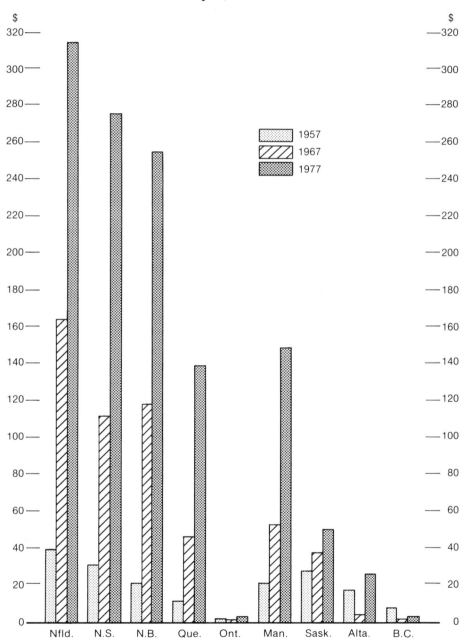

(the largest single component), established programs, and grants in lieu of taxes. See Appendix 1 to Chapter 3 for data sources. See also the Appendix to Chapter 4 "Data on Explanatory Variables" for a discussion of our use of province-wide empirical measures for CMA's.

Natural Resource Revenues

Recall that differentials in natural resource rents (NRR) could enhance the fiscal attractiveness of some cities more than others because provincial fiscal capacity is not balanced completely through federal taxation and equalization. This was taken up in Chapter 2 in our review of the equity: efficiency debate as well as findings by Winer and Gauthier (1983).

When we refer to NRR, we are particularly interested in the impact of post-1973 oil price-hikes on oil revenues, fiscal capacity and policy in Alberta. To appreciate the magnitudes involved, consider Figure 3.3 which depicts changes in per capita levels of NRR between 1970 and 1977. We are also interested in the possible effects of the Alberta Heritage Savings Trust Fund. Following the rapid increase in world energy prices in 1973, the Alberta government increased the level and quality of services provided to Albertans while maintaining the most favourable regime of corporate, personal and sales taxes in Canada. Perceiving that such "stimulative action" could set off unprecedented migration to Alberta, the government decided to save a portion of its non-renewable resource revenues (ie., oil-related). Thus, until recently, 30% of the province's annual non-renewable NRR has been transferred to the Fund. The aim of the Fund is to (i) reduce inflationary pressures and over-stimulative fiscal spending, (ii) generate savings for future generations of Albertans, and (iii) allow investment to provide a source of income (perhaps capital), that could be used in the future to supplement other government revenues.[22]

In the case of Alberta, expenditures and policies hinging on NRR in Alberta could have affected migration to its metropolitan areas in four different ways. First, "unchecked" spending on fiscal-related services in the "early" years may have exerted a positive, direct "pull" on migrants. Second, formation of the Heritage Fund (to check spending), may have resulted in investments which are exerting a positive, direct "pull" on migration for employment. For example, the Fund has undertaken investments to establish a high calibre medical research community. Third,

Figure 3.3: Natural Resource Revenues Per Capita, 1971 Dollars

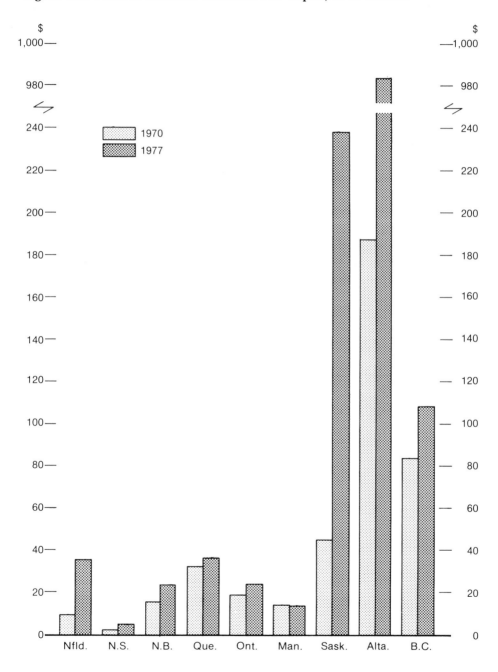

as capital accrues to the Fund, its potential as a stabilizing force in Alberta's economic growth over time, may exert a positive, indirect pull on migrants who perceive future benefits. Fourth, if the Fund results in a fiscal drag on the rest of the country, residents of other provinces may experience a positive, indirect "push" to move to Alberta.

Now, NRR could take on a 'core hypothesis' interpretation if inequities in provincial fiscal capacity were somehow to undermine the efficiency of the market mechanism to allocate labour to its best place of competitive advantage. Yet, there is no reason to suppose that the effects of NRR would not be widely felt through opportunities in the labour market as well. As Betcherman (1980) points out, the energy related "mega-projects" in the Canadian west are expected to make large demands for a variety of skilled occupations that are already in short supply across the country. If so, this would likely show up if NRR were evaluated simultaneously with JOB and WAGE variables; the coefficients on the latter would drop. This point was raised in a critique of Winer and Gauthier's (1983) results in Chapter 2.

In light of the above, we do not include NRR among our 'core hypothesis' variables; rather we qualify the hypothesized effects of NRR with a "disclaimer";

Hypothesis 15:
The greater the difference between city 'j' and 'i' in terms of its "home" province's natural resource revenues ($NRR_j > NRR_i$), the greater the probability of migration from 'i' to 'j' will be (M_{ij}). NRR is evaluated for post-1971 migration only.

Hypothesis 16:
NRR may not exert an independent effect on M_{ij} but may do so largely through its effects on labour market opportunities. This will show up if NRR is evaluated simultaneously with JOB and WAGE variables and the coefficients on the latter variables drop.

Our use and measurement of NRR is identical to that of Winer and Gauthier (1983). NRR is represented as the sum of provincial indirect taxes from the resource sector, and net profits of resource-related provincially owned Crown corporations per capita (ie., per provincial population), at the beginning of the migration period under study. Complete definitional details and data sources are provided in Appendix 1 to Chapter 3.

Additional Economic Considerations

Let us now consider a number of additional economic factors which may be relevant to understanding intermetropolitan migration in Canada. At this juncture our selection of variables becomes considerably more eclectic. Possibly, the best defence we can offer for considering them – aside from the economic rationale to be provided – is that most have not been evaluated previously in a Canadian context. In addition, two of the variables lend themselves to a 'core hypothesis' interpretation.

Home Ownership

Owners of homes tend to be less migratory than renters.[23] Investment in a large, bulky physical asset implies greater inertia if only because the asset must be liquidated prior to mobility (unless rented). Up to 1971, declining rates of home ownership in Canada might have implied that Canadians were at "greater risk" of mobility. Ownership of dwellings among highly migratory 25-34 year-olds was showing a decline from approximately 50% in 1961 to 42.8% in 1971. After 1971, however, ownership rates among 25-34 year-olds jumped almost 10% to 51.6% in 1976 and remained at 50.4% in 1981. Why the turnaround, and what might the implication for migration be?

There can be little doubt that the turnaround in ownership rates stems from the 1972 restructuring of Canada's tax system. Prior to 1972, tax incentives, rollover provisions and tax shelters were highly favourable to investments in rental housing. As Smith (1983) points out, this encouraged households to change their demand from home ownership to rental housing. After 1972, the situation changed dramatically. First, a capital gains tax was imposed on realized gains on all financial and real assets, except for a principal residence. Second, rollover provisions were terminated. Third, paper losses in real estate or investments in real estate as a tax shelter were eliminated. Fourth, part of the gain on real estate – excluding principal residence – became taxable.

Smith (1983) shows that the introduction of a capital gains tax on all assets – except the principal residence – conferred a substantial tax benefit on homeowners, since home ownership became the only vehicle by which a non-taxable capital gain could be realized. In addition, he argues that inflationary expectations increased the relative attractiveness of home ownership because it increased benefits of the exemption from capital gains tax and of the non-taxation of imputed net rent. The latter benefit rises because the increase in the imputed net rent arising from inflation is not taxed, while the increase in income necessary to pay the higher cost of equivalent housing is taxed.

Effects of the aforementioned tax revisions on the demand for housing are reflected in Table 3.1. Observe the jump in housing prices in 1973 and 1974 following the 1972 tax revisions (column 1). This reflects increased demand for existing housing stock. Observe also the drop in apartment starts (rental units) from 45.4% of all starts in 1971 to 32.7% in 1976 (column 2). Finally, observe that total dwelling starts minus apartment starts increased from about 127,000 in 1971 to 162,000 by 1973 and 183,000 by 1976. This increase corresponds roughly with the increased demand for new housing units.

If renters opted to become home owners in view of the 1972 tax revisions, their change in status would likely dampen their propensity to migrate. If present owners were motivated to hold onto their dwellings in view of inflationary expectations and attractive post-1972 price rises in housing, then their propensity to migrate may have declined as well. To my knowledge, the possible effects of tax-exempt housing on migration has not been previously evaluated. It leads to the following hypotheses:

Hypothesis 17:
The greater the incidence of home ownership (OWN) among younger people at place of origin 'i', the less the probability of migration from place 'i' to 'j' will be (M_{ij}).

Core Hypothesis 18:
OWN will exert a greater negative impact on post-1971 migration.

OWN is measured per thousand population of the Census Metropolitan Area specific to those in the age group 25-34 years. It is represented as an average rate over the migration period under study. This age group has been selected as (i) it is likely to be highly sensitive to housing market financial conditions – more so than, say, older more established individuals, and (ii) most 25-34 year-olds have taken up private residence as distinct from living with their parents. See Appendix 1 to Chapter 3 for definitional details and data sources.

TABLE 3.1: Changes in the Housing Market, 1970 - 83

	Prices of existing single detached dwellings	Apartment starts	All dwelling starts
	(1)	(2)	(3)
	% change from previous year	000's	000's
1970	0.6	91.9	190.5
1971	6.7	106.2	233.7
1972	5.5	103.7	249.9
1973	14.5	106.5	268.5
1974	35.6	74.0	222.1
1975	20.1	70.4	231.5
1976	14.6	89.3	273.2
1977	6.9	93.3	245.7
1978	1.5	77.3	227.7
1979	9.3	58.4	197.0
1980	−0.9	48.3	158.6
1981	2.0	61.6	178.0
1982	3.9	53.2	125.9
1983	9.8	44.1	162.6

Source: Canada Mortgage and Housing.

Cost of Housing

As a rule of thumb, payments for housing used to absorb about 25% of the average North American's income and up to 40% of the income of the poor. Thanks to inflation during the late 1970's and early 1980's, the general rule of thumb today may be more in order of 40%.[24] Housing thus represents a large component of the consumer budget and asset portfolio.

Housing markets vary considerably between Census Metropolitan Areas (CMA's). In some CMA's, such as Vancouver, prices have fluctuated over short periods of time to the extent that a "middle-class" four-bedroom house with a market value of, say, $100,000 in 1978 was demanding a market price of $200,000 by mid-1981. Since most migrants travel in household or family units, and in view of the almost universal desire to own one's own home, it is reasonable to expect individuals considering migration to be aware of the cost of housing in different CMA's. Furthermore, when housing prices are on the rise it can be assumed that rental prices are on the rise as well. (In both Canada and the United States, neither housing nor rental prices are incorporated in the consumer price index, though they lead increases in the cost of living.)

The price of housing may affect migration in two ways. On the one hand, higher absolute housing prices at place 'j' are likely to deter in-migration. To cite an actual example, a professor earning $38,000 per year and owning a four-bedroom house valued at $80,000 in eastern Canada was offered a position at the University of British Columbia in 1981 at $45,000 per year. He declined the offer when he discovered that an equivalent house in Vancouver would cost him over $200,000. On the other hand, owner-occupiers may chose to remain at their present location if real estate speculation or the demand for housing as an infla- tionary hedge were to boost the value of their housing stock. As noted previously, owner-occupiers in high growth areas would be in a favourable position, particularly after the 1972 revisions affecting capital gains tax.

Empirical evidence on the effects of housing costs on migration is extremely scant. In a study of interregional migration in the U.K., Gor- don (1982) reports that higher housing prices at destination deterred in- migration. In their study of interprovincial migration in Canada, Winer and Gauthier (1983) found that higher housing price indices in Alberta and British Columbia exerted a negative effect on migration to these prov- inces – as expected. A similar conclusion was reached by Mills et al. (1983) with respect to higher housing prices in Alberta and Saskatchewan – though their 1961-78 time-series data on incomes and prices do not ap- pear to have been adjusted for inflation. Then, of course, there is the widely cited work of Rossi (1980) which attaches a great deal of impor- tance to housing values in short distance and intra-urban migration.

The discussion above gives rise to the following hypotheses:

Hypothesis 19:
Asymmetry will be evident in the effect of housing price (HOUSE) on migration from city 'i' to 'j'. High values of HOUSE at destination will work to repel potential migrants. High values of HOUSE at origin will work to retain, rather than push people out.

Core Hypothesis 20:
HOUSE will exert a greater effect on M_{ij} after the 1972 revisions to Canada's tax system.

HOUSE is represented as the average estimated total cost of new housing units (land plus buildings) in Census Metropolitan Areas, at the beginning of the migration period under study. See Appendix 1 to Chapter 3 for data sources.

Dual Income-Earning Households

Most people migrate as members of households or families. In the past, the husband was most likely to be the sole breadwinner. Thus, economically motivated migration was likely to be contingent on job prospects, unemployment or income opportunities of the "male household head". Today, women and wives are far more prevalent in the labour force. Moreover, the organization of productive activity in metropolitan areas has become increasingly concentrated in services versus heavy manual labour or industrial-type work. Consequently, places offering good job opportunities for males may be ruled out as viable alternatives if job opportunities are not available for female household members as well.

The importance of the "dual income-earning" household on migration has been demonstrated by Mincer (1978). If, for example, the husband is unemployed, presence of a working wife relaxes pressure on job search and mobility. On the other hand, should a move be desirable, the wife's income may help to finance the move. Furthermore, the prospect of a working wife after a move will reduce the risk of "unsuccessful relocation" should the husband fail to find a job.

Unfortunately, shortcomings of available data rule out the evaluation of the dual income household hypothesis per se. However, if employment considerations are important to women, then we would expect migrants – who consist largely of individuals in families – to be attracted to places where higher rates of female labour force participation prevail. Thus, female labour force opportunities are represented as the proportion of women aged 15 to 64 years that are economically active in each CMA. Whether higher rates of female labour force participation at place of origin would serve to curtail migration (in view of its "cushioning effects"), or facilitate migration (through its possible "financing effects") is to be determined empirically.

The discussion above lends itself to the following hypothesis:

Hypothesis 21:
The greater the difference between city 'j' and 'i' (j/i) in female labour force opportunities (FEM$_j$ >FEM$_i$), the greater the probability of migrating from 'i' to 'j' will be (M$_{ij}$).

Our measure of FEM is represented as the number of women aged 15 years and older in the labour force per thousand women aged 15 years and over, at the beginning of the migration period under study. See Appendix 1 to Chapter 3 for details and qualifications.

Immigration

When Canada opens its doors to immigration, which is usually at times of low national unemployment, the majority of those who gain entry flock to the largest metropolitan areas. Were immigrants to compete for scarce jobs in some cities more than others, this might deplete employment opportunities for internal migrants and thus deter them from going to those cities. This is the interpretation adopted, though not tested, by Winer and Gauthier (1983, p.36). On the other hand, were immigrants to bring substantial savings and entrepreneurial talent with them, they might actually boost labour market opportunities at their new destination. This is the interpretation adopted here.

The possible effects of immigration on the creation of job opportunities can be examined in terms of production, consumption and economy-of-scale effects. On the production side, Clodman et al. (1982) point out that immigrants may fill critical shortages in the labour market thus allowing the industries concerned to experience growth. Such growth may lead to the expansion and creation of new jobs. Alternatively, immigrants might invest in, and start their own businesses which, in turn, might stimulate new jobs and opportunities. On the consumption side, the expenditure patterns of immigrants may differ from native born Canadians to the extent that greater demand for certain goods and services may promote growth in certain industries. In this respect, one need only think of specialized goods and services in ethnic communities such as Vancouver's "Chinatown" or Toronto's "Italian boroughs".

Hard evidence on the impact of immigrants on the labour market is fragmentary, but there are grounds for arguing that immigrants promote, rather than take away jobs by simply filling vacancies. Polèse

(1978), for example, reports that every new immigrant worker in Québec creates, in the first year, an additional labour demand equivalent to .22 workers due to consumption expenditures by him plus his family (a multiplier of 1.22). Adding more indirect expenditure impacts due to induced government spending, induced residential construction, and private investment by immigrants raises the regional employment multiplier per immigrant worker to 1.45.

Were the impact of immigrants on metropolitan employment limited to industrial-type jobs in, say, large establishments, it would be reasonable to assume that such effects would be "picked up" by our "industrial" employment growth variable (ie., JOBS in Hypotheses 7 and 8). However, there is reason to believe that immigrants create jobs "on the fringe" by pursuing self-employment activities. Canada's Department of Employment and Immigration conducted a longitudinal survey in 1974 on three immigrant cohorts which revealed that the number of self-employed immigrants had doubled over a three-year period. The survey revealed that after three years, 94 immigrant entrepreneurs in the first cohort had generated 516 jobs, whereas 101 immigrant entrepreneurs in the second cohort had generated 190 jobs, and 77 immigrant entrepreneurs in the third cohort had generated 146 new jobs (over a two-year period). These findings, combined with the multiplier effects noted above, suggest that immigration may indirectly enhance the attractiveness of CMA's in its own right.

Having said the above, it is important to acknowledge that the inclusion of immigration (IMMIG) in our model might also introduce problems. Suppose that CMA's appeal to immigrants and internal migrants equally. This would suggest that variations in IMMIG and M_{ij} might stem from the same set of causes. If so, the two variables would be jointly dependent; meaning that, at best, IMMIG would be co-linear with more legitimate independent (exogenous) variables in the model. In addition, any unmeasured factors would affect IMMIG and M_{ij} in the same way. These effects would, therefore, be spuriously captured by the IMMIG variable.

One means of checking on the problem implied above is to compare rates of IMMIG and rates of in-migration (from all sources to CMA's) over several time periods. Exemplary rates are provided below for Canada's five largest CMA's. These rates do not appear to be strongly correlated. Moreover, the correlation coefficient between IMMIG and migration to all of Canada's CMA's over four periods of time is only $r^2 = .18$ (significant at the level .01 of statistical significance).

CMA	Internal in-migration		Foreign immigration	
	1959 - 61	1976 - 81	1956 - 61	1976 - 81
Calgary	23.7	33.7	6.4	6.4
Edmonton	19.0	24.8	5.2	5.0
Montréal	6.6	5.1	4.1	2.3
Toronto	7.0	8.2	8.6	5.5
Vancouver	11.0	12.5	5.0	5.2

In view of the above, it is our position that IMMIG still merits evaluation *but* that caution should be exercised when interpreting empirical results in Chapters 4 and 5.

Hypothesis 22:
The greater the difference between city 'j' and 'i' in rates of immigration of the foreign born ($IMMIG_j > IMMIG_i$), the greater the probability of migration from 'i' to 'j' will be.

IMMIG is measured per thousand population of Census Metropolitan Areas during the migration period under study. Data measuring the "force" of recent immigration on CMA's as well as the rate of internal migration to and from CMA's have been collected for the same period of time by the Census of Canada. See Appendix 1 to Chapter 3 for definitional details and data sources.

Information, Fixed and Psychic Costs

Migration over long distances is said to involve psychic costs if migrants are separated from friends and relatives or are placed out of touch with unique amenities in their home region. Migration over long distances is also expected to involve fixed and informational costs, the former related to transportation, the latter to time and money devoted to accessing information on distant places. All three costs are usually represented by one variable – physical distance between places.
    This study also employs the traditional distance variable but with an important caveat. Distance is not interpreted largely as a fixed cost

variable as is standard practice in most economic studies. We now know that distance in North America exerts a far more powerful deterrent effect on place-to-place migration than could ever be accounted for by fixed costs alone (see Chapter 2).

Though distance is hypothesized to exert a negative effect on migration, we would also expect this effect to have diminished over time. As countries become wealthier, or in the case of wealthier individuals, we would expect (i) fixed costs of relocation to shrink relative to earnings, and (ii) psychic costs to diminish in view of improved telecommunications, news media and transport. To an extent, this expectation is borne out in studies which have measured the effects of distance on migration in countries at different levels of development. In relatively poor countries such as India, for example, Greenwood (1971) estimates the elasticity of distance at -1.97 for 1960 interstate migration flows. In a "middle-income country" such as Venezuela, Schultz (1982) estimates distance elasticities for males with no education at approximately -1.60, for males with primary education at -1.30, for males with secondary education at -.90, and for males with higher education at about -.65. These elasticities pertain to 1961 interstate migration in a context where education is likely to parallel socio-economic status rather closely. And, in a relatively rich country such as the United States, distance elasticities have been estimated at approximately -.90 for 1956-60 interstate migration by Greenwood (1968) and at -.80 for 1965-70 intermetropolitan migration by Fields (1979).

Our distance hypotheses then, are;

Hypothesis 23:
The greater the distance ($DIST_{ij}$) between city 'i' and 'j' the less the probability of migration from 'i' to 'j' will be (M_{ij}).

Hypothesis 24:
$DIST_{ij}$ will exert a smaller impact on M_{ij} today than in the past.

Note that hypothesis 24 is not represented as a 'core hypothesis'. One reason is that a change in tastes is not necessary to bring about declining relevance of DIST in the migrant's utility calculus. Second, we have no evidence that public policy has influenced the relationship between DIST and M_{ij}, and thus individual attitudes toward DIST. Rather, the *meaning* of the variable is likely to have changed in view of improved transport and telecommunications. Indeed, if over time, transport and communications costs per mile have been declining, then a reduced coefficient on $DIST_{ij}$ (ie., in regression analysis), may be perfectly compatible with stability in the migration relationship over time.

It is also important to acknowledge that coefficients on distance (in regression analysis) could be sensitive to the spatial structure of the metropolitan urban system itself. Suppose that growing proportions of all migrants, over time, were moving between CMA's in the Canadian west and that long-distance migration between eastern and western CMA's had declined. Suppose also that distance had less of a deterrent effect on inter-CMA migration in the Canadian west due to better roads, communications, etc. In this case, a decline in the overall impact of DIST on M_{ij} in Canada over time would really be attributable to a shift in migration fields. Preliminary analysis of Canadian migration fields over time suggests this is not likely to be relevant to the evaluation of Hypothesis 24. See the methodological Appendix to Chapter 4, "Age and Spatial Structure".

$DIST_{ij}$ is represented by the road mileage between Census Metropolitan Areas, and has been calculated once only for 1970.

Another means of representing psychic costs and informational barriers to migration in Canada, is to consider the effects of differences in language and culture. Recall from Chapter 2 that studies of interprovincial migration in Canada have established that commonality of French or English language, or culture, is strongly and positively correlated with migration between two places. By implication, language differentials or discrimination between ethnic groups may diminish migration by restricting access to labour force opportunities or adding to psychic costs. The study by Robinson and Tomes (1982) concludes that French origin exerts effects on migration in Canada that cannot be explained by economic considerations alone.

Hypothesis 25:
The greater the commonality of language/ethnicity ($LANG_{ij}$) between two cities 'i' and 'j', the greater the probability of migration from 'i' to 'j' will be (M_{ij}).

Core Hypothesis 26:
$LANG_{ij}$ will exert more of an impact on M_{ij} today than in the past in view of the separatist and language policies pursued by the government of Québec (ie., Bill 101).

Is Hypothesis 26 realistic? The answer is "yes" if it is reasonable to assume that separatist-type policies have not been effectively counteracted by integrative-type policies. By "separatist" policies we refer to events leading up to the enactment of language Bill 101, as well as its effects thereafter. Bill 101 is acknowledged to have aggravated language barriers between the province of Québec and predominantly English-speaking provinces, particularly between 1976-81 (see Chapter 2).[25] By "integrative" policies, we refer to policies which have sought to promote bilingualism in Canada. These have progressed slowly – though the French immersion program for civil servants has enjoyed an element of success. Futhermore, one development which seems to have detracted from the "push" for bilingualism stems from relaxed language requirements for university entrance or graduation. Credits in French language courses are no longer formal requirements in most Canadian universities. The result is that university enrolments in French have dropped in English-speaking parts of the country.

Hypothesis 26 merits 'core hypothesis' interpretation because separatist-type policies – including French language requirements – may be affecting attitudes toward jobs and opportunities in Québec. In addition, if the capacity to communicate in French has become a prerequisite to employment in Québec for "nationalistic" reasons rather than for job-related reasons per se, then the market mechanism may be prevented from allocating labour to its best place of competitive advantage. Thus, we would expect events in Québec to have accelerated migration of English-speaking Montréalers to anglophone centres and, more significantly, to have reduced migration in the other direction.

$LANG_{ij}$ is represented in our empirical work as a "dummy variable". The dummy variable takes a value of '1' if 50% or more of the population of both city 'i' and 'j' share the same ethnic origin; '0' otherwise. Thus $LANG_{ij}$ for migration between Montréal and Québec is assigned '1'; for Montréal to Vancouver '0'; and for Toronto to Vancouver '1'.

Social and Amenity Considerations

Crime

In some countries crime rates not only differ substantially between cities but differences are broadcast widely. In Canada, crime rates may vary between CMA's but one is rarely confronted with the rumour that city A is far more dangerous than city B. Evidence on the effect of crime rates on migration in Canada is non-existent. For the United States, a few studies report that differential crime rates exert mixed or uncertain effects on migration, especially when evaluated in the presence of economic variables.[26]

Assuming that information concerning differentials in violent crime will bear more on migration decisions than, say, fraud, traffic violations, etc., we hypothesize the following;

Hypothesis 27:
The greater the differential between city 'j' and 'i' in rates of violent crimes ($CRIME_j > CRIME_i$), the less the probability of migration from 'i' to 'j' will be.

CRIME is represented as a rate per thousand population of each Police Metropolitan Area at the beginning of the migration period under study. CRIME is represented by a composite of all murders, homicides, sexual offences, assaults which are not indecent, and robberies. See Appendix 1 to Chapter 3 for sources and qualifications.

Climate/Geography

Canadian metropolitan areas differ widely in terms of proximity to geographical assets such as mountains or oceans. The problem with representing such considerations in studies of migration, however, is that they elude meaningful quantification. Imagine trying to quantify the attractiveness of 'mountains plus ocean' surrounding Vancouver versus 'bigger mountains and expansive prairie' on the fringe of Calgary. CMA's also differ widely in terms of length of seasons, warmth of summer and harshness of winter. In this case, however, indices of climate can be constructed which may figure in the migrant's utility calculus.

Our position is that climate considerations are likely to be most relevant to the relatively wealthy and the elderly. In the case of the relatively wealthy, climate and the pursuit of leisure would seem to go hand-in-hand. In the case of the elderly, climate may be important not only for the pursuit of leisure (among the retired), but for health reasons as well. The elderly are clearly more fragile and are exposed to greater risk of accidents or sickness in extremely cold climates. For example, fatalities of old people during harsh winter months are commonplace in the Prairie provinces but are virtually unheard of in, say, Victoria, British Columbia. Moreover, long periods of snowfall or ice-covered roads and walkways may be viewed with glee by children but they are likely to be viewed as a menace by the elderly.

To date, only one study in Canada has evaluated surrogates of climate on migration in Canada. Simmons (1980) found that higher "mean January temperature" was positively correlated with net migration to "urban-centred" regions, but was not significantly correlated with rates of in-migration or out-migration. Note that in this study, however, effects of climate at places of origin *and* destination were not evaluated simultaneously. In contrast, several studies on migration in the United States have examined the effects of climate indices such as average days or centimetres of rainfall, freezing days, days of sunshine, etc. While results are not conclusive, climate considerations have been shown to be relevant to migration to certain areas such as Florida or California, or to the migration of the elderly or retired.[27]

With the above in mind, several indices of climate have been ruled out in favour of a measure of snowfall (SNOW). SNOW not only reflects the total amount of frozen precipitation but snowfall tends to accumulate when freezing weather prevails.

Hypothesis 28:
The greater the differential in city 'j' and 'i' in centimetres of (SNOW$_j$ > SNOW$_i$) the less the probability of migration from 'i' to 'j' will be.

SNOW is represented by the average number of centimetres of snow at weather stations in or around each Census Metropolitan Area, during winter months. Measurements of SNOW have been averaged over 1965 and 1980, with values ranging from 31 to 296 cm between CMA's. See Appendix 1 to Chapter 3 for definitional details and data sources.

Selectivity Considerations

Universals in empirical studies of migration are that the propensity to migrate from place 'i' declines with age and increases with education.[28] These findings marry well with predictions of the human capital model since (i) older people have less time to capitalize on earnings differentials attributable to migration, and (ii) the more educated have greater accessibility to opportunities in distant labour markets. It is also apparent that age and education exert independent effects on migration even when labour market opportunities are controlled.[29]

Demographers refer to education and age as "selectivity variables" in the sense that younger, more educated persons are thought to be more dynamic, viable elements of a population. If there is a high incidence of young, educated people in an origin population, that population is expected to "send out" more of its members in pursuit of opportunities elsewhere.

Age considerations are seldom represented in aggregate models of migration unless (i) age distributions vary considerably between provinces, states or cities, or (ii) the demographic structure of a population has changed over time. With respect to the first point, preliminary analysis of age distributions among CMA's reveals almost identical proportions of youth in each city. Thus, it is not necessary to control for age distribution in the analysis of our cross-sectional data. The second point is relevant to testing our 'core hypothesis'. If a population ages over time, producing more elderly who are not in the labour force, then fewer of its members would likely migrate for work-related reasons (eg., an increase in retirement migration). Were this to apply to Canada, the age structure would have to be controlled while determining if and why work-related reasons were declining as influences in intermetropolitan migration.

Again, preliminary analysis of Canada's age structure over time suggests this consideration is not likely to be relevant. On the one hand, the proportion of Canada's population aged 60 or over has remained relatively constant at 11.0% between 1956-61, 11.3% between 1966-71 and 12.7% between 1976-81. On the other hand, the share of Canada's population aged 15-29 increased from approximately 23% between 1956-61 to 28% between 1976-81, the majority of which are likely to be in the labour force. Growth of this cohort could alter employment opportunities and risks of unemployment at different CMA's – thus discouraging migration for work-related reasons – but we control for this consideration by introducing specific measures of employment and unemployment.

In contrast to age variables, education variables usually are represented in aggregate models. Some places are more favourably endowed than others with educational institutions or families containing more educated members (eg., in more prosperous cities).

Hypothesis 29:
The greater the prevalence of higher educated persons (EDUC) in city
'i', the greater the probability of migration from 'i' to 'j' will be.

EDUC is represented as the number of persons with "some university, a university degree, or a university degree plus additional education" per thousand CMA population, at the beginning of the migration
period under study. See Appendix 1 to Chapter 3 for data sources and
qualifications.

Summing Up

The generalized cost/benefit framework set forth in the beginning of this
chapter (equations 1 through 4), has now been given substance in the
form of 29 hypotheses covering 21 empirical measures. The major
theoretical constructs, empirical variables and hypotheses to be evaluated
are summarized in Table 3.2. Complete definitional details and data
sources are provided in the Appendix to Chapter 3.
In all cases, selection of the variables in Table 3.2 has been guid-
ed by theory or empirical precedent. This means that our empirical findings can be compared – in general terms – with those of previous studies.
At the same time, however, this study should set empirical precedents
of its own for three reasons. First, it is the first study to evaluate any
of the variables listed in Table 3.2 in the context of intermetropolitan
migration in Canada. Second, it is the first study to evaluate several
variables in any migration context in Canada (eg., crime rates, home
ownership, immigration). Third, it provides the first evaluation of the
changing impact of "traditional" market versus "non-traditional" public
sector variables on migration in a society that is undergoing change over
time.
Equally important to formulating theory and selecting empirical
variables is the "functional form" of the statistical model to be tested.
Choice of an appropriate functional form involves several methodological
decisions. Too often these are neglected or underplayed in studies of
migration. Time and again this has resulted in a loss of information or
estimation error. These and related issues are taken up in the Appendix
to the following chapter. The reader is advised to consult this important Appendix before taking on our empirical results.

TABLE 3.2: Summary of Explanatory Variables and Hypothesized Relationships

Variable	Empirical measure	Symbol	Hypothesized sign	
			Destination	Origin
Labour market component				
Earnings opportunities	Industrial wage	WAGE 1	+	−
	composite; wage	WAGE 2	+	−
	variants (1) through (4)	WAGE 3	+	−
		WAGE 4	+	−
Employment opportunities	Industrial composite of employment growth	JOBS	+	−
Unemployment	Unemployment rate	UNEMP	−	+
The business cycle	Residential building construction	DS	+	−
Government transfers, fiscal structure				
Unemployment insurance	UIC benefits	UIGEN	+	+ or − (?)
	UIC availability if unemployed	UIPROB	+	+ or − (?)
Government fiscal policy	Federal government transfers to provinces	GRANT	+	−
Natural resource revenues	Resource revenues	NRR	+	−
Additional economic considerations				
Home ownership	Ownership among 25-34 year-olds	OWN	NA	−
Cost of housing	Cost of new housing units	HOUSE	−	−
Dual income-earning households	Female labour force participation	FEM	+	−
Immigration	Immigration of foreign born	IMMIG	+	−
Information, fixed and psychic costs				
	Distance	DIST	−	−
	Commonality of language	LANG	−	−
Social and amenity considerations				
Crime	Crimes of violence	CRIME	−	+
Climate severity	Total snowfall	SNOW	−	+
Selectivity considerations				
Education	Proportion of highly educated	EDUC	NH	+

Note: NH signifies "no hypothesized effect"; NA signifies "no account".

Footnotes

1. To illustrate, say, that it is appropriate to represent Q_j solely by an average yearly wage of $5,000 versus an average yearly wage at place 'i' of $4,500. Assume that the costs of migrating are, on average, $1,000. If potential migrants assessed the returns to migration in terms of a short planning horizon of only year, then according to equation (2), ($5,000 – $4,500) – $1,000 < 0. If income were the only thing that mattered, the result would dictate "do not migrate". However, were migrants to expect that the wage differential would persist for, say, 10 years, then 10 ($5,000 – $4,500) – $1,000 > 0, which clearly exceeds the initial monetary barriers to migration. The discount factor 'r' enters the equation so that the expected gain of $5,000 over the 10-year period can be translated into a present value (ie., adjusted for inflation).

2. See Liu (1975, 1980), Graves (1980), Porell (1982), Martin and Lichter (1983), Roseman (1983).

3. See Greenwood and Sweetland (1972).

4. This point is developed in OECD (1982). Union effects are not likely to increase in this respect in the future since the proportion of the workforce that belongs to unions is falling in both Canada and the U.S.

5. See Cornwall (1981), OECD (1982).

6. See Wachter (1974), Piore (1983).

7. In keeping with Kerr (1954), our view is that labour markets are more likely to function as a system of "structured" versus "structureless" markets. In a structured market, jobs are filled by promotion and by the transfer of workers who have already gained entry to an "internal labour market". Internal labour markets are said to exist because tasks are becoming increasingly specific to jobs and require specific on-the-job training. Such training, which has to be financed by the employer, ties the worker to the firm because the latter cannot sell the acquired skills on the open market and the former wants to obtain returns from his investment on human capital for the longest period of time. Thus, jobs in structured markets may be shielded from the direct influence of competitive forces in the labour market (eg., fluctuating wage rates). In contrast, pricing and allocation decisions in the "external" or "structureless" market are said to be controlled directly by economic variables with no attachment between the worker and the employer *except the wage*. See Addison and Siebert (1979).

    A similar perspective on North American labour markets maintains that it is useful to dichotomize the economy into a primary and a secondary sector where workers and employers operate according to different behavioural rules; that wages are determined by different factors in the secondary sector than in the primary sector; and that economic mobility is marked by pervasive unemployment because unlike those with job-specific training or high human capital endowments, workers in secondary labour markets are not "protected" during periods of economic slack. See Cain (1976) and Piore (1979). A primary labour market is said to consist of jobs in large firms and/or unionized occupations which tend to offer several of the following traits; high wages, good working conditions, employment stability, chances of advancement, equity, and due process in the administration of work rules. In contrast, a secondary labour market is said to have jobs which, relative to those in the primary sector, are decidedly less attractive. They tend to involve low wages, poor working conditions, considerable variability in employment, little chance of promotion, and often arbitrary management. Economic mobility of workers in this sector is likely to be marked by pervasive unemployment because, unlike those with job specific training or high human capital endowments, secondary workers are not "protected" during periods of economic slack. See Cain (1976) and Piore (1979).

8. See Rogerson and MacKinnon (1981).

9. If migrants do not adjust for cost of living differences, they may suffer from "money illusion". Rabianski (1971) deflated nominal earnings by cost of living differentials to arrive at real earnings, but found that both nominal and real earnings perform equally well in his study of U.S. migration. Renas and Kuman (1978) contend that although migrants consider money income and the cost of living in their locational decisions, they do not consider real income in such decisions. Cebula (1980), reports much the same thing. He points out that "retirement migrants", for example, may not be interested in earnings but may be interested in the independent effect of cost of living differences on their fixed incomes. His results show that cost of living differentials - treated independently of income - exert a significant influence on net migration to U.S. metropolitan areas.

10. See Todaro (1969, 1976, 1980). Todaro submits that formulating the probability variable (or expected wages), in this way avoids the "all or nothing" problem of having to assume that the migrant either earns the average income at place 'j' or earns nothing in the periods immediately following migration to 'j'.

11. See Fields (1976).

12. To illustrate how equation (10) would measure earnings over a one-year period, suppose that there is no unemployment at place 'j' during the entire year. In this case, W4 would equal the average wage W_j multiplied by T' or, say, 52 weeks. As with previous wage variants W2 and W3, this total yearly earnings figure would also be adjusted for the relevant cost of living differential (CPI_j). In contrast, suppose that unemployment was 100% at place 'j'. In this case $W4_j$ is determined by multiplying the average unemployment insurance benefit payment times the total average number of weeks that the "average" unemployed worker is permitted to collect (T"). In the absence of employment earnings, yearly earnings are now represented solely by total unemployment insurance income, adjusted by the relevant cost of living differential (CPI_j).

13. W3 or W4 could be further refined to measure "take home pay". Such a variant would thus take into consideration differential tax rates.

14. See Greenwood (1981) and Fields (1976, 1979). Bartel (1979) also shows that job mobility plays a dominant role in the decision to migrate. On the other hand, in a review of several studies, Alperovich et al. (1977) show that weak results on wage variables vis-à-vis employment variables can be partially attributed to "simultaneous equations bias."

15. See OECD (1982).

16. This speculation has been countered and qualified by Schlottmann and Herzog (1981).

17. That is, economic theory predicts that geographic mobility in the economy as a whole should be pro-cyclical, increasing at the peak of the business cycle when job opportunities are abundant and decreasing in a recession when jobs are scarce.

18. See Shaw (1974a).

19. A review of relevant studies and additional empirical evidence is provided in Shaw (1978, 1980, 1983; Chapter 2).

20. The 1979 changes to Canada's unemployment insurance program were introduced in two steps. In January 1979, the benefit rate declined from 66.6% to 60% of insurable earnings. There were also two minor amendments removing from coverage those working fewer than 20 hours per week and requiring high-income earners to repay a portion of benefits received. On July 1, 1979, additional qualification requirements were imposed upon new entrants and repeaters. The new entrants and re-entrants, defined as those with fewer than 14 weeks of work in the year preceding their qualifying period, were required to have at least 20 weeks of insured employment to qualify for benefits as compared to 10 or 14. See Beach and Kaliski:1983.

21. In addition to unemployment insurance variables, several studies on intermetropolitan migration in the U.S. evaluate transfer variables such as welfare payments. Again the evidence is far from conclusive, though a review of studies by Cebula (1979) gives the impression that such considerations are relevant to explaining migration. In addition, Schlottmann and Herzog (1982) report that taxes or "fiscal pressure" has the expected effect on net migration.

22. See Collins (1980) for a good review of the issues involved.

23. See Shaw (1975, Chapter 2).

24. See Clemhout and Neftci (1981), Weinstein (1981).

25. At the same time, however, it is likely that the implementation of Bill 101 contributed to migration between Québec City or Montréal and predominantly English-speaking cities, as anglophones are known to have left Québec province in relatively large numbers in and around 1977.

26. See Porell (1982).

27. See Kau and Sirmans (1977/78), Cebula (1979), Clark and Ballard (1980), Schlottmann and Herzog (1981). Renas and Kuman (1983) undertake a comprehensive review and evaluation which provides more impressive support for climate variables than has existed in the past.

28. See Shaw (1975), Schwartz (1976).

29. See Morgan (1975/76), Schlottmann and Herzog (1981).

Chapter 4
Aggregate Results

Introduction

Just as migration theory incorporates assumptions that must be justified, the empirical model estimated here employs assumptions that demand to be understood. Choices concerning estimation procedures can affect empirical results. These choices include how rates of intermetropolitan migration should be normalized; whether explanatory variables should be evaluated in a linear or a logarithmic form; whether a symmetrical or an asymmetrical model should be employed; how "simultaneity" and "aggregation" bias might be minimized; how to deal with problems of "return" or "repeat" migration; and whether controls are needed for changing age and spatial structure.

Not wishing to deal with these and related issues superficially, we have devoted an entire appendix to the discussion of an appropriate "functional form" for empirical estimation. The Appendix, entitled "Appropriate Model Specification and Data" also contains important information on the strengths and weaknesses of our empirical data. In brief, the Appendix to this chapter tells us the following about our empirical model. First, the determinants of migration from place 'i' to 'j' are evaluated in the context of a polytomous logistic model. In keeping with the polytomous model of migration is represented as the ratio of the probability of moving (P_{ij}) between place 'i' and 'j' and the probability of *staying* at 'i' (P_{ii}). Second, in keeping with most applications of the polytomous model, own migration measure 'P_{ij}/P_{ii} (hereafter, M_{ij})

is disaggregated by personal characteristics of migrants. This evaluation is carried out in Chapter 5 when migration flows are disaggregated by the migrant's level of education (more on this later). Third, in keeping with most applications of the polytomous model, we adopt a double-log specification and employ ordinary least squares regression. Fourth, explanatory variables are evaluated separately to allow for possible asymmetries in the effects of origin and destination characteristics (ie., $\ln X_i \pm \ln X_j$ rather than in ratio format $\ln X_i / \ln X_j$).

In addition to the above, various steps or precautions have been taken to test for, or to minimize "aggregation" and "simultaneity" bias. With respect to aggregation bias, migration flows have been grouped into different geographical areas (eastern versus western Canada), disaggregated into smaller geographical units than in past studies (Census Metropolitan Areas versus provinces), and disaggregated by personal characteristics of migrants (education). Again, this is undertaken in Chapter 5. With respect to simultaneity bias, explanatory variables have been measured at the beginning of the migration period to reduce interaction between migration and its possible causes. This procedure is not possible when yearly migration data are derived from administrative tax or family allowance files (as in Winer and Gauthier:1983). Moreover, vague "explanatory" variables which run the risk of being intercorrelated with more precise "explanatory" variables have been excluded (eg., population size, migrant stock).

The empirical models evaluated in this and the subsequent chapter follow the sequence indicated in Table 4.1. Model 1 represents a very basic economic model (à la Sjaastad). Model 2 adds our employment variable under the assumption that wages per se do not adjust to equilibriate the demand and supply of labour. Model 3 adds our unemployment and educational selectivity variables. The latter variable broadens the human capital dimension of the wage/employment model. Model 4 corresponds to our idea of a relatively full "traditional" market model. It adds residential dwelling starts under the assumption that some dimensions of the business cycle and housing market are likely to escape our "industrial" wage and employment measures. Model 5 adds our public sector or fiscal component in the form of unemployment insurance and federal equalization payments. Recall that expected differences in the performance of Models 4 and 5 have been expressed formally as 'core hypotheses' in Chapter 3. Finally, Models 6 and 7 add several additional economic, social and climatic variables. These models do not include all variables listed in Table 3.2 (Chapter 3); reasons for this will be given as we go along.[1]

There are three advantages to presenting empirical results along the lines indicated by Table 4.1. First, we can examine the "explanatory" or predictive power of simpler versus more expanded models. This will allow us to roughly follow the theoretical arguments set forth in Chapter 3. Second, we can identify variables which do and do not exhibit *consistency* in their explanatory power as additional variables are added to the equation. For example, if both wages and jobs exert *independent* effects on migration, then Model 2 (with jobs added) should produce a coefficient on its wage variable similar to the coefficient on the wage variable estimated by Model 1 (without jobs). Essentially, this procedure facilitates checks for multicollinearity (see the Appendix to Chapter 4). Third, by systematically developing a family of models, we allow the reader to select a predictive/explanatory model best suited to his own research/policy needs.

In the process of evaluating our 'core hypothesis' we will be looking for changing patterns of regression *coefficients* over time. To what extent are they unstable reflecting changing relevance of variables in the migration process? In this context, growth or decline in the "impact" of a 'core hypothesis' variable on migration over time would be implied if (i) its *coefficient* increases (decreases) but the *value* of the variable per se remains constant (all else constant), (ii) its coefficient remains constant but the value of the variable per se increases or decreases (all else constant), (iii) its coefficient increases and its value increases (all else constant), or (iv) its coefficient remains constant and its level remains constant but other influences in the model decline in importance. While we plan to emphasize changing coefficients, it is also important to recognize that aspects of our 'core hypothesis' might also be true when a variable's coefficient remains exactly the same in different time periods. For example, reduced out-migration from the Atlantic provinces in the 1970's could be quite compatible with stable coefficients for, say, wages and unemployment insurance over time, but might be caused by the much higher *values* of unemployment insurance payments in the 1970's (see Hypotheses 10, 11, 12).

The Wage Variants

Recall from Chapter 3 that our first concern is to identify an appropriate wage variant for the labour market component of our migration model. Four possible wage variants have been specified;

TABLE 4.1: Overview of Variables Included in the Empirical Models[1]

Variables	Model						
	1	2	3	4	5	6	7
$DIST_{ij}$	X	X	X	X	X	X	X
$WAGE1_i$	X	X	X	X	X	X	X
$WAGE1_j$	X	X	X	X	X	X	X
$LANG_{ij}$	X	X	X	X	X	X	X
$JOBS_i$		X	X	X	X	X	X
$JOBS_j$		X	X	X	X	X	X
$UNEMP_i$			X	X	X	X	X
$UNEMP_j$			X	X	X	X	X
$EDUC_i$			X	X	X	X	X
DS_i				X	X	X	X
DS_j				X	X	X	X
$UIGEN_i$					X	X	X
$UIGEN_j$					X	X	X
$UIPROB_i$					X	X	X
$UIPROB_j$					X	X	X
$GRANT_i$					X	X	X
$GRANT_j$					X	X	X
NRR_i					X	X	X
NRR_j					X	X	X
$CRIME_i$						X	X
$CRIME_j$						X	X
$SNOW_i$						X	X
$SNOW_j$						X	X
OWN_i						X	X
FEM_i							X
FEM_j							X
$IMMIG_i$							X
$IMMIG_j$							X

[1] Mean values for all variables are provided in Appendix 5.

- WAGE1 = nominal wages
- WAGE2 = WAGE1 adjusted for cost of living differentials
- WAGE3 = WAGE2 adjusted for the probability of unemployment
- WAGE4 = WAGE3 adjusted for the probability of receiving unemployment insurance if unemployed

Each wage variant has been evaluated in the context of Model 1, excluding the variable "commonality of language" ($LANG_{ij}$). Table 4.2 presents results for four time frames (wages have, of course, been

TABLE 4.2: Performance of the Wage Variants

Migration period	Wage variant tested	Explanatory variables									R^2	Observations
		$DIST_{ij}$	$W1_i$	$W1_j$	$W2_i$	$W2_j$	$W3_i$	$W3_j$	$W4_i$	$W4_j$		
1956 - 61	WAGE1	−.589 (6.523)	−.920 (1.228)	3.041 (3.964)							.209	272
	WAGE2	−.602 (6.747)			−.868 (.991)	3.307 (3.771)					.202	272
	WAGE3	−.578 (6.400)					−.795 (1.067)	3.233 (4.313)			.216	272
	WAGE4	−.585 (6.461)							−.878 (1.143)	3.147 (4.062)	.211	272
1966 - 71	WAGE1	−.497 (6.795)	−1.311 (1.898)	3.317 (4.800)							.240	272
	WAGE2	−.501 (7.017)			−1.163 (1.615)	3.884 (5.394)					.252	272
	WAGE3	−.489 (6.728)					−1.081 (1.578)	3.598 (5.252)			.249	272
	WAGE4	−.491 (6.736)							−1.121 (1.599)	3.548 (5.059)	.244	272
1971 - 76	WAGE1	−.491 (6.206)	.082 (.109)	.682 (.915)							.141	272
	WAGE2	−.490 (6.239)			.266 (.318)	.506 (.605)					.139	272
	WAGE3	−.483 (6.069)					.122 (.163)	.824 (1.108)			.142	272
	WAGE4	−.481 (6.058)							.149 (.195)	.873 (1.144)	.142	272
1976 - 81	WAGE1	−.398 (4.829)	−1.122 (1.172)	.694 (.727)							.087	272
	WAGE2	−.399 (4.838)			−1.241 (1.330)	.826 (.888)					.088	272
	WAGE3	−.391 (4.768)					−.966 (1.013)	1.785 (1.873)			.095	272
	WAGE4	−.397 (4.820)							−1.158 (1.121)	.806 (.781)	.086	272

adjusted for inflation – see Appendix 1 to Chapter 3). These results convey that adjustments to WAGE1 (ie., to produce WAGE2, 3 or 4), add little to the explanatory capacity of Model 1. To illustrate, consider the migration period 1956-61 and the performance of our model when it includes WAGE1 (ie., $W1_i$ and $W1_j$) versus WAGE4 (ie., $W4_i$ and $W4_j$). Both models – which also include $DIST_{ij}$ – account for approximately 21% of the variance in migration between CMA's (ie., $R^2 = .209$ versus .211). In addition, the size, sign and statistical significance of the regression coefficients on $W1_i$ and $W1_j$ versus $W4_i$ and $W4_j$ are highly similar. The same impression emerges when we compare the performance of the model containing WAGE1 versus WAGE4 for the other migration periods 1966-71, 1971-76 and 1976-81. The explanatory power of the models differs over these periods (ie., different R^2 levels), but the performance of the regression coefficients on the WAGE variants *within* each period is highly similar. WAGE3 construes a slight advantage in three of the four migration periods but hardly enough to justify its lengthy data computation. Furthermore, as we shall see, combining unemployment and wages separately is superior to combining unemployment and wages in multiplicative fashion (à la WAGE3).

Impressions concerning the performance of WAGE1 remain unchanged when migration flows are disaggregated by region (east versus west) or by educational attainment of the migrants themselves (results not presented here). Furthermore, WAGE1 performs as well or better than WAGE2, 3 or 4 when additional explanatory variables are included in the estimating equation. Consequently, our findings confirm Hypothesis 4 (simple wage variants [ie., nominal or actual wages] represent the present value of expected net earnings benefits to migration as well as more complex, multiplicative variants).

Traditional Market Models

We turn now to an evaluation of Models 1 through 4. Data on our dependent and independent variables are grouped into one general pooling (1,088 observations for the four migration periods covering 1956-81), a pre-1971 pooling (544 observations for two time periods covering 1956-71), and a post-1971 pooling (544 observations for two time periods covering 1971-81).

Mean values for all variables and a correlation coefficient matrix for the 1956-81 pooled data are presented in Appendix 5. The pre-1971 versus post-1971 data poolings are conducive to evaluating our 'core hypothesis'. Recall that the major hypothesis running throughout this study is that the influence of traditional labour market variables on migration is undergoing change. On the one hand, improvements in productivity and higher standards of living may be prompting the pursuit of leisure activities to the extent that earnings differentials per se figure less in the migrant's utility calculus. On the other hand, fiscal and social security-type programs may be cushioning the effects of, say, unemployment on earnings, thereby reducing pressure on individuals to migrate for income reasons alone. By organizing our intermetropolitan migration data according to pre-1971 and post-1971 periods, we can evaluate the effects of distinct policy and economic developments that took effect after 1971. These include (i) the 1971 revision of the Unemployment

Insurance Act, (ii) increased generosity of federal transfers to the Atlantic provinces, (iii) effects of the post-1971 oil price increases on fiscal capacity of the western provinces, including the establishment of the Alberta Heritage Fund, and (iv) restructuring of Canada's tax system and its likely effects on home ownership.

The pre-1971 and post-1971 data poolings are also conducive to evaluating whether models estimated on pooled data over a long time span (1956-81) produce coefficients comparable to those estimated for more recent time frames (1976-81). If they do not, then past studies which have pooled cross-sectional and time-series data over relatively long time spans, could be questioned from the standpoint of current policy relevance. Winer and Gauthier (1983), for example, base their estimates on all-pooled data covering the years 1951-78 in one part of their study and 1968-77 in another. *In consideration of the different time frames in this study, all income measures have been adjusted for inflation.*

Again, focusing on Model 1 – which contains WAGE1 – we find that the results presented in Table 4.3 confirm several of our hypotheses. First, observe that origin and destination wages are highly significant in the pre-1971 period but not so in the post-1971 period. Coefficients are flagged with an asterisk if they carry the expected sign, significant at the .01 level.[2] Observe also that the explanatory import of Model 1 is considerably less for the post-1971 period. This lends tentative support to Core Hypothesis 3 (earnings considerations exert a smaller impact on migration "today" than in the past).

Second, observe that origin and destination wages exhibit the expected sign (ie., positive effect at destination and negative effect at origin), but that their effects are asymmetrical in order of magnitude. The positive coefficient on $WAGE1_j$ is both larger and more statistically significant than the negative coefficient on $WAGE1_i$. This implies that destination wages outperform origin wages in their contribution to the explanatory power of the equation. These findings agree with most studies of migration and confirm Hypothesis 1 (the greater the differential in earnings between cities, the greater M_{ij} will be) and Hypothesis 2 (asymmetry is evident in the impact of origin and destination earnings on M_{ij}).

Third, distance exhibits the expected negative effect. However, its coefficient and statistical significance are considerably smaller in the post-1971 period (elasticity -.455) than in the pre-1971 period (elasticity -.533). If we refer back to Table 4.2 we find that the elasticity on

TABLE 4.3: Empirical Models 1 and 2: Aggregate Results

	Time frame					
	1956 - 81 pooled		Pre-1971		Post-1971	
	R.C.	't' value	R.C.	't' value	R.C.	't' value
Model 1						
Intercept	−2.289	−	−6.144	−	.481	−
$DIST_{ij}$	−.509	(13.455)*	−.553	(10.197)*	−.455	(8.562)*
$WAGE1_i$	−.939	(3.490)*	−1.130	(2.838)*	−.392	(.775)
$WAGE1_j$	2.004	(7.452)*	3.126	(7.853)*	.800	(1.584)
$LANG_{ij}$	1.161	(11.367)*	1.065	(7.339)*	1.246	(8.746)*
R^2	.263		.308		.222	
Fvalue	96.395		59.933		38.459	
Observations	1,088		544		544	
Model 2						
Intercept	−3.339	−	−8.076	−	−2.415	−
$DIST_{ij}$	−.525	(14.255)*	−.575	(11.154)*	−.459	(8.795)*
$WAGE1_i$	−1.217	(4.507)*	−1.666	(4.125)*	−.266	(.522)
$WAGE1_j$	2.485	(9.205)*	4.033	(9.994)*	1.250	(2.455)*
$LANG_{ij}$	1.127	(11.350)*	1.092	(7.929)*	1.184	(8.346)*
$JOBS_i$	−.001	(.069)	−.009	(.414)	−.013	(.693)
$JOBS_j$	.117	(8.216)*	.170	(7.818)*	.088	(4.596)*
R^2	.306		.379		.253	
Fvalue	79.403		54.595		30.232	
Observations	1,088		544		544	

Note: R.C. = regression coefficient;
   * = sign as expected and statistically significant at .01 level.

$DIST_{ij}$ fell to -.398 during the 1976-81 period. These findings provide confirmation of Hypothesis 23 (distance has a negative effect on M_{ij}) and Hypothesis 24 (distance exerts a smaller impact on migration "today" than in the past). Confirmation of Hypothesis 23 is universal whereas Hypothesis 24 has received scant attention in the empirical literature. Exceptions include Courchene (1970) and Vanderkamp (1971).

Model 1 also contains a "dummy" variable to capture the effects of "commonality of language" between pairs of CMA's. This variable exhibits the expected positive effect. Thus, Hypothesis 25 (the greater the commonality of language/ethnicity between two cities, the greater the probability of migration between them will be) is confirmed. This finding is in agreement with Courchene (1970), Robinson and Tomes (1982), and Winer and Gauthier (1983).

Observe also, that both the size of the coefficient on $LANG_{ij}$ and its statistical significance are larger for the post-1971 period than the pre-1971 period. This suggests *tentative* support for Core Hypothesis 26 ($LANG_{ij}$ exerts more of an impact on migration "today" than in the past in view of separatist and language policies pursued by the government of Québec).

Recall that Model 1, as evaluated in Table 4.3, parallels that of early Sjaastad-type models. Laber and Chase (1971) employed such a model and claimed to explain 50-60% of the variance in interregional migration in Canada. Our results are quite different. Model 1 explains no more than $R^2 = .308$ of the variance in intermetropolitan migration. In fact, when time periods are disaggregated (see Table 4.2), the best Model 1 can do (with WAGE1 and $DIST_{ij}$, but without $LANG_{ij}$), is $R^2 = .209$ for 1956-61, $R^2 = .240$ for 1966-71, $R^2 = .141$ for 1971-76, and $R^2 = .087$ for 1976-81. In our view, the discrepancy in "explanatory power" between our model and the version estimated by Laber and Chase is likely to stem from problems of "aggregation bias". As illustrated in the Appendix to Chapter 4 ("More on Aggregation Bias") models which use regional or provincial data may give distorted impressions about labour market determinants of migration (see, however, footnote 11, Chapter 1). Our claim is simply that the estimates reported here on wage and distance effects are likely to be far more accurate and realistic than those of previous studies of migration in Canada.

Model 2 (Table 4.3) incorporates our employment variable, JOBS. Observe, via comparison with Model 1, that the explanatory power of the equation increases without seriously disturbing the elasticities or statistical significance of the remaining variables. Hypothesis 5 (the greater the differential in growth of JOBS between cities, the greater M_{ij} will be) is thus tentatively confirmed. In addition, our expectation of asymmetry in the effects of destination versus origin employment is confirmed. Indeed, as in most studies, asymmetry in the effects of origin and destination variables (ie., origin typically weak), is so prevalent throughout this study that we shall not draw attention to it again. (Explanations for asymmetry are taken up in the Appendix to Chapter 4.)

Core Hypothesis 6 (employment considerations exert a smaller effect on migration "today" than in the past) is also tentatively confirmed. This is evident in a comparison of the pre- and post-1971 results where the positive coefficient on JOBS at destination is both larger and more significant during the pre-1971 period. Note also that the addition of JOBS to Model 2 increases its explanatory power about 7% for the pre-1971 period compared with only 3% for the post-1971 period.

Model 3 differs from Model 2 in that unemployment (UNEMP) and educational selectivity considerations (EDUC$_i$) have been added (Table 4.4). In both the pre- and post-1971 period, destination UNEMP exhibits the expected negative sign at statistically significant levels. Our interpretation of Model 3 is that it provides tentative support for Hypothesis 7 (high unemployment at city 'j' will deter in-migration, and high unemployment at city 'i' will promote out-migration), as well as additional support for Core Hypothesis 6. First, with respect to Hypothesis 7, the effects of unemployment at destination (UNEMP$_j$) exhibit the expected sign ($-$) during both pre- and post-1971 periods at statistically significant levels – though the coefficient is larger and more significant during the latter period. In contrast, the coefficient on unemployment at origin (UNEMP$_i$) exhibits an unexpected sign during the pre-1971 period, and switches signs between the pre-1971 and post-1971 periods. It also exhibits an almost negligible coefficient for post-1971 migration (which is not statistically significant). Effects on UNEMP$_i$ may be obscured then for the reasons discussed in the formulation of Hypothesis 7. Second, if UNEMP can be interpreted as a control for economic slack in the labour market, then consistency in the falling coefficients on JOBS$_j$ over time in Model 2 (without unemployment) as well as in Model 3 (with unemployment) suggests further confirmation of Core Hypothesis 6 – as it applies to JOBS that is. Attention is drawn to this point in view of our introductory comments to the section on "Fiscal Variables" in Chapter 3.

Educational selectivity (EDUC$_i$) at origin also exerts the expected positive effect. Thus Hypothesis 29 (the greater the incidence of higher educated persons in city 'i', the greater M$_{ij}$ will be) receives tentative confirmation. Addition of UNEMP and EDUC adds about 3% to the explanatory power of Model 3 over Model 2. As noted above, however, unemployment is more significant during the post-1971 period. This is to be expected since unemployment problems began to take on greater significance across the country as of about 1974.

TABLE 4.4: Empirical Models 3 and 4: Aggregate Results

	Time frame					
	1956 - 81 pooled		Pre-1971		Post-1971	
	R.C.	't' value	R.C.	't' value	R.C.	't' value
Model 3						
Intercept	−3.626	—	−10.285	—	−2.570	—
$DIST_{ij}$	−.517	(13.696)*	−.561	(10.626)*	−.452	(8.559)*
$WAGE1_i$	−.982	(3.192)*	−1.365	(3.041)*	−.081	(.157)
$WAGE1_j$	2.363	(7.431)*	4.206	(9.248)*	1.150	(2.181)*
$LANG_{ij}$	1.044	(10.433)*	.982	(7.124)*	1.092	(7.650)*
$JOBS_i$	−.015	(1.014)	−.023	(.961)	−.031	(1.520)
$JOBS_j$	.102	(7.045)*	.157	(6.928)*	.075	(3.835)*
$UNEMP_i$	−.143	(.951)	−.456	(2.480)	.027	(.099)
$UNEMP_j$	−.771	(5.046)*	−.508	(2.723)*	−1.138	(4.158)*
$EDUC_i$	.721	(4.654)*	.832	(3.792)*	.886	(3.760)*
R^2	.331		.401		.286	
Fvalue	59.136		40.829		23.808	
Observations	1,088		544		544	
Model 4						
Intercept	−.407	—	−9.456	—	−5.753	—
$DIST_{ij}$	−.558	(15.431)*	−.596	(13.020)*	−.494	(9.202)*
$WAGE1_i$	−1.270	(4.133)*	−.959	(2.350)*	−.190	(.370)
$WAGE1_j$	1.299	(4.089)*	2.181	(5.132)*	1.191	(2.289)*
$LANG_{ij}$	1.077	(11.333)*	1.100	(9.132)*	1.071	(7.602)*
$JOBS_i$	−.020	(1.426)	−.019	(.915)	−.027	(1.358)
$JOBS_j$	.093	(6.758)*	.138	(6.983)*	.073	(3.802)*
$UNEMP_i$	−.273	(1.796)	−.341	(2.019)	.060	(.203)
$UNEMP_j$	−.355	(2.352)*	−.067	(.397)	−.685	(2.342)*
$EDUC_i$	.814	(5.112)*	1.153	(5.376)*	.822	(3.453)*
DS_i	−.315	(2.742)*	−.185	(1.231)	.067	(.347)
DS_j	1.161	(10.940)*	1.790	(13.384)*	.767	(4.043)*
R^2	.401		.558		.308	
Fvalue	65.388		61.141		21.489	
Observations	1,088		544		544	

Note: R.C. = regression coefficient;
* = sign as expected and statistically significant at .01 level.

Model 4 adds residential dwelling starts (DS). This variable appears to make a significant, independent, contribution to the explanatory power of the equation. It does so without distorting coefficients on most of the other explanatory variables. Accordingly, Hypothesis 8 (the greater the differential between cities in building cycles – as represented by residential dwelling starts – the greater M_{ij} will be) receives tentative confirmation. Core Hypothesis 9 (building cycles exert a smaller impact on M_{ij} "today" than in the past) also receives tentative confirmation.[3]

In our view, Model 4 can be construed as a relatively full "traditional" economic model of migration. It contains the usual wage, employment and unemployment variables; it contains an adjustment for physical and psychic costs or barriers to migration ($DIST_{ij}$, $LANG_{ij}$); it contains a human capital or selectivity variable ($EDUC_i$); and it contains an indicator of business cycle and housing activity (DS). Another variable which we intended to add to Model 4 measures prices in the housing market (HOUSE). The problem with housing prices, however, is that we found them to be highly intercorrelated with wages, dwelling starts and education.[4] Thus, when HOUSE is added to Model 4 (results not presented here), coefficients on the other explanatory variables are observed to switch sign with nothing being added to the explanatory power of the equation in the process. Accordingly, Hypothesis 19 (housing prices will exert independent effects on M_{ij}) and Core Hypothesis 20 (housing prices will exert a greater effect on M_{ij} after the 1972 revisions to Canada's tax system) cannot be adequately evaluated in this study.

So where do we stand? When *all* data are pooled, our "traditional" market model – as represented by Model 4 – accounts for approximately 40% of the variation in M_{ij} (Table 4.4). In the pre-1971 period, it accounts for a respectable 56% of the variance in M_{ij} versus only 31% in the post-1971 period (see Figure 4.1). Judging from differentials in explanatory power over the two time frames as well as differences in coefficients on the important variables, we have reason to conclude that one dimension of our 'core hypothesis' has received a good measure of support. That is, the influence of "traditional" market variables on migration seems to have shrunk in more recent years. The provocative question now is, "What is squeezing them out?". Are fiscal variables exercising a greater influence on migration during the post-1971 period than during the pre-1971 period? Or, might the changing performance of "traditional" economic variables simply be put down to transitional phenomena associated with adverse cyclical conditions.

Figure 4.1: A Schematic Representation of the Explanatory Power of Models
1 Through 4

Pre-1971 Migration

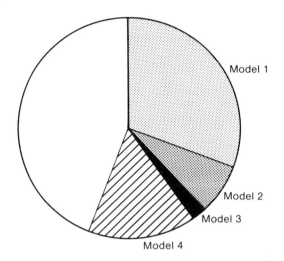

Post-1971 Migration

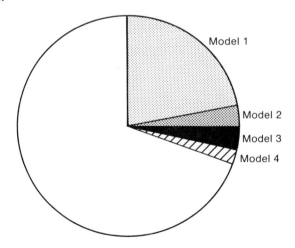

Model 1 = Distance, Wages, Commonality of Language
Model 2 = Model 1 plus Jobs
Model 3 = Model 2 plus Unemployment and Educational Selectivity
Model 4 = Model 3 plus Residential Building Construction

Traditional Market Model with Fiscal Component

Recall from Chapter 3 that the variables in our fiscal component include federal equalization and related payments to provinces (GRANT), unemployment insurance transfers to persons (UIGEN, UIPROB), and natural resource revenues accruing to resource rich provinces (NRR). According to Core Hypotheses 12 and 14, GRANT, UIGEN and UIPROB are expected to exert a greater impact on post-1971 migration in view of post-1971 policy developments. In contrast, NRR has not been given a 'core hypothesis' interpretation; Hypothesis 16 states that natural resource revenues accruing to provinces may not exert an *independent* effect on M_{ij} but may do so largely by augmenting employment and wage opportunities.

Model 5 builds on Model 4 by adding the four variables noted above. Results are presented in Table 4.5. First impressions are that variables in our fiscal component make a significant contribution to the explanatory power of the equation during the post-1971 period. They add approximately 13% to the explanatory power of the equation at a time when federal policy boosted the generosity of both unemployment insurance and equalization grants. Five of the six coefficients on our 'core hypothesis' variables (GRANT, UIGEN, UIPROB) carry the expected sign, four of them are statistically significant, and three exhibit significant negative signs at place of origin (ie., the place at which individuals decide to migrate or not). In contrast, during the pre-1971 period they contribute only 4% to the explanatory power of the equation. Two of the 'core hypothesis' variables carry the expected sign at significant levels and only one has the expected negative sign at place of origin.

On closer inspection, however, we observe that addition of the fiscal variables to Model 5 is not problem free. They affect the size of the coefficient on the wage variable, particularly during the post-1971 period. This implies intercorrelation between fiscal and wage variables. Correlation coefficient matrices (not presented here) convey that the higher the wage level, the higher the level of unemployment insurance generosity (ie., high wage areas offer higher levels of protection). In addition, the higher the wage level, the less federal equalization grants are likely to be. Disadvantages of the wage distortion do seem to be outweighed, however, by advantages of adding the fiscal variables to Model 5. For the post-1971 period, the explanatory power of the equation is not only enhanced, but signs on 11 variables are as expected and statistically significant. This compares with only seven variables for Model 4.

TABLE 4.5: Empirical Model 5: Aggregate Results

	time frame					
	1956 - 81 pooled		Pre-1971		Post-1971	
	R.C.	't' value	R.C.	't' value	R.C.	't' value
Model 5						
Intercept	−3.962	—	8.371	—	6.044	—
$DIST_{ij}$	−.590	(16.873)*	−.657	(14.355)*	−.529	(10.411)*
$WAGE1_i$	−3.733	(3.504)*	−6.435	(2.724)*	−14.192	(5.667)*
$WAGE1_j$	3.704	(3.505)*	1.394	(.588)	12.957	(5.311)*
$LANG_{ij}$	1.261	(13.273)*	1.343	(10.310)*	1.151	(8.022)*
$JOBS_i$	−.008	(.546)	−.009	(.370)	−.015	(.787)
$JOBS_j$	.077	(5.616)*	.164	(7.336)*	.042	(2.280)*
$UNEMP_i$	−.268	(1.746)	−.283	(1.504)	.222	(.635)
$UNEMP_j$	−.462	(3.019)*	−.039	(.210)	−.960	(2.755)*
$EDUC_i$	.729	(4.199)*	.862	(3.932)*	.984	(3.215)*
DS_i	.097	(.807)	.035	(.233)	.428	(1.780)
DS_j	1.481	(13.321)*	1.912	(14.652)*	−.094	(3.90)
$UIGEN_i$	−3.595	(3.537)*	−6.489	(2.736)*	−14.842	(5.832)*
$UIGEN_j$	1.257	(1.241)	−2.336	(.983)	15.064	(6.260)*
$UIPROB_i$	−.265	(1.289)	−.457	(1.054)	−.643	(1.772)
$UIPROB_j$	−1.065	(5.155)	.465	(1.078)	−.179	(.496)
$GRANT_i$	.064	(2.178)	.135	(3.628)	−.113	(2.281)*
$GRANT_j$	.133	(4.618)*	.175	(4.842)*	.113	(2.240)*
NRR_i	NA		NA		.197	(2.593)
NRR_j	NA		NA		.018	(.245)
R^2	.459		.595		.440	
F value	53.439		45.470		21.744	
Observations	1,088		544		544	

Note: R.C. = regression coefficient;
    * = sign as expected and statistically significant at .01 level.
  NA = no account of variable in this regression.

Observe that the performance of NRR in the post-1971 regression does not accord with Hypothesis 15 (the greater the difference between city 'j' and 'i' in terms of its "home" province's NRR, the greater M_{ij} will be). Rather, the coefficient on NRR_j is opposite to what is expected and is not statistically significant. The same applies to the coefficient on NRR_i though it is statistically significant. Were we to remove

NRR from Model 5, we would observe a drop in the R^2 value of only .006 (results not presented here). Furthermore, were we to evaluate NRR in the presence of "traditional" market variables only (ie., Model 4), we would observe that the coefficients on wages, jobs and residential construction would drop below statistically significant levels (results not presented here). The implication is that NRR is intercorrelated with these variables as conveyed by Hypothesis 16 (NRR may not exert an independent effect on M_{ij} but may do so largely through its effects on labour market opportunities).

Impressions concerning the performance of NRR are not altered when it is evaluated in the context of "disaggregated" migration flows (Tables 4.8 and 5.8) or in the context of more "exploratory" models not reported on here. Our conclusion then, is that natural resource revenues – as measured by NRR – is *not* a useful variable for understanding the determinants of intermetropolitan migration in Canada. If natural resource revenues are affecting migration, they are likely to be doing so through investment and expenditure effects on the labour and housing market rather than through independently perceived fiscal advantages. On this point, our results disagree with those reported by Winer and Gauthier (1983). We have decided, therefore, to drop NRR from all further models in our "building block" sequence (ie., Models 6 and 7).

Summing up, the results in Table 4.5 on Model 5, tentatively confirm Hypothesis 13 (the greater the difference between cities in access to federal government equalization transfers to provinces [GRANT], the greater M_{ij} is likely to be).[5] In addition, they tentatively confirm Hypothesis 10 (the greater the difference between city 'i' and 'j' in the generosity [UIGEN] and ease of obtaining unemployment insurance [UIPROB], the less the probability of M_{ij} is likely to be). Furthermore, results on Model 5 versus Model 4, are consistent with the idea that fiscal variables are at least partially responsible for the "failure" of migrants to respond as strongly to more "traditional" market variables during the post-1971 period (see Figure 4.2). This implies tentative confirmation of Core Hypothesis 12 (UI benefits will serve to dampen M_{ij} more after the generous 1971 revisions to Canada's Unemployment Insurance Act), and Core Hypothesis 14 (federal government equilization payments will have more of an effect on M_{ij} after 1971 in view of increased allocations to eastern Canada).

Figure 4.2: A Schematic Representation of the Explanatory Power of Model
4 Versus Model 5

Pre-1971 Migration

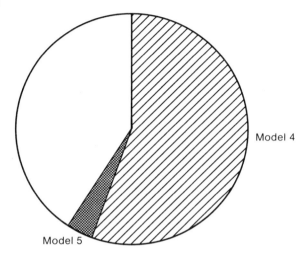

Post-1971 Migration

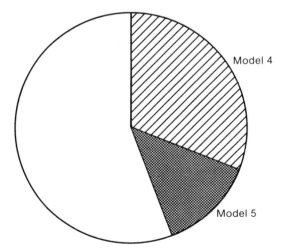

Model 5 = Model 4 plus fiscal variables.

A Fuller Model?

Several variables which were discussed in Chapter 3 under the ruberic "additional economic variables" or "social and amenity considerations" remain to be evaluated. These include home ownership (OWN), female labour force opportunities (FEM), immigration (IMMIG), a measure of violent crime (CRIME), and a measure of climate (SNOW).

One difference between the remaining variables and those evaluated in Models 1 through 5 is that they have been selected on rather eclectic grounds. Compared with wages and employment growth, for example, their hypothesized effects can be justified far less on theoretical grounds or in terms of empirical precedent. Another problem with these variables is that the gap between the "theoretical concepts" we have in mind and most of our empirical measures is rather wide. For example, we use female activity rates (FEM) to proxy dual income-earning households, and we use a measure of snowfall (SNOW) as a surrogate for the effects of climate. In contrast, the correspondence between most of our theoretical concepts and empirical variables in Models 1 through 5 is considerably tighter (or, at least, we use empirical surrogates that are generally accepted). A third potential problem is that some of our additional economic considerations may be collinear with important variables already in Models 1 through 5. This problem was discussed in Chapter 3 with respect to our immigration variable (IMMIG).

All this is to say that the addition of variables to Model 5 to produce a "fuller model" does not necessarily imply that we will be producing a better model. Rather, estimation of Models 6 and 7 should be construed as more of an exploratory exercise.

Model 6 in Table 4.6 builds on Model 5 by adding our measure of crime (CRIME), climate (SNOW) and home ownership (OWN). Previous scrutiny of correlation coefficient matrices conveyed that these three variables were not seriously intercorrelated with our "traditional" market or fiscal variables. Therefore, we interpret them as relatively independent influences. By implication the same cannot be said about FEM, and IMMIG; this will be taken up in the context of Model 7 in Table 4.7.

Observe from Table 4.6 that the addition of CRIME, SNOW and OWN augment the "explanatory power" of Model 6 over Model 5 but by a small margin. R^2 values increase by 4.6% for the all-pooled data, 7.1% for the pre-1971 period, and 3.2% for the post-1971 period. Observe also that most of the variables show signs that are contrary to expectation.

TABLE 4.6: Empirical Model 6: Aggregate Results

| | Time frame | | | | | |
| | 1956 - 81 pooled | | Pre-1971 | | Post-1971 | |
	R.C.	't' value	R.C.	't' value	R.C.	't' value
Model 6						
Intercept	1.302	—	27.761	—	11.076	—
$DIST_{ij}$	−.681	(18.882)*	−.793	(17.114)*	−.545	(10.621)*
$WAGE1_i$	−2.346	(2.130)*	−8.094	(3.461)*	−11.353	(5.826)*
$WAGE1_j$	1.576	(1.412)*	−1.565	(.673)	8.619	(4.402)*
$LANG_{ij}$	.991	(9.590)*	.949	(6.846)*	.957	(6.242)*
$JOBS_i$	.008	(.530)	.020	(.844)	−.002	(.137)
$JOBS_j$	.091	(6.787)*	.200	(9.323)*	.015	(.799)
$UNEMP_i$	−.213	(1.444)	−.096	(.536)	−.018	(.047)
$UNEMP_j$	−.498	(3.345)*	−.199	(1.123)	−.282	(.763)
$EDUC_i$	.884	(4.798)*	1.050	(4.409)*	.902	(2.467)*
DS_i	.047	(.393)	−.150	(.974)	.684	(3.162)
DS_j	1.363	(12.668)*	1.600	(12.588)*	.093	(.428)
$UIGEN_i$	−2.480	(2.373)*	−8.542	(3.639)*	−12.527	(6.176)*
$UIGEN_j$	−.079	(.076)	−4.284	(1.868)	11.999	(6.045)*
$UIPROB_i$	−.109	(.536)	−.748	(1.751)	−.669	(2.000)*
$UIPROB_j$	−.883	(4.332)	.258	(.601)	−.463	(1.333)
$GRANT_i$	.103	(3.509)	.180	(4.915)	−.056	(1.143)
$GRANT_j$	.172	(5.913)*	.203	(5.776)*	.055	(1.128)
$CRIME_i$	−.045	(.683)	−.050	(.612)	−.071	(.628)
$CRIME_j$	.379	(5.761)	.419	(5.226)	.601	(5.276)
$SNOW_i$	−.129	(1.501)	−.175	(1.495)	−.282	(2.218)
$SNOW_j$	−.600	(7.529)*	−.768	(7.591)*	−.107	(.858)
OWN_i	.354	(2.027)	.598	(3.021)	.281	(.633)
R^2	.505		.656		.472	
Fvalue	49.404		45.143		21.162	
Observations	1,088		544		544	

Note: R.C. = regression coefficient;
  * = sign as expected and statistically significant at the .01 level.

Indeed, $CRIME_j$ at place of destination shows a positive sign at statistically significant levels. $SNOW_j$ does exhibit the expected negative sign at destination at significant levels for the all-pooled and pre-1971 data but it is not significant in the post-1971 regression. A tentative conclusion then is that none of the hypotheses concerning the expected effects of CRIME (Hypothesis 27), SNOW (Hypothesis 28) or OWN (Hypothesis 17 and Core Hypothesis 18), are confirmed.

Turning now to Model 7, we observe that the addition of immigration (IMMIG) and female activity rates (FEM) boosts the "explanatory power" of the model considerably. R^2 values increase over those obtained by Model 6 by approximately 13% for the all-pooled data and 24% for the post-1971 period. Moreover, both variables exhibit the expected sign at place of destination, usually at high levels of statistical significance. In the process, however, coefficients on some of the important fiscal and labour market variables are observed to change. This applies particularly to the unemployment insurance variables (UIGEN, UIPROB) and unemployment (UNEMP) in the post-1971 period. Thus, the increase in "explanatory power" is accompanied by lost rigor or specificity. We conclude then that Hypothesis 21 (the greater the differential in female labour force opportunities [FEM], between cities, the greater M_{ij} will be) has received *tentative* confirmation but that its effects on M_{ij} cannot be interpreted as entirely independent. The same applies to Hypothesis 22 (the greater the differential in rates of immigration of the foreign born between cities, [IMMIG], the greater M_{ij} will be).

Migration During the 1976-81 Period

To focus on more recent patterns of migration, Models 1 through 7 have also been calibrated on data pertaining to 1976-81 only. Our general impression is that the results presented in Table 4.8 are largely consistent with those reported in Tables 4.2 to 4.7. A crude comparison of results on Models 5 and 7 for the 1976-81 period versus different time frames can be made as follows;

Differences are, however, evident in the magnitudes of coefficients on individual explanatory variables over the different time frames. This implies that models calibrated on "early data" are not likely to serve as a reliable guide to predicting more current migration patterns. To a large extent, this conclusion is consistent with our 'core hypothesis'.

TABLE 4.7: Empirical Model 7: Aggregate Results

	Time frame					
	1956 - 81 pooled		Pre-1971		Post-1971	
	R.C.	't' value	R.C.	't' value	R.C.	't' value
Model 7						
Intercept	−9.898	—	52.002	—	−45.257	—
$DIST_{ij}$	−.648	(20.709)*	−.759	(16.869)*	−.563	(13.885)*
$WAGE1_i$	−1.067	(.972)	−12.370	(4.649)*	−5.522	(3.232)*
$WAGE1_j$	.318	(.289)	−4.688	(1.813)	4.337	(2.565)*
$LANG_{ij}$	.804	(8.701)*	.705	(5.106)*	.944	(7.770)*
$JOBS_i$	−.015	(1.172)	.021	(.772)	−.008	(.515)
$JOBS_j$	.043	(3.537)*	.129	(5.327)*	.014	(.958)
$UNEMP_i$	−.623	(4.345)	.030	(.154)	.041	(.129)
$UNEMP_j$	.407	(2.909)	.313	(1.676)	2.056	(6.801)
$EDUC_i$	.691	(3.559)*	1.101	(4.024)*	.827	(2.595)*
DS_i	−.040	(.375)	−.402	(2.183)*	.517	(3.129)
DS_j	.543	(5.327)*	.816	(4.994)*	.210	(1.172)
$UIGEN_i$	−.419	(.439)	−11.624	(4.685)*	−7.306	(4.269)*
$UIGEN_j$	−1.294	(1.356)	−7.284	(3.054)	4.869	(2.916)*
$UIPROB_i$	−.021	(.119)	−.889	(2.002)*	−.172	(.639)
$UIPROB_j$	−.781	(4.430)	−.982	(2.195)	.015	(.056)
$GRANT_i$	.104	(3.565)	.135	(3.429)	.051	(1.143)
$GRANT_j$	.250	(9.161)*	.242	(6.535)*	.278	(6.597)*
$CRIME_i$	.004	(.075)	−.102	(1.159)	−.102	(1.154)
$CRIME_j$	.017	(.290)	.118	(1.356)	.127	(1.380)
$SNOW_i$	−.230	(2.626)	.002	(.012)	−.184	(1.701)
$SNOW_j$	−.194	(2.514)*	−.050	(4.488)*	.250	(2.260)
OWN_i	.369	(2.358)	.774	(3.599)	.447	(1.304)
FEM_i	.499	(.859)	−1.672	(1.879	1.485	(1.679)
FEM_j	1.365	(2.552*	.780	(.974)	3.667	(3.995)*
$IMMIG_i$	−.097	(.989)	.500	(2.836)	−.012	(.092)
$IMMIG_j$	1.252	(12.899)*	.914	(5.297)*	1.527	(12.822)*
R^2	.636		.689		.711	
Fvalue	68.479		43.984		46.905	
Observations	1,088		544		544	

Note: R.C. = regression coefficient;
    * = sign as expected and statistically significant at .01 level.

TABLE 4.8: Empirical Models 1 to 7: 1976-81 Results

	Model 1 R.C.	Model 1 't' value	Model 2 R.C.	Model 2 't' value	Model 3 R.C.	Model 3 't' value	Model 4 R.C.	Model 4 't' value	Model 5 R.C.	Model 5 't' value	Model 6 R.C.	Model 6 't' value	Model 7 R.C.	Model 7 't' value
Intercept	8.724	—	12.981	—	22.788	—	15.333	—	-124.907	—	-47.668	—	-110.764	—
$DIST_{ij}$	-.415	(5.339)*	-.431	(5.999)*	-.423	(6.407)*	-.482	(6.842)*	-.612	(9.288)*	-.591	(8.599)*	-.568	(10.295)*
$WAGE1_i$	-1.550	(1.733)	-1.631	(1.933)	-1.651	(2.017)*	-1.486	(1.767)	-2.400	(.483)	-4.453	(1.415)	-3.597	(1.290)
$WAGE1_j$	.269	(.298)	-.505	(.599)	.059	(.076)	.633	(.785)	39.438	(8.909)*	23.550	(7.655)*	16.758	(5.237)*
$LANG_{ij}$	1.237	(5.901)*	1.171	(6.035)*	1.017	(5.641)*	.999	(5.579)*	1.250	(7.181)*	1.265	(5.845)*	.981	(5.537)*
$JOBS_i$			.020	(.766)	.024	(.852)	.025	(.886)	.009	(.367)	.020	(.652)	-.006	(.219)
$JOBS_j$			.177	(6.911)*	.126	(5.137)*	.126	(5.170)*	.117	(5.461)*	.125	(4.535)*	.054	(2.070)*
$UNEMP_i$					-.061	(.165)	.088	(.219)	.535	(.710)	.425	(.402)	.522	(.510)
$UNEMP_j$					-2.713	(7.346)*	-2.340	(5.885)*	-6.308	(8.376)*	-5.820	(6.299)*	-2.398	(2.810)*
$EDUC_i$					-.139	(.321)	.140	(.323)	.442	(.909)	.314	(.429)	1.080	(1.305)
DS_i							.209	(.876)	.478	(1.659)	.437	(1.463)	.602	(2.509)
DS_j							.580	(2.415)*	-.844	(2.926)	-1.219	(4.159)	-.522	(2.020)
$UIGEN_i$									-2.520	(.492)	-4.549	(1.304)*	-6.477	(2.391)*
$UIGEN_j$									40.803	(9.528)*	26.508	(8.315)*	13.484	(4.411)*
$UIPROB_i$									-.668	(.871)	-.738	(.840)	-.912	(1.264)
$UIPROB_j$									5.084	(6.754)*	4.628	(5.783)*	3.085	(4.690)*
$GRANT_i$									.168	(1.457)	.168	(1.489)	.299	(2.132)
$GRANT_j$									.218	(1.891)	.067	(.607)	.411	(2.976)*
$CRIME_i$											-.091	(.365)	-.116	(.594)
$CRIME_j$											.117	(.477)	-.358	(1.844)
$SNOW_i$											-.127	(.752)	-.237	(1.562)
$SNOW_j$											-.303	(1.800)	.106	(.567)
OWN_i											-.174	(.224)	.548	(.805)
NRR_i									-.038	(.351)				
NRR_j									-.420	(4.182)				
FEM_i													3.152	(1.548)
FEM_j													5.171	(2.604)*
$IMMIG_i$													-.290	(1.320)
$IMMIG_j$													1.184	(6.321)*
R^2	.191		.315		.433		.446		.625		.606		.770	
Fvalue	15.786		20.309		22.187		18.998		22.093		17.416		30.289	
Observations	272		272		272		272		272		272		272	

Note: R.C. = regression coefficient;
* = sign as expected and statistically significant at .01 level.

	Time frame			
	1956 - 81	Pre-1971	Post-1971	1976 - 81
Number of coefficients estimated in Model 5	17	17	19	19
Number showing expected sign	13	13	14	13
Number showing expected sign plus statistically significant	10	8	10	7
R^2	.459	.595	.440	.625
Number of coefficients estimated in Model 7	26	26	26	26
Number showing expected sign	18	15	17	16
Number showing expected sign plus statistically significant	9	12	10	11
R^2	.635	.689	.714	.770

Summing Up

Results in this chapter provide tentative confirmation of several of our hypotheses concerning the determinants of intermetropolitan migration in Canada. First, our most provocative hypothesis – which has been described in Chapters 1 and 3 as our 'core hypothesis' – has received confirmation in two ways. On the one hand, our representation of a "traditional" market model is less relevant to explaining intermetropolitan migration in Canada in recent years than in the past. This judgment is based on results of Model 4 in Table 4.4. On the other hand, changes in fiscal variables after 1971, are more relevant to explaining migration in recent years. This judgment is based on Model 5 which adds several fiscal variables to Model 4 (see Table 4.5). Our interpretation – in keeping with our 'core hypothesis' – is that fiscal variables such as unemployment insurance and federal equalization grants are partially responsible for crowding out the influence of more "traditional" labour market variables on migration.

Second, our procedure of adding explanatory variables to a "bare bones" Sjaastad-type formulation (ie., Models 1 through 4) conveys that the influence of the labour market on migration is not adequately represented by wage rates and distance. That measures of employment growth, unemployment and residential construction make an independent contribution to the estimating equation suggests that rigidity, if not segmentation, is at work in the Canadian labour market.

Third, our evaluation of alternative wage variants suggests that little is gained by computing more complex income/employment indicators in multiplicative fashion. Possibly, migrants themselves do not perform intricate adjustments to their earnings expectations in multiplicative fashion because they do not possess the information required to do so. Another possibility is that migrants are "risk averse", meaning that they may assign separate weights to, say employment and wages. If so, then an increase in, say, job probability (or reduced unemployment probability) might weigh more heavily than an equivalent increase in wage rates in the migrant's utility calculus. A multiplicative wage variant such as WAGE4 neglects this possibility.

Fourth, asymmetry is strongly evident in the effects of our variables measured at destination and origin. Typically, destination effects dominate origin effects in wages ($WAGE1_j$), employment ($JOBS_j$), unemployment ($UNEMP_j$), residential dwelling starts (DS_j), immigration ($IMMIG_j$), female activity rates (FEM_j), and federal equalization grants ($GRANT_j$). As noted previously this finding conforms with results of a great many other studies; rationale for it have been presented in the methodological Appendix to Chapter 4.

Fifth, our results convey that economic variables – be they "traditional" market or fiscal variables – dominate as influences in intermetropolitan migration in Canada. By comparison, non-economic measures such as crime or climate, perform poorly.

Sixth, our results differ from those presented by Winer and Gauthier (1983) on the influence of natural resource revenues (NRR) on migration to the Canadian west. Migrants may well be attracted to the Canadian west due to NRR-related developments but the real mover is more likely to be higher NRR-related incomes and growth of jobs than NRR-related money or fiscal illusion. In addition, our results disagree with Winer and Gauthier's (1983) interpretation that immigration is likely to have a negative effect on internal migration by virtue of absorbing scarce jobs in the labour market. Our results imply that immigration to CMA's is strongly and positively correlated with M_{ij}. While problems of multicollinearity cannot be ruled out, it seems reasonable to assume that immigrants exert a positive influence on CMA economies and that these, in turn, exert a draw on internal migrants.

Finally, our empirical estimates offer two advantages over previous studies of migration in Canada. One advantage is that they derive from units of analysis far more homogeneous than, say, provinces or regions.

Recall from the Appendix to Chapter 4 that Miller's model accounted for 88% of the variance when *interstate* migration data were used versus only 49.6% when *intermetropolitan* data were used. Recall also that Laber and Chase's model explained about 50-60% of the variance in *interregional* migration in Canada compared with only 30% when we estimated a similar version in the context of *intermetropolitan* migration. Our point, then, is that most of the empirical coefficients estimated in Models 1 through 6 are likely to serve as a more reliable guide to the "true" significance of several determinants of long-distance migration in Canada such as wages, employment growth, unemployment, distance (see, however, footnote 11 to Chapter 1). A second advantage is that our empirical estimates have been calculated over different time frames rather than one long time frame. Thus, they reflect the realities of important socio-economic changes during more recent times. This is important from the standpoint of predicting migration in the near future.

Footnotes

1. To dispell any confusion over our estimation procedures, the "building block" approach alluded to here neither prescribes nor is aligned with stepwise regression.

2. Studies of migration which employ regression techniques usually judge significance of explanatory variables 'X' as determinants of dependent variable 'Y' (the variable to be explained), on the basis of Student 't' tests. If the regression coefficient for a particular explanatory variable 'X' exceeds a critical Student 't' value, it is said to be "statistically significant". More precisely, if the ratio of the regression coefficient for 'X' exceeds its standard error (or residual variance) by a specified amount (usually a ratio of two or more), the researcher concludes that 'X' cannot be rejected as a significant correlate of variations in 'Y'. In the studies reviewed in Chapter 2, as well as our own empirical work, Student 't' values have been calculated at the .01 level of significance. This means that if the ratio of the regression coefficient for 'X' to its standard error exceeds the Student 't' level corresponding to a .01 level of significance, chances of accepting an incorrect hypothesis (that X is a significant determinant of Y) are less than 1 in 100.

    Correct usage of the term "statistical significance", however, requires that the data in question derive from a sample, which is normally distributed. Thus, if 'X' is judged to be statistically significant at the .10 level, it also implies that there is less than a 1 in 100 chance that it constitutes an erroneous or unrepresentative sample from the population at large. (It follows that as the size of the sample (eg., a sample of migrants) approaches the total population (all migrants), the chances of an erroneous or unrepresentative sample approach zero.) In regression studies involving cross-sectional or time-series migration data, observations for empirical study often tend not to be a sample. Rather, they often consist of *all* observations available, or some portion of all observations, but not selected randomly. Thus, statements concerning statistical significance at the .01 level are unorthodox. More appropriately, they imply that the researcher has employed a broad, well-known criterion to (i) reject or accept a particular variable in terms of its ability to account for variations in 'Y', and (ii) make comparisons between variables in terms of the rigor by which they are able to acount, differently, for variations in 'Y'.

3. Moreover, if residential dwelling starts (DS) can be interpreted as a partial control for economic slack in the labour market (ie., business cycles), then consistency in the falling coefficients on WAGE and JOBS in Model 3 without DS and Model 4 with DS provides further confirmation of Core Hypothesis 3 (WAGE effects) and 6 (Job effects).

4. The simple correlation coefficient between $HOUSE_i$ and $WAGE_i$ is .660; $HOUSE_i$ and DS_i is .433; $HOUSE_i$ and $EDUC_i$ is .666; $HOUSE_i$ and NRR_i is .418; $HOUSE_i$ and FEM_i is .656; $HOUSE_i$ and $UIGEN_i$ is .490.

5. It is worthy of note that our measure of GRANT was disaggregated into two submeasures "general purpose transfers" (GPT) and "specific purpose transfers" (SPT). Overall, GRANT was highly correlated with both GPT and GST. Such disaggregations, therefore, construed no advantage.

Chapter 5
Disaggregated Results

Introduction

To what extent do the results reported in Chapter 4 apply to different regions in Canada? Do they apply equally to migrants who differ in terms of, say, levels of education or income? If they do, can we reasonably assume that migrants in different places or with different characteristics are strongly homogeneous in their response to socio-economic influences. Recall that strong homogeneity implies that one theoretical/empirical model might work equally well for all; that requirements for disaggregated data can be relaxed; and that a highly aggregate empirical model might be used as a reliable policy guide for predicting the behaviour of different target groups.

To test for homogeneity, or rather the lack of it, we stratify our sample in two ways. First, data for all time periods are grouped into an eastern versus western region. Our eastern region consists of 320 observations covering 1956-81; these include migration flows originating from Saint John, St. John's, Halifax, Montréal and Québec City. Our western region consists of the same number of migration flows originating from Victoria, Vancouver, Calgary, Edmonton and Winnipeg. Migration flows originating from CMA's in centrally located Ontario have been excluded in the interests of polarizing "origin" CMA's as much as possible on an "east:west continuum".

Second, migrants are stratified into three educational subgroups. These are, (i) migrants with an educational attainment less than a grade 12 diploma, (ii) those with grade 12 diploma or more, but less than university graduation, and (iii) those with university graduation or more (eg., BA, MA, PHD). This stratification makes use of 1976-81 data only, with a resulting sample size of 272 observations for each education group.

Rather than stratify migrants by level of education, we might have selected income as a stratifying variable (eg., as in Winer and Gauthier:1983). Differences in the two variables are likely to be marginal in the context of metropolitan Canada, however, since levels of income are highly correlated with levels of education. This applies particularly to urban wage and salary workers. In addition, our selection of education as a stratifying variable is preferable to income for this study because it is more directly aligned with notions about the interrelationship between human capital and employment. Following the arguments in Chapter 3 pertaining to segmented labour markets and wage rigidities, we are interested in the response of workers with different human capital endowments to "traditional" market versus fiscal variables.

Now, in view of our interest in workers with different human capital endowments, we would prefer to limit our evaluation to those in the labour force per se. Recall that all previous estimates reported in this study pertain to migration rates for the general population (males and females aged five years and over). With this in mind, the 1976-81 migration data which are analyzed here have been further disaggregated to apply only to males aged 15 years and over. Males of this age group correspond more closely to traditional notions of the active labour force.

The first part of this chapter presents results on Models 1 through 7 by region. (See Table 4.1, Chapter 4, for an overview of the variables involved.) The second part takes up results on the educational subgroups. It is possible to summarize points of interest rather directly since our presentation closely parallels that of the previous chapter.

Results by Region

Judging from the results in Tables 5.1 and 5.2 on Models 1 through 4, significant differences are evident in the determinants of migration to and from CMA's located in the Canadian West and East. First, as might be expected, commonality of language ($LANG_{ij}$) is much more significant for migration from eastern than western CMA's (ie., larger coefficient as well as more statistically significant). For migration flows originating from the west, commonality of language is likely to be relatively

TABLE 5.1: Empirical Models 1 and 2: Regional Results

	Region			
	West (1956 - 81)		East (1956 - 81)	
	R.C.	't' value	R.C.	't' value
Model 1				
Intercept	6.638	—	−4.405	—
$DIST_{ij}$	−1.185	(11.357)*	−.209	(2.296)*
$WAGE1_i$	−.535	(.782)	1.722	(2.891)
$WAGE1_j$	.976	(1.590)	−.643	(1.062)
$LANG_{ij}$	.169	(.670)	1.695	(10.629)*
R^2	.327		.276	
Fvalue	38.296		30.062	
Observations	320		320	
Model 2				
Intercept	5.199	—	−3.987	—
$DIST_{ij}$	−1.147	(11.266)*	−.246	(2.742)*
$WAGE1_i$	−1.085	(1.592)	.873	(1.345)
$WAGE1_j$	1.715	(2.765)*	.131	(.210)
$LANG_{ij}$	.118	(.480)	1.625	(10.365)*
$JOBS_i$	.028	(.962)	−.048	(1.465)
$JOBS_j$	.127	(4.467)*	.100	(3.893)*
R^2	.369		.313	
Fvalue	30.466		23.752	
Observations	320		320	

Note: R.C. = regression coefficient;
 * = sign as expected and statistically significant at .01 level.

unimportant as only 40 inter-CMA migration flows originating from the west do not share a common language out of a total of 320. In contrast, 144 inter-CMA migration flows originating from the east do not share a common language. The difference in the coefficient on $LANG_{ij}$ arises because M_{ij} between Montréal and Québec City (common $LANG_{ij}$ = 1) and M_{ij} between English-speaking CMA's (common $LANG_{ij}$ = 1) is greater than that between French- and English-speaking CMA's in the east (common $LANG_{ij}$ = 0).

TABLE 5.2: Empirical Models 3 and 4: Regional Results

	Region			
	West (1956 - 81)		East (1956 - 81)	
	R.C.	't' value	R.C.	't' value
Model 3				
Intercept	12.335	—	.038	—
$DIST_{ij}$	−1.179	(11.915)*	−.231	(2.633)*
$WAGE1_i$	−4.535	(1.955)*	−.853	(.845)
$WAGE1_j$	1.425	(2.245)*	.122	(.195)
$LANG_{ij}$	−.123	(.507)	1.587	(10.347)*
$JOBS_i$	.080	(1.858)	−.083	(2.535)*
$JOBS_j$	.103	(3.624)*	.095	(3.682)*
$UNEMP_i$	.336	(.567)	−.405	(1.265)
$UNEMP_j$	−1.407	(4.549)*	.419	(1.499)
$EDUC_i$	3.183	(2.944)*	1.613	(3.861)*
R^2	.414		.365	
Fvalue	24.306		19.815	
Observations	320		320	
Model 4				
Intercept	14.473	—	3.013	—
$DIST_{ij}$	−.967	(9.714)*	−.356	(3.902)*
$WAGE1_i$	−5.320	(1.974)*	−1.535	(1.265)
$WAGE1_j$	.559	(.908)	−.212	(.345)
$LANG_{ij}$	.056	(.243)	1.545	(10.327)*
$JOBS_i$	.103	(2.371)	−.109	(3.347)*
$JOBS_j$	.095	(3.546)*	.091	(3.608)*
$UNEMP_i$	.355	(.537)	−.484	(1.459)
$UNEMP_j$	−.873	(2.846)*	−.049	(.170)
$EDUC_i$	3.040	(2.780)*	1.562	(3.759)*
DS_i	−.269	(.798)	−.137	(.602)
DS_j	1.379	(6.231)*	.893	(4.330)*
R^2	.479		.403	
Fvalue	25.785		18.876	
Observations	320		320	

Note: R.C. = regression coefficient;
     * = sign as expected and statistically significant at .01 level.

Second, distance (DIST$_{ij}$) exerts a larger negative effect on migration *from* the west. Similar results are found in Winer and Gauthier's (1983) Tables 4.2 and 4.5. Why this should be so is difficult to say. Possibly, it stems from the fact that migration in Canada has always been, on balance, westward. If potential migrants in the east are more likely to have friends and relatives in the west (ie., past migrants from the east), this consideration may reduce informational costs, psychic costs to moving and initial settlement costs (all of which are proxied by DIST$_{ij}$).

Third, Models 3 and 4 convey that wage, unemployment and dwelling starts are more relevant to understanding migration from western Canada than from eastern Canada. If Model 4 is interpreted as a relatively full "traditional" market model, we observe that it accounts for almost 8% more variance in M$_{ij}$ *from western Canada than from* the east.

Why would Model 4 be less relevant to understanding migration from CMA's in eastern Canada? The answer, in keeping with our 'core hypothesis' is that fiscal influences exert a far greater impact on migration to and from eastern Canada (see also Figures 3.1 and 3.3 in Chapter 3). Consider the results in Table 5.3 on Model 5. This is evident when our measures of unemployment insurance (UIGEN, UIPROB) and our measure of federal equalization grants (GRANT) are added to Model 4 to produce Model 5. (Note that NRR is not evaluated since data on our east/west disaggregation include observations over the entire 1956-81 period whereas NRR data are available for the post-1971 period only). These variables add approximately 7% to the explanatory power of the equation for eastern Canada versus only 3% for western Canada. Observe also that three of the coefficients on the fiscal variables carry the expected sign and are statistically significant for eastern Canada whereas none are statistically significant for western Canada (though five carry the expected sign). Finally, comparison of the coefficients (elasticities) on the significant fiscal variables in the eastern region reveals that each is appreciably larger than its counterpart in western Canada. These results are in agreement with arguments first set out by Courchene (1970), and provide further support for the 'core hypothesis' of this study.

Results on our so-called "fuller models" are presented in Table 5.4 (Model 6) and Table 5.5 (Model 7). Recall from Chapter 4 that Model 6 adds only those variables which can be assumed to be relatively independent of our "traditional" market and fiscal variables (ie., CRIME, SNOW and OWN). These variables perform much the same way as they

TABLE 5.3: Empirical Model 5: Regional Results

	Region			
	West (1956 - 81)		East (1956 - 81)	
	R.C.	't' value	R.C.	't' value
Model 5				
Intercept	7.474	—	1.955	—
$DIST_{ij}$	−.867	(8.287)*	−.520	(5.324)*
$WAGE_i$	−5.733	(1.610)	−6.191	(2.520)*
$WAGE_j$	2.677	(1.086)	4.702	(2.020)*
$LANG_i$	.256	(1.007)	1.534	(8.050)*
$JOBS_i$	.029	(.490)	−.101	(2.998)*
$JOBS_j$	.085	(3.074)*	.073	(2.873)*
$UNEMP_i$	−.108	(.126)	−.600	(1.553)
$UNEMP_j$	−.803	(2.458)*	−.407	(1.388)
$EDUC_i$	2.269	(1.568)	1.014	(2.193)*
DS_i	.132	(.307)	−.003	(.014)
DS_j	1.659	(6.927)*	1.279	(6.044)*
$UIGEN_i$	−3.032	(1.323)	−5.374	(2.464)*
$UIGEN_j$	1.558	(.649)	3.197	(1.463)
$UIPROB_i$	−.567	(1.142)	−1.011	(2.017)*
$UIPROB_j$	−.849	(1.850)	−.806	(2.271)
$GRANT_i$	−.039	(.375)	.300	(1.803)
$GRANT_j$	.060	(.951)	.204	(3.672)*
NRR_i	NA		NA	
NRR_j	NA		NA	
R^2	.506		.472	
Fvalue	18.199		15.897	
Observations	320		320	

Note: R.C. = regression coefficient;
  * = sign as expected and statistically significant at .01 level;
Note: NA = no account of variable in this regression.

did when Model 6 was applied to our aggregate data in Chapter 4. $CRIME_j$ at destination carries an unexpected sign at statistically significant levels whereas OWN_i carries the expected sign but at levels below statistical significance. Thus, Hypothesis 27 (the greater the differential in rates of violent crime between cities, the less M_{ij} will be) remains rejected. The same applies to Hypothesis 17 and Core Hypothesis 18

TABLE 5.4: Empirical Model 6: Regional Results

	Region			
	West (1956 - 81)		East (1956 - 81)	
	R.C.	't' value	R.C.	't' value
Model 6				
Intercept	34.599	—	16.952	—
$DIST_{ij}$	−.647	(6.328)*	−.750	(6.130)*
$WAGE1_i$	−5.023	(.834)	−9.268	(3.294)*
$WAGE1_j$	−1.795	(.699)	2.816	(1.184)
$LANG_{ij}$	−.479	(1.919)	1.304	(6.524)*
$JOBS_i$	.026	(.332)	−.132	(3.487)*
$JOBS_j$	.103	(3.990)*	.086	(3.401)*
$UNEMP_i$	.852	(.808)	.119	(.191)
$UNEMP_j$	−1.010	(3.360)*	−.535	(1.845)
$EDUC_i$	2.931	(1.179)	1.340	(2.571)*
DS_i	.213	(.482)	.510	(1.590)
DS_j	1.533	(6.985)*	1.292	(6.198)*
$UIGEN_i$	−.417	(.154)	−4.840	(2.208)*
$UIGEN_j$	−1.235	(.492)	2.158	(.970)
$UIPROB_i$	−.946	(1.573)	−.830	(1.467)
$UIPROB_j$	−.470	(1.010)	−.550	(1.543)
$GRANT_i$	.013	(.111)	.838	(1.594)
$GRANT_j$	.076	(1.269)	.218	(3.828)*
$CRIME_i$	−.082	(.224)	1.082	(1.340)
$CRIME_j$	.599	(4.779)	.374	(3.164)
$SNOW_i$	.062	(.178)	7.89	(.742)
$SNOW_j$	−1.162	(6.560)*	−.550	(3.085)*
OWN_i	−3.050	(1.597)	−.410	(.365)
R^2	.603		.514	
Fvalue	20.487		14.257	
Observations	320		320	

Note: R.C. = regression coefficient;
    *   = sign as expected and statistically significant at .01 level.

concerning the effects of home ownership on migration. In contrast, results on our climate variable, $SNOW_j$, suggest that Hypothesis 28 (the greater the differential in centimetres of snowfall between cities, the less M_{ij} will be) should be reconsidered. Recall that this hypothesis was rejected in Chapter 4 though $SNOW_j$ did exhibit the expected sign at

TABLE 5.5: Empirical Model 7: Regional Results

	Region			
	West (1956 - 81)		East (1956 - 81)	
	R.C.	't' value	R.C.	't' value
Model 7				
Intercept	.851	—	−53.263	—
$DIST_{ij}$	−.600	(7.632)*	−.782	(7.349)*
$WAGE_i$	8.096	(1.125)	−1.886	(.552)
$WAGE_j$	−3.115	(1.295)	−3.248	(1.282)
$LANG_{ij}$	−.860	(4.431)	1.181	(6.900)*
$JOBS_i$	.068	(1.081)	−.122	(3.271)*
$JOBS_j$	.051	(2.478)*	.063	(2.831)*
$UNEMP_i$	−.564	(.601)	.617	(.946)
$UNEMP_j$	.322	(1.251)	.782	(2.802)
$EDUC_i$	−1.680	(.587)	−1.569	(1.200)
DS_i	.419	(1.140)	.609	(2.106)
DS_j	.547	(3.032)*	.566	(2.947)*
$UIGEN_i$	1.303	(.583)	1.516	(.680)
$UIGEN_j$	−3.083	(1.525)	−3.482	(1.597)
$UIPROB_i$	−.429	(.875)	−.059	(.106)
$UIPROB_j$	−.238	(.670)	−1.065	(3.101)
$GRANT_i$	.161	(1.712)	−.293	(.558)
$GRANT_j$	.225	(4.190)*	.282	(5.014)*
$CRIME_i$	−.391	(.999)	.349	(.405)
$CRIME_j$	.098	(.968)	−.019	(.181)
$SNOW_i$	.897	(1.390)	.186	(.185)
$SNOW_j$	−.791	(5.332)*	−.127	(.756)
OWN_i	−.431	(.230)	.913	(.879)
FEM_i	−5.268	(1.750)	12.399	(3.028)
FEM_j	3.391	(3.090)*	−.288	(.251)
$IMMIG_i$	−1.821	(2.903)	.399	(1.612)
$IMMIG_j$	1.412	(7.897)*	1.495	(7.692)*
R^2	.775		.658	
Fvalue	37.189		20.782	
Observations	320		320	

Note: R.C. = regression coefficient;
   * = sign as expected and statistically significant at .01 level.

significant levels for the all-pooled data and the pre-1971 period. In view of its performance in Table 5.4 where it exhibits the expected negative effect at significant levels for both the western and the eastern regions, we suggest that Hypothesis 28 merits tentative confirmation.

Turning now to results on Model 7 (Table 5.5), we find that the performance of female labour force opportunities (FEM) and immigration (IMMIG) accords more with expectation for the western than the eastern region. For the western region, they boost the "explanatory power" of the equation by approximately 17% over Model 6. In addition, both variables exhibit the expected sign at both origin and destination, two of the expected signs are statistically significant, and the remaining two approach statistical significance. In contrast, FEM and IMMIG perform "poorly" in the eastern region. While they boost the "explanatory power" of the equation by approximately 14% over Model 6, only one coefficient ($IMMIG_j$) exhibits the expected sign. Furthermore, signs on several other variables in the equation are reversed in the process (ie., as compared with Models 5 and 6). Why these variables should perform so differently between the two regions is not clear. Our conclusion is that Hypothesis 21 (the greater the differential in female labour force opportunities [FEM] between cities, the greater M_{ij} will be) and Hypothesis 22 (the greater the differential in rates of immigration of the foreign born, [IMMIG] between cities, the greater M_{ij} will be) should continue to be regarded as confirmed. As in Chapter 4, however, their utility in boosting "true" explanatory power is likely to be confounded by problems of multicollinearity.

Results by Education

When migrants are grouped by levels of education, results of Models 1 through 7 provide several additional insights into the migration process in Canada. Recall that the migrants in these regressions consist of males aged 15 years and over. Males in this age group correspond more closely to traditional notions of the active labour force. Recall also that these regressions pertain to inter-CMA migration flows for the period 1976-81 only.

The most striking impression to emerge from these regressions is that the results *across* educational subgroups are remarkably similar. For example, in Model 1, only $DIST_{ij}$ and $LANG_{ij}$ carry the expected sign at statistically significant levels for each educational group (Table 5.6). Moreover, R^2 values are similar for each group. To a large extent, the same pattern emerges with respect to significant variables in Models 2 through 7 (see Tables 5.7 to 5.10).

Another impression is that our "redefinition" of migrants to correspond more closely with traditional notions of the active labour force has but a minimal effect on the performance of Models 1 through 7. That is, when Models 1 through 7 are calibrated on migration rates for the general population versus those of labour force ages, results are highly similar. This is evident when results on Model 5 for migrants of labour force ages are compared with results on Model 5 for migrants in the general population. (See Tables 5.7 and 4.7, both of which pertain to the 1976-81 period.) Observe that identical variables in both tables carry the expected sign at statistically significant levels. R^2 values are also similar. This implies that a "structural analysis" of the migratory behaviour of both the general population and those of labour force ages is equally well suited to unravelling the major determinants of migration in Canada. Of course, this generalization is demonstrated only in the context of intermetropolitan migration for the period 1976-81.

Having said the above, it is also true that some of the empirical coefficients in Models 1 through 7 do show slight differences between educational groups. Without attempting to ascertain whether the differences are profound or not, let us note a few in the interests of placing them in the context of ongoing research. First, note that the coefficient (elasticity) on distance in Models 1 through 4 (Tables 5.6 and 5.7) increases in both size and significance with higher levels of education. These results agree with McInnis (1971). They are also in keeping with findings of Winer and Gauthier (1983) where the negative coefficient on distance is observed to increase among migrants in higher income groups.

Our results on distance disagree, however, with conclusions drawn by Marr et al. (1978). They also seem counterintuitive. Recall from Chapter 2 that Marr et al. (1978), following Schwartz (1976), propose that distance should exert less of a negative or "barrier" effect on the migration of more educated persons since such individuals are (i) likely to be better informed, (ii) may have greater ability to make use of information, (iii) may experience lower psychic costs of migration, and (iv) are more likely to have a job waiting upon relocation (eg., job transfers).[1] Yet, it is also possible that more educated persons are more inert if they own greater amounts of real estate (home and recreational

TABLE 5.6: Empirical Models 1 and 2: Males Aged 15+ by Education Groups, 1976 - 81 Data

	Education groups					
	Less than Grade 12		Grade 12 but less than university degree		University degree or more	
	R.C.	't' value	R.C.	't' value	R.C.	't' value
Model 1						
Intercept	9.6451	—	4.675	—	14.625	—
$DIST_{ij}$	−.350	(3.747)*	−.466	(5.208)*	−.485	(5.501)*
$WAGE1_i$	−1.948	(1.789)	−1.499	(1.439)	−1.797	(1.751)
$WAGE1_j$	.269	(.193)	1.163	(1.117)	−.374	(.365)
$LANG_{ij}$	1.346	(5.338)*	1.192	(4.937)*	1.183	(4.976)*
R^2	.139		.168		.169	
Fvalue	10.785		13.430		13.530	
Observations	272		272		272	
Model 2						
Intercept	14.190	—	9.328	—	18.203	—
$DIST_{ij}$	−.368	(4.207)*	−.484	(5.289)*	−.498	(6.048)*
$WAGE1_i$	−2.017	(1.964)*	−1.556	(1.597)	−1.703	(1.760)
$WAGE1_j$	−.658	(.642)	.284	(.292)	−1.188	(1.230)
$LANG_{ij}$	1.274	(5.393)*	1.120	(4.997)*	1.128	(5.069)*
$JOBS_i$	.017	(.548)	.014	(.482)	−.020	(.684)
$JOBS_j$	.198	(6.362)*	.201	(6.786)*	.186	(6.319)*
R^2	.253		.291		.280	
Fvalue	14.976		18.105		17.199	
Observations	272		272		272	

Note: R.C. = regression coefficient;
    * = sign as expected and statistically significant at .01 level.

land), greater amounts of fixed capital (businesses, law or medical practices), or occupy more senior positions with head office locations in Canada's largest CMA's (eg., Toronto). Furthermore, if segmented labour markets are operating, those with higher levels of education may be in jobs where specific on-the-job training inhibits easy entry or exit (and thus, geographic mobility). These questions merit further research.

TABLE 5.7: Empirical Models 3 and 4: Males Aged 15+ by Education Groups, 1976 - 81 Data

	Education groups					
	Less than Grade 12		Grade 12 but less than university degree		University degree or more	
	R.C.	't' value	R.C.	't' value	R.C.	't' value
Model 3						
Intercept	25.176	—	20.212	—	25.898	—
$DIST_{ij}$	−.361	(4.625)*	−.475	(6.332)*	−.494	(6.355)*
$WAGE1_i$	−1.978	(2.145)*	−1.459	(1.651)	−1.681	(1.835)
$WAGE1_j$	.089	(.096)	.976	(1.107)	−.658	(.720)
$LANG_{ij}$	1.079	(5.042)*	.926	(4.512)*	.991	(4.660)*
$JOBS_i$	.021	(.719)*	.012	(.447)	−.017	(.582)
$JOBS_j$	.130	(4.463)*	.138	(4.950)*	.136	(4.738)*
$UNEMP_i$	.137	(.312)	−.153	(.363)	.129	(.295)
$UNEMP_j$	−3.631	(8.282)*	−3.325	(7.913)*	−2.576	(5.913)*
$EDUC_i$	NA		NA		NA	
R^2	.409		.427		.366	
Fvalue	22.785		24.521		18.974	
Observations	272		272		272	
Model 4						
Intercept	20.011	—	13.747	—	21.174	(2.619)
$DIST_{ij}$	−.403	(4.799)*	−.525	(6.531)*	−.532	(6.372)*
$WAGE1_i$	−1.939	(2.013)*	−1.297	(1.407)	−1.667	(1.741)
$WAGE1_j$	.561	(.583)	1.455	(1.578)	−.204	(.214)
$LANG_{ij}$	1.067	(4.986)*	.910	(4.442)*	.980	(4.606)*
$JOBS_i$	.022	(.743)	.013	(.471)	−.016	(.560)
$JOBS_j$	.129	(4.461)*	.138	(4.958)*	.137	(4.734)*
$UNEMP_i$	.196	(.410)	−.012	(.027)	.169	(.357)
$UNEMP_j$	−3.327	(7.003)*	−3.014	(6.625)*	−2.285	(4.837)*
$EDUC_i$	NA		NA		NA	
DS_i	.074	(.263)	.199	(.731)	.048	(.171)
DS_j	.473	(1.647)	.484	(1.764)	.452	(1.588)
R^2	.415		.435		.372	
Fvalue	18.459		20.054		15.462	
Observations	272		272		272	

Note: R.C. = regression coefficient;
  * = sign as expected and statistically significant at .01 level;
  NA = no account of variable in this regression.

A second notable difference between educational groups is that the coefficient on $LANG_{ij}$ decreases in both size and significance with higher levels of education (see Models 1, 5 and 7). This agrees with findings reported by Marr et al. (1978). There are several reasons why $LANG_{ij}$ may represent less of a barrier to the migration of the more educated. One reason is that the highly educated typically occupy more senior business or service positions where English is an accepted, or at least a functional, working language. Another reason is that highly educated anglophones are more likely to have had some French language training than poorly educated anglophones. Finally, more highly educated persons tend to travel more and this may produce a more cosmopolitan attitude to residence in places of different cultural/ethnic composition.

Third, Models 3 and 4 convey that those with lower educational attainment are somewhat more responsive to wages and unemployment. While $WAGE1_j$ cannot be said to perform well for any of the educational groups (as in the post-1971 pooling), $WAGE1_j$ does exhibit the expected sign at a higher level of statistical significance for the least educated. As for unemployment, $UNEMP_j$ exhibits the expected sign for all groups. However, elasticity and statistical significance are larger for the least educated. Our interpretation of these results accords with segmented labour market theory that workers endowed with less human capital face the greatest risk of unemployment. Moreover, it is likely that such workers would be less able to buffer the costs of incurring unemployment through accumulated assets.

Fourth, employment opportunities at destination (JOBS) would appear to be equally relevant to the migration decisions of all education subgroups. This is not unexpected insofar as the maximization of future earnings requires that a job be secured first — regardless of one's human capital (education).

Addition of the fiscal variables in Model 5 (Table 5.8) has a similar impact across all educational groups, the exception being that the coefficient on $GRANT_j$ appears to influence the behaviour of lower educated migrants more. Since these migrants are likely to have lower average incomes, GRANT may be exerting a desirable effect as a measure of federal equalization policy. As for our measure of natural resource revenues (NRR), we observe that it exhibits an unexpected negative sign at destination at statistically significant levels. Again, we have an indication that this variable has limited utility for explaining inter-CMA migration. If NRR were to be dropped from Model 5 (results not presented here), the R^2 value would fall by less than 2% for each educational group.

TABLE 5.8: Empirical Model 5: Males Aged 15+ by Education Groups, 1976 - 81 Data

| | Education groups | | | | | |
| | Less than Grade 12 | | Grade 12 but less than university degree | | University degree or more | |
	R.C.	't' value	R.C.	't' value	R.C.	't' value
Model 5						
Intercept	−143.778	−	−126.542	−	−105.507	−
$DIST_{ij}$	−.566	(6.644)*	−.652	(8.538)*	−.613	(7.492)*
$WAGE1_i$	3.117	(.537)	−3.667	(.705)	−2.895	(.519)
$WAGE1_j$	39.413	(6.868)*	44.407	(8.638)*	38.063	(6.905)*
$LANG_{ij}$	1.352	(5.992)*	1.259	(6.230)*	1.147	(5.290)*
$JOBS_i$	.019	(.692)	.029	(1.178)	−.016	(.603)
$JOBS_j$	.121	(4.362)*	.128	(5.149)*	.131	(4.913)*
$UNEMP_i$	.336	(.345)	−.780	(.894)	.379	(.405)
$UNEMP_j$	−6.817	(6.981)*	−7.254	(8.293)*	−6.847	(7.299)*
$EDUC_i$	NA		NA		NA	
DS_i	.286	(.769)	.211	(.634)	.339	(.949)
DS_j	−.819	(2.191)	−1.114	(3.328)	−1.163	(3.236)
$UIGEN_i$	4.334	(.773)	−3.148	(.627)	−1.581	(.293)
$UIGEN_j$	39.577	(7.126)*	44.738	(8.997)*	41.143	(7.715)*
$UIPROB_i$	−.119	(.122)	.756	(.865)	−.203	(.216)
$UIPROB_j$	4.225	(4.328)*	5.329	(6.094)*	5.919	(6.312)*
$GRANT_i$	.169	(1.127)	.029	(.214)	−.026	(.182)
$GRANT_j$	.463	(3.094)*	.339	(2.538)*	.029	(.204)
NRR_i	−.155	(1.183)	.053	(.456)	−.069	(.549)
NRR_j	−.429	(3.296)	−.454	(3.895)	−.378	(3.023)
R^2	.534		.606		.533	
Fvalue	16.117		21.582		16.030	
Observations	272		272		272	

Note: R.C. = regression coefficient;
      *   = sign as expected and statistically significant at .01 level;
      NA = no account of variable in this regression.

Model 6, as applied to the educational groups (Table 5.9), tells us nothing new about CRIME, SNOW or OWN, except that $CRIME_j$ at destination now exhibits the expected negative sign for all groups and is statistically significant for the highest educated migrants. Possibly, $CRIME_j$ is more important to higher educated migrants because they are

TABLE 5.9: Empirical Model 6: Males Aged 15+ by Education Groups, 1976 - 81 Data

	Education groups					
	Less than Grade 12		Grade 12 but less than university degree		University degree or more	
	R.C.	't' value	R.C.	't' value	R.C.	't' value
Model 5						
Intercept	−41.687	−	−66.108	−	−31.172	−
$DIST_{ij}$	−.532	(6.085)*	−.606	(7.688)*	−.606	(7.191)*
$WAGE1_i$	−4.815	(1.203)	−.891	(.524)	−5.923	(1.538)
$WAGE1_j$	23.352	(6.004)*	28.200	(8.039)*	23.684	(6.323)*
$LANG_{ij}$	1.469	(5.733)*	1.430	(6.187)*	1.050	(4.254)*
$JOBS_i$	.012	(.335)	.035	(1.082)	−.006	(.165)
$JOBS_j$	.133	(3.815)*	.133	(4.219)*	.146	(4.318)*
$UNEMP_i$	1.122	(.895)	−.757	(.699)	−.012	(.010)
$UNEMP_j$	−6.563	(5.566)*	−6.704	(6.303)*	−6.567	(5.783)*
$EDUC_i$	NA		NA		NA	
DS_i	.271	(.715)	.404	(1.180)	.161	(.441)
DS_j	−1.271	(3.415)	−1.547	(4.608)	−1.441	(4.019)
$UIGEN_i$	−3.236	(.775)	−2.765	(.735)	4.020	(1.000)
$UIGEN_j$	25.032	(6.215)*	30.236	(8.322)*	27.792	(7.164)*
$UIPROB_i$	−.942	(.865)	.499	(.508)	.034	(.032)
$UIPROB_j$	3.919	(3.848)*	4.926	(5.364)*	5.516	(5.625)*
$GRANT_i$	.166	(1.157)	−.016	(.121)	−.041	(.296)
$GRANT_j$	.323	(2.284)*	.166	(1.298)*	−.127	(.931)
$CRIME_i$	.072	(.280)	−.292	(1.034)	.028	(.091)
$CRIME_j$	.072	(.230)	.149	(.529)	−.039	(.131)
$SNOW_i$	−.214	(1.016)	.189	(.997)	−.245	(1.207)
$SNOW_j$	−.366	(1.714)	−.208	(1.077)	−.236	(1.146)
OWN_i	−.972	(1.504)	−.846	(1.451)	.566	(.910)
R^2	.526		.593		.522	
Fvalue	13.208		17.354		13.009	
Observations	272		272		272	

Note: R.C. = regression coefficient;
 * = sign as expected and statistically significant at .01 level;
 NA = no account of variable in this regression.

likely to have greater asset holdings to protect. This kind of interpretation borders on pure speculation, however. Thus, in keeping with our results in Chapter 4, we continue to reject the hypotheses pertaining to these variables.

TABLE 5.10: Empirical Model 7: Males Aged 15+ by Education Groups 1976 - 81 Data

	Education groups					
	Less than Grade 12		Grade 12 but less than university degree		University degree or more	
	R.C.	't' value	R.C.	't' value	R.C.	't' value
Model 7						
Intercept	−100.278	−	−174.148	−	−115.343	−
$DIST_{ij}$	−.499	(6.512)*	−.584	(8.986)*	−.576	(8.220)*
$WAGE1_i$	−6.800	(1.694)	1.512	(.444)	−4.878	(1.329)
$WAGE1_j$	19.084	(4.850)*	22.180	(6.640)*	17.845	(4.958)*
$LANG_{ij}$	1.234	(5.273)*	1.166	(5.868)*	.803	(3.751)*
$JOBS_i$	.012	(.334)	.002	(.075)	−.022	(.696)
$JOBS_j$	.046	(1.337)*	.057	(1.934)	.060	(1.887)
$UNEMP_i$	1.293	(1.074)	.390	(.328)	.662	(.565)
$UNEMP_j$	−2.663	(2.239)	−3.099	(3.071)*	−2.606	(2.396)*
$EDUC_i$	NA		NA		NA	
DS_i	.367	(1.063)	.665	(2.272)	.335	(1.064)
DS_j	−.516	(1.500)	−.826	(2.830)	−.665	(2.113)
$UIGEN_i$	−5.540	(1.441)	−3.522	(1.079)	−5.193	(1.479)
$UIGEN_j$	12.772	(3.350)*	17.375	(5.368)*	14.260	(4.088)*
$UIPROB_i$	−1.091	(1.119)	.186	(.224)	.411	(.461)
$UIPROB_j$	2.155	(2.293)*	3.305	(4.143)*	3.752	(4.365)*
$GRANT_i$	.135	(.683)	.331	(1.962)	.124	(.684)
$GRANT_j$	.838	(4.245)*	.568	(3.390)*	.340	(1.886)
CRIME	−.019	(.069)	−.272	(1.137)	.016	(.061)
CRIME	−.345	(1.234)	−.313	(1.318)	−.518	(2.028)*
SNOW	−.171	(.782)	−.079	(.428)	−.392	(1.958)
SNOW	−.069	(.316)	.171	(.911)	.157	(.777)
OWN	−.743	(1.210)	−.542	(1.039)	.767	(1.365)
FEM_i	−.040	(.015)	7.048	(2.851)	3.669	(1.378)
FEM_j	8.379	(2.950)*	6.212	(2.577)*	7.316	(2.816)*
$IMMIG_i$	.169	(.625)	−.536	(2.338)*	−.264	(1.069)
$IMMIG_j$	.890	(3.289)*	1.106	(4.819)*	1.131	(4.573)*
R^2	.644		.729		.676	
Fvalue	17.804		26.513		20.544	
Observations	272		272		272	

Note: R.C. = regression coefficient;
       * = sign as expected and statistically significant at .01 level;
     NA = no account of variable in this regression.

Finally, turning to Model 7 in Table 5.10, we again find little that is new. As in past applications of Model 7 which contain FEM and IM-MIG, the addition of these variables boosts the "explanatory power" of the regression considerably. A difference here, however, is that coefficients on the fiscal variables do not seem to be as seriously distorted as in previous estimations of Model 7 (eg., on aggregated and regional data).

Concluding Notes

Three general conclusions emerge from the empirical results presented in this chapter. First, most variables which exhibited the expected sign and which were statistically significant in Chapter 4 (aggregate results), retain "explanatory power" when our sample is stratified into two regions. The same applies when our 1976-81 data are stratified by education. Second, our 'core hypothesis' receives additional confirmation when our sample is disaggregated by region. Third, when our 1976-81 data – pertaining to males aged 15 years and over – are stratified by education, the fiscal variables make a strong showing. In fact, they make a stronger and more consistent showing when migration pertains to the population of labour force ages than to the general population (as in Chapter 4). In the case of unemployment insurance, which is most relevant to individuals in the active labour force, this is as it should be.

Our procedure of evaluating Models 1 through 7 in the presence of disaggregated data has been valuable insofar as it reflects on possible limitations of the homogeneity assumption. That is, principal determinants of intermetropolitan migration in Canada may stand out as being more relevant to some migration flows than to others. This is important for policy-makers interested in influencing the migration behaviour of specific target groups to or from specific places.

Footnote

1. Recall in Chapter 2 that the study by Marr et al. (1978) was criticized for its use of the reciprocal of distance (1/D) which was subsequently log transformed.

Chapter 6
Summary and Discussion of Findings

Introduction

Above all, we have has sought to decipher major determinants of migration among Census Metropolitan Areas (CMA's) in Canada. In the process, several hypotheses have been evaluated concerning the changing nature of migration determinants in a society which is evolving over time. Recall from Chapter 1 that the major hypothesis running throughout this study – our 'core hypothesis' – is that the influence of "traditional" labour market variables on migration is undergoing change. On the one hand, improvements in productivity, labour-saving technology, and higher standards of living may be prompting the pursuit of leisure activities to the extent that earnings differentials per se figure less in the migrant's utility calculus. In addition, segmented labour markets, firm-specific training, unions and professional licensing may be dampening the responsiveness of potential migrants to perceived earnings differentials. On the other hand, fiscal and social security-type programs may be cushioning the effects of, say, unemployment on earnings, thereby reducing pressure on individuals to migrate for income reasons alone. Such developments may not only diminish the influence of labour market variables per se on migration, they may subtract from the range of options open to policymakers to influence migration.

Thus far, three major findings of this study have been summarized in Chapter 1. First, we pointed out that our 'core hypothesis' could not be rejected. Our findings are consistent with the idea that (i) the influence of "traditional" market variables on intermetropolitan migration such as wages, employment opportunities, and business activity, has contracted over time, and (ii) that fiscal variables, involving unemployment insurance or federal equalization grants, may have partially displaced "traditional" market variables as influences of recent migration. These findings are not likely to be undermined by changes in Canada's demographic and spatial structure over time. Second, we concluded that our search for determinants of intermetropolitan migration in Canada has been largely successful. We have formulated an empirical model which, in various forms, exhibits a considerable degree of consistency in its ability to explain both aggregate and disaggregated migration flows. In this study, disaggregations have been performed by stratifying our sample into two geographical regions (east versus west), and by stratifying migrants into three educational subgroups. Third, we concluded that the empirical estimates deriving from this study should serve as a more reliable guide to the "true" significance of several determinants of migration in Canada than has been available in the past. That is, superior empirical data on labour market variables and more appropriate units of analysis (eg., CMA's versus provinces) have facilitated more rigorous testing of hypotheses.

We turn now to a point-by-point summary of more detailed findings. Recall that a total of 29 hypotheses have been evaluated in this study. Relevant theoretical underpinnings and a formal statement of each hypothesis are set out in Chapter 3, whereas empirical findings from past inquiry are reviewed in Chapter 2.

Table 6.1 indicates rejection or confirmation of each hypothesis. Decisions concerning rejection or confirmation are based largely on *patterns* of regression coefficients across several models tested in Chapters 4 and 5. Do these patterns behave as expected when variables are evaluated in the context of aggregate migration flows (Chapter 4) and disaggregated migration flows (Chapter 5)? Do the variables in question perform consistently at statistically significant levels? If the answer is "yes", then the hypotheses pertaining to these variables would merit strong confirmation. (Complete definitional and source details on each variable in Table 6.1 are provided in Appendix 1 to Chapter 3.)

In addition to the above, decisions concerning rejection or confirmation have been influenced by the "theoretical rigor" of the models in which variables have been evaluated. Recall that a sequence of models has been tested in "building block" fashion. Some models (eg.,

TABLE 6.1: A Crude Classification of Hypotheses and Degree of Confirmation

Hypothesis	Model 4 Yes	Model 4 No	Model 5 Yes	Model 5 No	Model 7 Yes	Model 7 No	Overall degree of confirmation	Qualifying remarks
Core 1 The greater the differential in earnings (WAGE) between CMA's the greater M_{ij} will be.	X		X		X		Strong	Only for WAGE$_j$
2 Asymmetry will be evident in the impact of origin and destination earnings on M_{ij}.	X		X		X		Strong	
Core 3 Earnings will exert a smaller impact on M_{ij} "today" than in the past.	X			X		X	Moderate	
4 Simple wage variants will perform as well as more complex variants.	X		NA		NA		Strong	Only for JOBS$_j$
5 The greater the differential in employment (JOBS) between CMA's the greater M_{ij} will be.	X		X		X		Strong	
Core 6 Employment will exert a smaller impact on M_{ij} "today" than in the past.	X		X		X		Strong	
7 High unemployment (UNEMP) will deter in-migration at CMA 'j' and promote out-migration at CMA 'i'. Asymmetry will be evident.	X		X			X	Moderate	Only for UNEMP$_j$
8 The greater the differential between building cycles (DS) between CMA's the greater M_{ij} will be.	X		X		X		Strong	Only for DS$_j$
Core 9 Building cycles will exert a smaller impact on M_{ij} "today" than in the past.	X		X		X		Strong	Only for DS$_j$
10 The greater the difference between CMA 'i' and 'j' (i/j) in the: generosity of unemployment insurance (UIGEN); and the ease of obtaining unemployment insurance (UIPROB); the less migration from 'i' to 'j' will be.	NA		X		X		Strong	Only for UIGEN$_j$ / Only for UIPROB$_j$
11 Asymmetry will be evident in the impact of origin and destination unemployment insurance on M_{ij}.	NA			X	X		Weak	
Core 12 Unemployment insurance benefits will dampen M_{ij} more after the 1971 revisions to Canada's Unemployment Insurance Act.	NA		X		X		Strong	Only for UIGEN
Core 13 The greater the differential in federal equalization grants (GRANT) between CMA's the greater M_{ij} will be.	NA		X		X		Strong	Only for GRANT$_j$
Core 14 Federal equalization grants will have more of an effect on M_{ij} after 1971 in view of increased allocations to eastern Canada.	NA		X		X		Moderate	Only for GRANT$_j$
15 The greater the difference between CMA 'j' and 'i' in terms of its "home" province's natural resource revenue (NRR), the greater M_{ij} will be.	NA			X	NA		Not confirmed	
16 Natural resource revenues may not exert independent effects on M_{ij} but may do so largely through its effects on labour market opportunities.	NA		X		NA		Moderate	
17 The greater the differential in home ownership (OWN) between CMA's among younger people, the less M_{ij} will be.	NA		NA			X	Not confirmed	
Core 18 Home ownership will exert a greater negative impact on post-1971 migration.	NA		NA			X	Not confirmed	
19 Asymmetry will be evident in the effect of housing prices (HOUSE) on M_{ij}.	Disqualified		NA		NA		Disqualified	

TABLE 6.1: A Crude Classification of Hypotheses and Degree of Confirmation – Concluded

Hypothesis	Model 4 Yes	Model 4 No	Model 5 Yes	Model 5 No	Model 7 Yes	Model 7 No	Overall degree of confirmation	Qualifying remarks
Core 20 Housing prices will exert a greater effect on M_{ij} after 1972 revisions to Canada's tax system.	Disqualified		NA		NA		Disqualified	
21 The greater the differential in female labour force opportunities (FEM) between CMA's the greater M_{ij} will be.	NA		NA			X	Moderate	Only for FEM_j
22 The greater the differential in rates of immigration of the foreign born (IMMIG) between CMA's the greater M_{ij} will be.	NA		NA		X		Strong	Only for $IMMIG_j$
23 The greater the distance ($DIST_{ij}$) between CMA's the less M_{ij} will be.	X		X		X		Strong	
Core 24 Distance will exert a smaller impact on M_{ij} "today" than in the past.	X		X		X		Strong	
25 The greater the commonality of language/ethnicity ($LANG_{ij}$) between CMA's, the greater M_{ij} will be.		X	X		X		Strong	
Core 26 Language considerations will exert more of an impact on M_{ij} "today" than in the past in view of the separatist and language policies pursued by the government of Québec.		X	X		X		Moderate	
27 The greater the differential in rates of violent crime (CRIME) between CMA's the less M_{ij} will be.	NA		NA			X	Not confirmed	
28 The greater the differential in centimetres of snowfall per year (SNOW) between CMA's, the less M_{ij} will be.	NA		NA		X		Moderate	Only for $SNOW_j$
29 The greater the incidence of higher educated persons (EDUC) in CMA 'i' the greater M_{ij} will be.	X		X		X		Strong	

Note: NA = no account of variable in the regression; Disqualified = resting of variable ruled out for reasons given in the text.

Model 7) are afflicted by problems of multicollinearity more than others (eg., Model 4). This implies that the "true" performance of a particular variable in a "rigorous" model may be distorted when it is evaluated in a "less rigorous" model. Some judgment is therefore required about the adequacy of Model X versus Y when ultimately deciding to reject or accept a particular hypothesis.

With the above in mind, we have assessed the validity of hypotheses in the context of different empirical models. In Table 6.1, Model 4 can be interpreted as a relatively full "traditional" market model of migration. Estimates deriving from this model are not likely to be confounded by problems of multicollinearity. Model 5 adds our public sector variables. These variables distort the coefficient on our WAGE variable though it still retains its expected sign at statistically significant levels. Model 7 adds our so-called "additional variables", some of which clearly introduce problems of multicollinearity.

Note that Table 6.1 provides an overall assessment of "confirmation", ranging from "strong" to "not confirmed". Observe also that our assessment is accompanied by qualifying remarks. In most cases, qualifications pertain to asymmetries in the effects of, say, wages or employment opportunities at destination versus origin CMA's. As noted in our methodological Appendix to Chapter 4, and now in our own results, asymmetry is so prevalent in the effects of explanatory variables that most hypotheses should be qualified to this effect in the process of model building.

Detailed Findings

To render our classification of results in Table 6.1 more intelligible, detailed findings can be summarized as follows;

1) Use of a broadly conceived costs/returns model seems well suited to deciphering major determinants of intermetropolitan migration in Canada. Our empirical version has been "filled out" to the extent that explanatory variables in the model can best be described in terms of three components. One component consists of "traditional" market variables, another "public sector" or fiscal variables, whereas the third component consists of a mélange of "additional" economic and non-pecuniary variables. Our method of analysis has been to perform tests, in "building block" fashion. First, we have examined the relevance of the "traditional" market component. Then we have "added on" the "public sector" component. Finally, we have evaluated the relevance of all three components combined.

Our "traditional" market component has been expanded beyond an early Sjaastad-type formulation (1960), insofar as employment, unemployment and business cycle indicators have been added to "traditional" wage and distance variables. This follows from the assumption that rigidities and segmentation in the labour market are likely to permit high wages and job vacancies to co-exist with unemployment. Our results confirm that our expanded version "out-performs" a more narrowly construed Sjaastad version.[1]

2) When evaluating the "traditional" market component of our costs/returns model, we found that it explains more variance in intermetropolitan migration previous to 1971 than after 1971. This finding was anticipated in the form of our 'core hypothesis'. It does not imply, however, that migration has necessarily become less of an economic event. After 1971, "public sector" variables, consisting largely of economic influences, appear to have assumed greater importance in metropolitan migration patterns. Thus, when our "public sector" component is combined with our "traditional" market component our model performs considerably better. The same does not apply when non-pecuniary variables are added to the model (eg., crime or climate variables). In short, "traditional" market models of migration are not likely to be as relevant to understanding migration in Canada "today" as in the past, but their relevance can be enhanced by taking public sector or fiscal influences into consideration as well.

3) Turning to individual variables in the "traditional" market component of our model, we found strong indications of asymmetry in origin and destination effects of wages, employment opportunities, unemployment, residential construction, etc. Typically, destination effects dominate origin effects. Thus, a high wage at destination 'j' is likely to exert a greater "pull" on place 'i' to 'j' migration (M_{ij}) than is an equally high wage at origin 'i' likely to retard M_{ij}. This finding agrees with most studies on interprovincial migration in Canada and intermetropolitan migration in the United States. (Rationale have been provided in the Appendix to Chapter 4.) Lack of symmetry in origin and destination effects is clearly out of keeping with assumptions of the macro-adjustment model of migration (see Chapter 2 "Appropriate Theory").

4) In the process of selecting relevant variables for the "traditional" market component of our model, four alternative wage variants were specified. We found that (i) WAGE1 – which represents nominal average weekly wages – performs as well if not better than (ii) WAGE2 which adjusts *nominal* wages for cost of living differentials to produce real wages, or (iii) WAGE3 which further adjusts WAGE2 for the possible effects of being unemployed if remaining at CMA_i or migrating to CMA_j, or (iv) WAGE4 which further adjusts WAGE3 to allow for the possibility that an unemployed individual will receive unemployment insurance compensation.

Our results on nominal wages (WAGE1) agree with conclusions reached by Grant and Vanderkamp (1976) on the superiority of nominal wage measures over expected wage differentials. Furthermore, to assume that potential migrants perform the types of calculations implied by, say, WAGE4 may involve unrealistic assumptions about the availability of required information. We suggest that migrants may be "risk averse", implying that an increase in job probability (or reduced unemployment probability), may weigh more heavily than an equivalent increase in wage rates in their utility calculus. If so, it would be more appropriate to consider employment opportunities in conjunction with wage differentials, rather than multiplicatively as in WAGE4.

5) Our findings confirm that both employment opportunities and unemployment contribute to our understanding of migration, independently of wages. Again, this implies that high wages may exist side-by-side with unemployment etc. These results conform with expectations of segmented labour market theory. They are also consistent with results of several studies on intermetropolitan migration in the United States (Fields:1979, Greenwood:1981).

With respect to unemployment, we find that unemployment at destination exerts a significant deterrent effect on migration (as expected), whereas origin effects are indeterminate. In confirming that unemployment is a useful variable for understanding migration in Canada, our results run counter to those of Grant and Vanderkamp (1976). And, by emphasizing significant destination versus origin effects, our results also run counter to Courchene (1970), Marr et al. (1978), and Winer and Gauthier (1983). This implies that we should reject a conclusion advanced in our literature review in Chapter 2, p. 46 that measures of unemployment at origin might be retained as potentially more useful while discarding unemployment at destination.

6) To our knowledge, this is the first study of migration in North America to systematically evaluate the impact of residential construction on place-to-place migration. Recall that residential construction is used as a business cycle indicator to represent economic influences not likely to be "picked up" by more traditional economic variables. It makes a strong, independent contribution to explaining variations in rates of intermetropolitan migration in Canada. Findings on this variable agree with results of other studies undertaken by the author (see Chapter 3, footnote 19).

7) Turning to the "public sector" component of our model, we have been most interested in the following fiscal measures; increased generosity of unemployment insurance after 1971; changes in federal equalization grants after 1971; and, natural resource revenues accruing to the Canadian west, particularly oil-related revenues after the 1973 OPEC price hikes. On the one hand, our results suggest that unemployment insurance and federal equalization grants exerted stronger effects on migration after 1971 than before 1971. Unemployment insurance is represented by two variables; generosity of unemployment insurance (UIGEN) and the probability of obtaining unemployment insurance if unemployed (UIPROB). In most cases, UIGEN "out-performs" UIPROB. It typically exhibits the expected negative sign at origin for both pre-1971 and post-1971 migration, and it often exhibits the expected positive sign at destination for post-1971 migration. Moreover, it is more relevant to explaining migration to and from CMA's in eastern than western Canada. This conforms with expectation since average federal unemployment insurance transfers to persons are larger relative to average incomes in eastern Canada than in western Canada.

　　　To a lesser extent, conclusions about the relevance of unemployment insurance apply to federal equalization grants. In this case, however, the "pull" effects of equalization grants at destination are observed to be stronger than their retention effects at origin. This finding differs from results reported by Courchene (1970) that the major effect of federal transfers is to dampen out-migration.

　　　On the other hand, we were not able to ascertain that natural resource revenues (NRR) exert an independent effect on intermetropolitan migration. Rather, our evidence is more consistent with the idea that NRR influences migration to, say, Calgary and Edmonton through its income or job augmenting effects. Thus, we disagree with Winer and

Gauthier (1983) that migrants perceive and are drawn to the Canadian west by NRR-related fiscal benefits. Furthermore, our results cannot be aligned with the idea that negative effects of equalization and transfer payments to the Canadian east have been overstated, that existing programs are helping to prevent westward rent-seeking, and that complete horizontal fiscal balance is probably justified to further prevent inefficient rent-seeking.

8) When evaluating the "traditional" market component of our model, or the "traditional" market plus the "public sector" component, we usually included measures of distance, language/ethnicity, and educational selectivity. While distance always exhibits the expected negative effect, its significance as a cost/information barrier to migration has been observed to decline over time. A similar finding was reported by Courchene (1970). Our interpretation is that pecuniary costs of migration in Canada have become smaller, relative to earnings, and that improved telecommunications, etc., are working to erode psychic costs of migration.

That commonality of language/ethnicity exerts the expected positive effect on migration is in keeping with findings of several previous studies (Courchene:1970, Robinson and Tomes:1982, Winer and Gauthier:1983). In addition, our language/ethnicity measure is observed to exert a greater effect on migration after 1971. This variable is most relevant to explaining lower rates of migration to and from Montréal and Québec City. In addition, our results are consistent with the hypothesis that the pursuit of separatist policy and implementation of language Bill 101 have increased the importance of this variable after 1971. Thus our language/ethnicity measure not only proxies cultural differences and difficulties of accessing information, but possible job or language discrimination as well.

As expected, our measure of educational selectivity exerts a positive effect on intermetropolitan migration in Canada. That is, the greater the prevalence of educated people at CMA 'i', the more CMA 'i' is likely to emit migrants. This finding conforms with human capital expectations since migration to places of better advantage is viewed as an important means of augmenting lifetime earnings. Its relevance to understanding migration has been confirmed in several studies of intermetropolitan migration in the United States (Morgan:1975/76; Schlottmann et al.:1981).

9) The so-called third component of our expanded costs/returns model adds on several additional economic and non-pecuniary variables. Two of these variables, female activity rates and rates of foreign immigration, perform as expected and make a notable contribution to "explaining" variations in intermetropolitan migration. In the process, however, they distort coefficients on other variables in the Model (Model 7). This suggests problems of multicollinearity and that any conclusions concerning the relevance of these variables should be highlighted as being extremely tentative. Female activity rates have been used to proxy the prevalence of employment opportunities for women in different cities in view of the prevalence of dual income-earning households in Canada. Our results are consistent with the idea that migrants, most of whom relocate as members of households or families, are attracted to places where larger shares of women are in the labour force.

As for immigration, this is the first study to evaluate its effects on place-to-place migration in Canada. It is clearly the most significant variable in our so-called third component. Our results on this variable are consistent with the idea that foreign immigrants generate employment and income multiplier effects at CMA's to the extent that those CMA's become more attractive to domestic migrants. Thus, our interpretation and findings run counter to the (untested) hypotheses advanced by Winer and Gauthier (1983) that immigrants – through competition in the labour force – are likely to discourage in-migration of domestic migrants.

10) This is the first study of migration in Canada to evaluate effects of crime rates and one of the few studies to evaluate climate. In both our aggregate and disaggregated tests, crime rates perform poorly as determinants of intermetropolitan migration. This finding agrees with several studies of intermetropolitan migration in the United States where crime rates exert mixed and uncertain effects, especially when economic variables are controlled for (Porell:1982). While our climate variable performs poorly in aggregate tests, it performs as expected when migration flows are disaggregated by geographical region. Several studies of place-to-place migration in the United States report that climate considerations are relevant as well (see Renas et al.:1983).

11) This is also one of the few studies to evaluate the effects of housing prices and home ownership on migration in Canada. Unfortunately, problems of intercorrelation between housing prices and several other

explanatory variables (wages, dwelling starts) were sufficiently great as to prescribe that this variable be dropped from consideration. As for home ownership, it did not exhibit the expected deterrent effect on migration. This comes as a surprise because tax revisions in Canada after 1971 were accompanied by substantial jumps in home ownership among highly migratory age groups (25-35 year-olds). Aggregation bias may be responsible for this finding. If so, evaluation of home ownership *specific* to the migratory behaviour of, say, 25-to-35 year-olds might well yield the expected result. This question must be left to future research.

12) When evaluating components of our model using regionally disaggregated data, we found that coefficients on several variables changed. For example, language/ethnicity considerations are much more important to migration to and from CMA's in eastern than western Canada. In contrast, distance emerges as a greater deterrent of migration to and from CMA's in western than eastern Canada. A similar finding emerges in Winer and Gauthier's study (1983).

With respect to the "traditional" market component of our model we also found that wages, unemployment and dwelling starts are more relevant to understanding migration to and from western Canada than to eastern Canada. The explanation, in keeping with our 'core hypothesis', is that more generous unemployment insurance benefits and equalization grants in the east may be working to displace "traditional" market influences. This interpretation receives some support when we observe the effects of public sector variables in combination with the "traditional" market component of our model. Three of six coefficients on the public sector variables (unemployment insurance, equalization grants), carry the expected sign and are statistically significant for eastern Canada. In contrast, none are statistically significant for western Canada.

13) Our model has also been evaluated using data on male migrants aged 15 years or more, disaggregated by three levels of education. One impression to emerge is that our "redefinition" of migrants to correspond more closely with traditional notions of the active labour force (ie., males aged 15 years and over), has but a minimal effect on the performance of our model. This implies that a "structural analysis" of the migratory behaviour of both the general population and those of labour force ages is equally well suited to unravelling the major determinants of migration in Canada. Another impression is that results *across* educational subgroups are remarkably similar. One has to look hard to find significant differences.

Having said the above, coefficients on some variables were observed to change. For example, distance exerts more of a deterrent effect on the migration of persons who have attained university degrees than persons with less than grade 12. This finding agrees with results reported by McInnis (1971). It is also consistent with results reported by Winer and Gauthier (1983) – that the deterrent effect of distance increases among those with higher incomes (ie., assuming that higher paid individuals tend also to have higher levels of education).

Our results on distance are, however, in disagreement with those reported by Marr et al. (1978) for Canada and Schwartz (1976) for the United States. These authors propose that distance should exert less of a negative effect on the highly educated since such individuals are likely to be better informed, may have greater ability to make use of information, may experience lower psychic costs of migration, and are more likely to have a job waiting upon relocation. While we agree with this rationale, we also anticipate that the highly educated may encounter inertia effects to long-distance migration in cases where they own greater amounts of real estate (home and recreational land), greater amounts of fixed capital (business, law or medical practices), or occupy senior positions with head office locations in Canada's largest CMA's (eg., Toronto). In other terms, individuals with fewer ties and less wealth (who may also be the least educated), may be prone to migrate longer distances. This question merits further research.

We also found that language/ethnicity exerts less of a deterrent effect on the migration of the more educated. As this variable pertains largely to migration to and from Montréal and Québec City, we suggest that highly educated anglophones are more likely to have had some French language training than poorly educated anglophones; that the highly educated are likely to occupy more senior business or service positions where English remains a functional, working language, regardless of language policy; and that more highly educated persons tend to travel more and that this may result in a more cosmopolitan attitude to residing in communities with a different ethnic/cultural composition.

Finally, our results give the impression – far from conclusive however – that those who are least well educated may be somewhat more responsive to wage and unemployment differentials. This stands to reason if only because this "class" of migrants is likely to have fewer resources available to buffer the costs of, say, unemployment (eg., accumulated wealth). It is significant from a human capital perspective because migration for employment represents a human capital investment just as an investment in education does. If migration of the least educated for higher incomes or jobs benefits such individuals, it may also work to reduce income inequalities within and between CMA's in the process.

From Modelling to Policy

Fiscal variables matter in Canadian migration to the extent that they appear to be "crowding out" the impact of more traditional market variables. This implies that traditional tools of manpower policy for influencing migration between metropolitan labour markets, such as job creation, skill enhancement, or wages may be less effective currently than they might have been in the past.

Our results can also be aligned with views espoused by Courchene and others that market forces that would naturally work to induce migration from low to high income regions (and thus equalize earned incomes across the country) are being short-circuited by a fiscal structure that subsidizes residence in regionally depressed regions. We find no evidence to support the position espoused by Boadway and Flatters, that failure to institute complete horizontal fiscal balance will allow rent-seeking migrants to pursue surplus fiscal capacity in the Canadian west.

Our results should not, however, be construed as the "final word" on the desirability of completely unrestricted migration. Following Myrdal (1975), Polèse (1981) maintains that migrants embody not only labour but also other sources of growth such as capital, education and "advances in knowledge", not to mention their possible effects on scale economies. He also suspects that migrants embody these sources of growth at a proportionately higher level than the population of in-migration regions. If so, then over a given period, in-migrants will raise the per capita income of that region and increase the disparity gap relative to the sending region (if that region has a lower per capita income). With this in mind, he submits that state transfer payment schemes, which may in fact discourage people from moving, may not be as detrimental to regional economic disparities as "Courchene-type arguments" maintain.

Any attempt to draw policy implications from the findings summarized in this study must also be cognizant of limitations of the modelling process itself. At the very least, this demands an understanding of the strengths and weaknesses of aggregate statistical models. It also involves philosophy of science questions. Have we identified "true" causes of migration, plausible determinants, or merely a handful of correlates? Are our findings aligned with impeccable theory, a reasonable explanatory framework, or speculative hypotheses? In addition, a discussion of policy implications cannot hope to be realistic unless it takes stock of the existing institutional framework. Can our results be aligned (or juxtaposed) with existing policies which prescribe a desired metropolitan form and content in Canada? Let us elaborate briefly on these important issues.

It was pointed out in Chapter 1 that our findings derive from secondary data (place-to-place migration from census sources), broad measures of "structural" differences between places of origin and destination (average employment growth, climate), and multivariate statistical techniques.[2] Guiding premises in our work are that (i) individuals are rational, (ii) that they seek to maximize their pecuniary and non-pecuniary well-being, (iii) that objectively measured differences between places convey information that is relevant to migration decision-making, and (iv) that – subject to information constraints – individuals will perceive and evaluate the desirability of "competing" places on this basis. These premises have been incorporated in the broadly conceived costs/returns model described in Chapter 3. It is on the basis of these premises that when objectively measured differences between places are correlated with migration, subjective motives concerning the desirability of these characteristics have been imputed to migrants.

It would not be correct to say that this approach identifies "true" causes or that it can be aligned with a fully developed theory about decision-making per se. Nor would it be correct to say that we have merely succeeded in identifying correlates of migration in the process of evaluating speculative hypotheses. More appropriately, this study identifies plausible determinants of migration. These can be aligned with a reasonable explanatory framework about how people judge the attractiveness of different places. Depending on the amount of information available or sought out, we propose that many determinants evaluated in this study operate directly whereas others will operate indirectly on the migrant's utility calculus. Some determinants operate directly in the sense that migrants will actually perceive "structural" or objectively measured characteristics of far away places (high house prices, climate), and will adjust their migration decisions accordingly. Other determinants are likely to operate indirectly, for example, as surrogates or general indicators of potential growth or development (capital investment or government equalization transfers). Then again, some determinants may enter the migration decisions of, say, highly informed individuals whose behaviour, in turn, may influence migration decisions of less informed individuals – via a demonstration effect.

Where then does the link between objective statistical inference and subjective decision-making become ambiguous? The answer can be illustrated as follows. Suppose our results lead us to believe that an X% increase (or decrease) in employment growth at city 'j' will bring about a Y% increase (or decrease) in migration from city 'i' to 'j'. To infer that policy modification of X will immediately bring about the predicted increase or decrease in Y assumes that (i) information will be sufficient, if not perfect, to permit prospective migrants to perceive the changed variables, (ii) prospective migrants will correctly re-estimate net pecuniary and non-pecuniary returns to migration in light of the perceived changes, and (iii) prospective migrants will adjust their migratory plans accordingly.

Problems with the assumptions above are threefold. First, we know that information is usually imperfect. Indeed, it is sufficiently imperfect that "return" and "repeat" migration are increasingly being studied in terms of disappointment and miscalculation of expected benefits (Grant and Vanderkamp:1982). Thus, in view of information constraints, some migrants might not perceive changes in variable X at all. A policy which changes X to bring about changes in Y may well have an impact smaller than that predicted by the empirical model. Second, as yet, we know very little about how individuals process available information. Is there a time lag involved? Who seeks out information and at what cost? Thus, efforts to change X to bring about a change in migration may be undermined by time lags or peculiarities of information processing. Third, empirical models of migration are only beginning to measure non-pecuniary variables in meaningful terms. This study has attempted to control some of these, but there can be no doubt that the correspondence between many of our theoretical and empirical constructs leaves much to be desired. At this stage of migration inquiry then, it is difficult to say with certainty that changes in variable X will exert a truly independent effect on migration because non-pecuniary variables have yet to be effectively controlled.

All this is to say that our empirical results provide a crude road-map about forces that influence the pace and direction of migration between metropolitan areas in Canada. While it can be realistically assumed – in keeping with established theory – that these forces affect the migrant's utility calculus either directly or indirectly, micro-elements of the decision-making process are only beginning to be deciphered.

Another important link between modelling and policy involves the institutional context in which our findings should be discussed. Suppose that existing policy sought to influence migration by manipulating wages only. In this context, the process of aligning our findings with policy would be straightforward. Since this study demonstrates that employment opportunities are important determinants of migration we could argue that policies ignoring this variable would be less successful than they otherwise might be. In contrast, suppose migration was operating laissez-faire; that there were no explicit policies operating on it directly. In this case it would be impossible to align our findings with existing policy. Rather we would be forced to contrive policy questions and to align them with views about how we believe the Canadian economy should develop. What is the relevant policy context in Canada?

Had this study been conducted 10 years ago, we would have immediately aligned our findings with research and policy concerns of the Ministry of State for Urban Affairs (hereafter MSUA). Launched in 1971, this ministry embarked on an ambitious program of urban development with the aim of consolidating a national urban strategy. Migration, as well as policies affecting it, were central concerns of MSUA. Today, MSUA does not exist. It was fully disbanded in 1979. Where then do we stand with respect to urban policy and planning in Canada? The answer as Weller (1982, p.41-46) puts it, is that;

– No explicit or implicit government policy or statement of a public nature, federal, provincial or local in origin, exists with regard to national settlement patterns, goals and objectives.

– No federal department (or agency) is responsible for rigorously evaluating or fully co-ordinating the impact of federal policies (and programs) on individual urban centres, much less on regional or national systems of such centres.

– No comprehensive models of national (or even regional or provincial) scope exist whereby policy variables with direct and indirect urban impacts can be assessed in the context of those impacts; nor are there any models of national (or even regional or provincial) scope which can incorporate urbanization process variables in their more macro-structural, spatial, or functional contexts.

- There is no forum or mechanism in place whereby the three levels of government (local, provincial and federal) seriously discuss on a regular basis circumstances and situations which bear on urbanization processes and urban systems at either national or provincial scales.

Weller (1982, p.44-45) goes on to lament this situation in view of many notable forces which are currently altering the face of urban Canada, including;

- The rush of migrants and immigrants to large cities in general and Ontario in particular in the late 1960's and early 1970's; and, in the late 1970's and early 1980's, a shift away from those centres and Ontario to smaller communities in general and western Canada in particular.

- A marked decline in growth (as opposed to development) in larger centres to the point where growth, or the avoidance of decline, is being actively pursued in most such centres across Canada.

- The changed attractiveness from downtown to suburban location for commercial development.

This means that many issues relevant to the welfare of metropolitan Canada are being taken up today more as "side issues" in the context of regional policy debates (eg., the equity:efficiency debate reviewed in Chapter 2). Needless to say, taking research cues from regional policy debates is hardly satisfactory if only because "regional perspectives" tend to blur the overwhelming importance of growth and change in and around metropolitan areas per se. As Bourne (1982, p. 282-83) puts it; "In most instances, provincial boundaries do not correspond to the boundaries of functional economic regions nor to the complex intermetropolitan and hierarchical organization of an urbanized economy . . . In the Canadian case the settled portion of the country has been subdivided into 125 regions, each centred on a metropolitan area or smaller centre but linked together as a spatial system . . . The urban centres in this system act as control points in the economy, sending out and receiving goods, capital, labour, and information. The mix of these components represents the particular chemistry of growth and

change in any modern economy . . . Its units of analysis are urban centred regions rather than regions of homogeneous economic activity and
land use. In this context, urban areas act to redesign the regions, rather
than the reverse".

   Bourne's point combines with Weller's synopsis to produce an in-
escapable conclusion. The many important developments affecting large
urban areas in Canada should, at the very least, be the subject of ongoing "urban impact assessment".[3] This study can be construed as one
form of "urban impact assessment" insofar as our results may lend
themselves to improved urban planning and policy in the future. Should
planners or policy-makers be interested in influencing migration among
Canada's metropolitan areas, our results suggest that the following pro-
positions merit further discussion and evaluation;

1) Attempts to influence migration between metropolitan labour markets
using traditional tools of manpower policy (wages, jobs), are likely to
be less effective "today" than they might have been in the past.

2) Unemployment and low incomes at place 'i' may constitute motivations to emigrate for employment or higher incomes, but availability of
unemployment insurance may dampen such motivation. The cushioning effects of unemployment insurance are most evident after 1971 when
benefits became increasingly generous, particularly in eastern Canada.
From a purely economic standpoint, unemployment insurance – which
construes obvious short-term benefits to the unemployed – may be under-
mining the market mechanism from efficiently allocating labour to its
best place of competitive advantage.

3) If equalization grants are partially intended to make poorer or lagg-
ing areas more attractive to migrants, then they seem to be succeeding.
This applies particularly to eastern Canada where equalization grants
grew substantially after 1971. Unlike unemployment insurance transfers,
equalization grants do not seem to retard emigration. Rather, they seem
to promote the population growth of metropolitan areas by stimulating
in-migration.

4) Increased migration to CMA's in the Canadian west, and particularly to Calgary and Edmonton, does not seem to be motivated by expected
fiscal benefits deriving from mushrooming natural resource revenues (ie.,

mainly oil-related). Rather, it appears that migrants have responded mainly to growth of employment opportunities and higher incomes that have been fed by growing resource revenues. The "boom" effects of natural resource revenues on jobs and incomes in the west has been partially offset by federal taxation and equalization programs. These, in turn, appear to have held rates of westward migration at levels lower than they otherwise might have been.

5) When a metropolitan area experiences a high rate of immigration of the foreign born, we can also expect it to exert more of a draw on domestic migrants. This generalization applies to internal migration before 1971 and after 1971, to CMA's in the Canadian west as well as in the east, and to migrants regardless of their level of education. In other terms, immigrants would appear to generate income and employment multiplier effects to the extent that policies directing them to particular CMA's are likely to bolster the attractiveness of those CMA's to domestic migrants.

6) Transportation and psychic costs of relocation are likely to represent less of a barrier to current migration than in the past. Not only are average relocation costs likely to be smaller relative to average household incomes, but psychic costs are likely to be diminishing in view of improved telecommunications, transport, etc.

7) Pursuit of separatist policy in Québec seems to be contributing to reduced migration to Montréal and Québec City as well as to higher rates of emigration from these cities. Migration from CMA's in "English" Canada to CMA's in "French" Canada has always been lower than between CMA's in "English" Canada or between CMA's in "French" Canada alone, but recent implementation of language Bill 101 has probably exacerbated the disparity. This is likely to undermine attempts to influence migration patterns to and from Québec via policy intervention in the labour market.

8) Finally, there is some evidence to suggest that individuals on the lower rungs of the educational/income ladder are somewhat more responsive to policies designed to influence migration through traditional labour market variables. If such individuals can be motivated to migrate to a metropolitan area offering better opportunities (eg., higher earnings) then the average welfare of all Canadians would likely benefit and the distribution of income at the origin metropolitan area would likely improve in the process.

We conclude this study by emphasizing that changing determinants of intermetropolitan migration in Canada should not be put down to any *specific* short list of public policies. Rather, the declining significance of "traditional" market variables and the growing significance of fiscal variables should be interpreted as more akin to a *general* shift in the structure and preferences of society. One aspect of this shift – starting with the Pearson years – has been the growing weight of government in the allocation of private benefits. And in this context, hindsight suggests that the influence of government activities on private decisions would cause changes in "traditional" determinants of migration – as our data suggests. Whether this is desirable can only be decided in terms of one's attitude to "bigger government" or in the context of the "equity:efficiency" debate as it applies to socio-economic events such as migration.

Footnotes

1. "Performance" is judged, crudely, in terms of numbers of variables exhibiting the expected sign at statistically significant levels plus the overall "explanatory" capacity of the equation (R^2).

2. Not only are survey data in short supply but statements of motives for migration must be interpreted with caution. As Ralston (1981, p. 58) puts it, "Where one accepts the migrant's own account of motives, one encounters the difficulty of distinguishing between "real" and "stated" motives and the further problem of the migrant's rationalization of the decision when cognitive dissonance has resulted from a choice between two alternatives. On the other hand, Ralston warns that when one imputes motives for migration on the basis of inference from structural factors there may be an over-emphasis on the rational element in the decision to migrate, to the neglect of differential perception and evaluation of objective factors. Debate on these and related issues is, of course, not new. It has been taken up in the context of several economic issues as well as migration (see Addison and Siebert:1979, p. 171, Nelson and Winter:1983).

3. A similar point has been developed by Clark (1983) with respect to interregional migration in the U.S. and implications of the President's national urban policy report "Urban America in the Eighties".

Appendices

Appendix 1 to Chapter 1

APPENDIX TABLE A.1.1 Population Growth of Census Metropolitan and Non-metropolitan Canada, 1951-81

Characteristics	Census metro-politan areas	Non-metropolitan areas	Total
		1971 Census boundaries	
Population			
1951	6,397,680	7,611,749	14,009,429
1956	7,747,301	8,333,490	16,080,791
1961	9,291,305	8,946,942	18,238,247
1966	10,684,482	9,333,398	20,014,880
1971	11,874,748	9,693,563	21,568,311
1976	12,582,574	10,410,030	22,992,604
1981	13,229,778	11,113,402	24,343,180
Percentage of Canada's population		per cent	
1951	45.7	54.3	100.0
1956	48.2	51.8	100.0
1961	50.9	49.1	100.0
1966	53.4	46.6	100.0
1971	55.1	44.9	100.0
1976	54.7	45.3	100.0
1981	54.3	45.6	100.0
Population growth rates			
1951 - 56	21.1	9.5	14.8
1956 - 61	19.9	7.4	13.4
1961 - 66	15.0	4.3	9.7
1966 - 71	11.1	3.9	7.8
1971 - 76	6.0	7.4	6.6
1976 - 81	5.1	6.8	5.9
1951 - 61	45.2	17.5	30.2
1961 - 71	27.8	8.3	18.3
1971 - 81	11.4	14.6	12.9
1951 - 81	106.8	46.0	73.8
Percentage of Canada's population growth			
1951 - 56	65.2	34.0	100.0
1956 - 61	71.6	28.4	100.0
1961 - 66	78.4	21.6	100.0
1966 - 71	76.6	23.4	100.0
1971 - 76	49.7	50.3	100.0
1976 - 81	47.9	52.1	100.0
1951 - 61	68.4	31.6	100.0
1961 - 71	77.6	22.4	100.0
1971 - 81	48.8	51.2	100.0
1951 - 81	66.1	33.9	100.0

Source: Censuses of Canada, Statistics Canada.

APPENDIX TABLE A.1.2 Selected Population Characteristics of Census Metropolitan Areas, 1951-81

Census Metropolitan Areas	Population				Intercensal population growth				Share of Canada's total metropolitan population	
	1951	1961	1971	1981¹	1956-61	1966-71	1976-81	1951-81	1981	1981-51
		1971 Census boundaries			%				%	ratio
Calgary	142,315	279,062	403,319	592,743	38.82	22.01	25.74	316.50	4.48	201.80
Chicoutimi	91,161	127,616	133,703	117,036	15.68	0.56	0.62	28.38	0.88	61.97
Edmonton	193,622	359,821	495,702	655,125	30.76	16.51	18.09	238.35	4.95	163.34
Halifax	138,427	193,353	222,637	243,283	13.42	6.07	2.01	75.75	1.84	85.19
Hamilton	281,901	401,071	498,523	542,095	17.44	8.99	2.40	92.30	4.10	92.97
Kitchener	107,474	154,864	226,846	273,994	20.31	17.98	5.45	154.93	2.07	123.21
London	167,724	226,669	286,011	289,710	15.45	12.74	4.76	72.73	2.19	83.58
Montréal	1,539,308	2,215,627	2,743,208	2,824,605	21.06	6.70	0.76	83.50	21.35	88.73
Ottawa-Hull	311,587	457,038	602,510	692,218	24.28	13.94	3.37	122.15	5.23	107.39
Québec City	289,294	379,067	480,502	536,065	15.43	9.98	3.88	85.30	4.05	89.60
Regina	72,731	113,749	140,734	164,313	24.70	6.27	9.68	125.92	1.24	108.77
St. Catharines - Niagara	189,048	257,796	303,429	274,257	10.63	6.30	-14.28	45.07	2.07	70.17
St. John's	79,758	106,666	131,814	150,635	15.23	12.15	6.55	88.87	1.14	91.93
Saint John	80,689	98,083	106,744	114,048	10.99	2.45	0.95	41.34	0.86	68.25
Saskatoon	55,679	95,564	126,449	154,210	31.04	9.10	15.26	176.96	1.17	134.48
Sudbury	80,543	127,446	155,424	150,154	18.13	13.66	-4.61	86.43	1.13	111.50
Thunder Bay	73,713	102,085	112,093	117,470	16.50	3.76	1.24	59.36	0.89	77.39
Toronto	1,261,861	1,919,409	2,628,043	3,006,506	22.10	14.77	7.24	138.28	22.73	115.26
Vancouver	568,172	826,798	1,082,352	1,268,183	19.06	16.00	8.78	116.35	9.59	104.69
Victoria	114,829	155,763	195,800	233,481	14.42	11.79	8.98	103.32	1.76	98.32
Windsor	182,619	217,215	258,643	258,833	4.20	8.53	-0.17	41.73	1.96	68.77
Winnipeg	357,229	476,543	540,262	570,814	15.46	6.19	0.71	59.79	4.31	77.24
Metropolitan Canada	6,397,680	9,291,305	11,874,748	13,229,778	19.93	11.14	5.14	106.79	100.00	100.0
All Canada	14,009,429	18,238,747	21,568,311	24,343,180	13.42	7.76	5.87	73.76	-	-

¹ The 1981 population figures adjusted to 1971 Census boundaries are based on preliminary analysis, yet to be finalized by Statistics Canada.

Source: Censuses of Canada, Statistics Canada.

APPENDIX TABLE A.1.3 Proportion of Canada's Population in Each Census Metropolitan Area, 1951-81

	1951	1956	1961	1966	1971	1976	1981
	CMA's as a percentage of Canadian population (1971 Census boundaries)						
Calgary	1.02	1.25	1.53	1.65	1.87	2.05	2.43
Chicoutimi	0.65	0.69	0.70	0.66	0.62	0.51	0.48
Edmonton	1.38	1.71	1.97	2.13	2.30	2.41	2.69
Halifax	0.99	1.06	1.06	1.05	1.03	1.04	1.00
Hamilton	2.01	2.12	2.20	2.29	2.31	2.30	2.23
Kitchener	0.77	0.80	0.85	0.96	1.05	1.13	1.13
London	1.20	1.22	1.24	1.27	1.33	1.20	1.19
Montréal	10.99	11.38	12.15	12.85	12.72	12.19	11.60
Ottawa-Hull	2.22	2.29	2.51	2.64	2.79	2.91	2.84
Québec City	2.06	2.04	2.08	2.18	2.23	2.24	2.20
Regina	0.52	0.57	0.62	0.66	0.65	0.66	0.67
St. Catharines – Niagara	1.35	1.45	1.41	1.43	1.41	1.39	1.13
St. John's	0.57	0.58	0.58	0.59	0.61	0.61	0.62
Saint John	0.58	0.55	0.54	0.52	0.49	0.49	0.47
Saskatoon	0.40	0.45	0.52	0.58	0.59	0.58	0.63
Sudbury	0.57	0.67	0.70	0.68	0.72	0.68	0.62
Thunder Bay	0.53	0.54	0.56	0.54	0.52	0.50	0.48
Toronto	9.01	9.78	10.52	11.44	12.28	12.19	12.35
Vancouver	4.18	4.32	4.53	4.66	5.02	5.07	5.21
Victoria	0.82	0.85	0.85	0.88	0.91	0.95	0.96
Windsor	1.30	1.30	1.19	1.19	1.20	1.13	1.06
Winnipeg	2.55	2.57	2.61	2.54	2.50	2.47	2.34
Metropolitan Canada	45.67	48.18	50.94	53.38	55.06	54.72	54.35

APPENDIX TABLE A.1.4 Change in the Proportion of Canada's Population in Each Census Metropolitan Area, 1951-81

	1951 - 56	1956 - 61	1961 - 66	1966 - 71	1971 - 76	1976 - 81
	CMA's as a percentage of Canadian population (1971 Census boundaries)					
Calgary	23.06	22.40	7.94	13.22	9.64	18.77
Chicoutimi	5.43	2.00	−5.06	−6.68	−18.40	−4.96
Edmonton	23.82	15.29	7.75	8.12	4.98	11.54
Halifax	7.29	0.00	−1.08	−1.57	0.48	−3.65
Hamilton	5.54	3.55	3.92	1.14	−0.39	−3.28
Kitchener	4.34	6.08	13.14	9.48	7.45	−0.40
London	1.98	1.79	1.99	4.61	−9.30	−1.05
Montréal	3.58	6.74	5.74	−0.99	−4.14	−4.83
Ottawa-Hull	2.82	9.58	5.43	5.74	4.26	−2.37
Québec City	−1.10	1.77	5.03	2.05	0.74	−1.88
Regina	9.26	9.95	6.09	−1.39	0.78	2.65
St. Catharines – Niagara	7.39	−2.46	0.90	−1.36	−1.11	−19.02
St. John's	1.11	1.60	0.41	4.07	0.61	0.63
Saint John	−4.58	−2.14	−3.20	−4.93	−0.72	−4.65
Saskatoon	14.11	15.53	10.51	1.24	−0.75	8.87
Sudbury	16.70	4.15	−2.23	5.48	−4.99	−9.91
Thunder Bay	3.56	2.72	−3.57	−3.72	−2.90	−4.38
Toronto	8.53	7.66	8.71	6.50	0.07	1.29
Vancouver	3.21	4.98	2.84	7.64	1.09	2.70
Victoria	3.28	0.89	2.53	3.67	4.56	1.04
Windsor	−0.56	−8.12	−0.02	0.71	−5.96	−5.71
Winnipeg	0.66	1.80	−2.72	−1.46	−1.58	−4.88
Metropolitan Canada	5.50	5.74	4.79	3.13	−0.60	−0.69

APPENDIX TABLE A.1.5 Selected Population Characteristics of the Seventeen Largest Census Metropolitan Areas, 1951-81

Census Metropolitan Areas	Rate of internal in-migration per 100 population				Rate of internal out-migration per 100 population				Rate of foreign in-migration per 100 population			
	1951-56	1966-71	1971-76	1976-81	1956-61	1966-71	1971-76	1976-81	1956-61	1966-71	1971-76	1976-81
Calgary	23.7	25.6	22.1	33.7	14.4	15.7	17.6	19.7	6.4	7.3	5.7	6.4
Edmonton	19.0	20.7	18.3	24.8	15.0	15.5	17.5	18.5	5.2	5.2	4.7	5.0
Halifax	14.1	18.1	15.5	14.9	15.8	17.1	15.9	16.8	2.2	2.9	2.4	1.5
Hamilton	8.6	11.4	9.3	9.6	7.6	8.5	9.7	10.2	5.3	5.7	3.8	2.1
Kitchener	14.8	19.8	15.9	13.6	7.8	13.0	13.8	14.0	4.6	7.8	5.9	2.6
London	16.0	18.5	14.6	16.7	13.2	13.8	16.2	17.0	5.0	5.9	4.9	2.2
Montréal	6.6	7.7	5.8	5.1	4.5	6.5	6.7	8.9	4.1	4.5	3.2	2.3
Ottawa-Hull	15.4	18.3	15.6	12.0	9.7	11.0	11.6	12.2	4.3	5.3	4.0	2.5
Québec City	7.3	14.0	11.6	9.0	5.3	7.8	8.8	9.2	.6	1.4	1.0	.7
St. John's	10.5	15.4	12.1	10.7	7.6	12.5	9.3	12.2	1.3	1.9	1.8	.9
Saint John	7.8	9.3	11.4	9.7	7.2	8.5	10.6	11.7	.9	.8	1.5	.7
Sudbury	12.1	18.2	9.4	7.6	13.4	13.9	15.8	15.9	2.9	2.9	1.3	.6
Toronto	7.0	9.3	6.3	8.2	6.6	9.0	10.7	8.9	8.6	11.4	8.7	5.5
Vancouver	11.0	16.3	11.1	12.5	8.3	9.1	11.8	10.9	5.0	7.7	6.9	5.2
Victoria	14.4	22.9	21.9	21.5	11.9	13.1	14.8	16.9	3.7	5.1	4.1	3.2
Windsor	6.0	8.8	5.6	6.5	8.7	8.4	10.9	10.9	2.8	5.5	2.8	2.4
Winnipeg	12.0	13.0	10.5	10.5	10.3	13.2	12.4	14.0	4.1	4.7	4.2	3.3
TOTAL	9.8	12.6	9.9	10.8	7.8	9.6	10.8	11.3	5.0	6.5	5.2	3.6

Note: The denominator in these rates is the CMA population at the beginning of the census period (ie., 1951, 1966, 1971, 1976) according to census boundaries which pertained at the time of each census.

Source: Calculated from Censuses of Canada, Statistics Canada.

APPENDIX TABLE A.1.5 Selected Population Characteristics of the Seventeen Largest Census Metropolitan Areas, 1951-81 – Concluded

Census Metropolitan Areas	Rate of internal net migration per 100 population				Rate of internal net migration plus foreign immigration per 100 population			
	1951-56	1966-71	1971-76	1976-81	1956-61	1966-71	1971-76	1976-81
Calgary	9.3	9.9	4.5	14.0	15.7	17.2	10.2	20.4
Edmonton	4.0	5.2	.8	6.3	9.2	10.4	3.9	11.3
Halifax	-1.7	1.0	-.4	-1.9	.5	3.9	1.8	-.4
Hamilton	1.0	2.9	-.4	-.6	6.3	8.6	3.4	1.5
Kitchener	7.0	6.8	2.1	-.4	11.6	14.6	8.0	2.2
London	2.8	4.7	-1.6	-.3	7.8	10.6	2.4	1.9
Montréal	2.1	1.2	-.9	-3.7	6.2	5.7	2.3	-1.5
Ottawa-Hull	5.7	7.3	4.0	-.2	10.0	12.6	8.0	2.3
Québec City	2.0	6.2	2.8	-.2	2.6	7.6	3.8	.5
St. John's	2.9	2.9	2.8	-1.5	4.2	4.8	4.6	-.6
Saint John	.6	.8	.8	-2.0	1.5	1.6	2.3	-1.3
Sudbury	-1.3	4.3	4.3	-8.3	1.6	7.2	5.6	-7.7
Toronto	.4	.3	.3	-.7	9.0	11.7	9.1	4.5
Vancouver	2.7	7.2	7.2	2.5	7.7	14.9	14.2	7.7
Victoria	2.5	9.8	9.8	4.6	6.2	14.9	13.9	7.8
Windsor	-2.7	.4	.4	-4.4	.1	5.9	3.2	-2.0
Winnipeg	1.7	-.2	-.2	-3.5	5.8	4.5	4.0	-.2
TOTAL	2.0	3.0	-.9	-.5	7.0	9.5	4.3	3.1

Note: The denominator in these rates is the CMA population at the beginning of the census period (ie., 1951, 1966, 1971, 1976) according to census boundaries which pertained at the time of each census.

Source: Calculated from Censuses of Canada, Statistics Canada.

Appendix 2 to Chapter 1

Concepts Used in Defining the Migration Status of the Canadian Population

MIGRATION STATUS

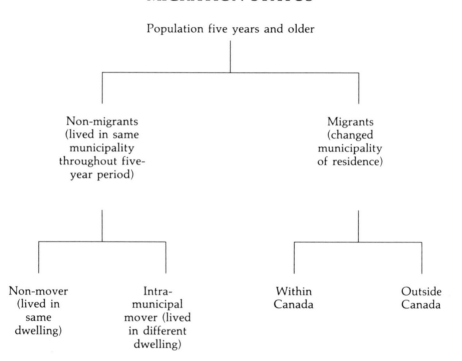

Population five years and older

Non-migrants (lived in same municipality throughout five-year period)

Migrants (changed municipality of residence)

Non-mover (lived in same dwelling)

Intra-municipal mover (lived in different dwelling)

Within Canada

Outside Canada

Migrants are persons who changed municipality of residence during the five-year period, June 1, 1976 – June 1, 1981.

Non-migrants are persons who were living in the same municipality throughout the five-year period.

Intra-municipal movers are persons who are living in the same municipality throughout the five-year period but who were living in different dwellings on June 1, 1976 and June 1, 1981.

It is important to note that unlike the 1971 Census bulletins or the 1961 Census monographs on migration, more recent definitions of migrants include people who had changed municipality of residence at least once between June 1, 1976 and June 1, 1981, but who reported themselves as residing in the same municipality at both dates. Except for this difference the concepts are the same as those used in 1971.

Appendix to Chapter 2

Reconciling Differences between Expected and Realized Income Returns to Migration

This appendix considers briefly an important economic dimension of the costs/returns model from the other side of the coin. Recall that the economists' neoclassical adjustment model predicts that labour will, on the whole, migrate from regions of low relative incomes and low labour demand to areas of high relative incomes and high labour demand. If this proceeds efficiently, the demand and supply for labour should tend toward equilibrium and wage rates should tend to equate across regions. Recall also that the economic aspects of individual migration decisions can logically be viewed within the milieu of human capital investment theory. Individuals are thought to move in anticipation of higher incomes and to do so they must invest in relocation. If the expectations of migrants are realized, then their investment should influence their resulting incomes in such a way that, after an appropriate period of adjustment, the level of their incomes should exceed that of stayers. In short, we expect individuals to migrate for higher incomes but do their pre- versus post-migration incomes confirm that they have done so?

A review of the literature provides, at best, mixed support for the "income expectations" hypothesis of the human capital model as stated above. Canadian studies by Courchene (1974) and Grant and Vanderkamp (1976) have examined tabular information to conclude that interprovincial and interregional migrants do experience positive income increases within a relatively short period of time. In contrast, mounting evidence from U.S. studies shows that returns to migration within five years after a move are either insignificant or negative (Yezer and Thurston:1976, Martin and Lichter:1983). The only studies reporting definite positive returns to migration pertain largely to "lifetime" migrants, usually defined as those living in a place different from their place of birth (ie., no time referent for their migration). However, as Grant and Vanderkamp (1980, 383) observe, the payoffs to lifetime migration cannot easily be construed as evidence for the human capital model because we cannot be sure that other changes such as increased training, education and experience over the lifetime have been adequately controlled. In addition, they claim that selectivity bias, which is a problem in all these types of studies, is more likely to be a serious problem when we analyze lifetime experiences.

In a more recent study, Grant and Vanderkamp (1980) admit to being perplexed by an absence of findings which indicate positive short-run gains to interregional migration in North America. They find it difficult to visualize that an optimizing migration decision would not have produced any positive payoff within the first five years after a move. Are we to accept that individuals are content to absorb negative income returns as well as sizeable investment costs to relocating? To help clarify the situation, they undertake an in-depth study using appropriate micro-data on migration.

The "new" results presented by Grant and Vanderkamp (1980) are likely to provoke our thinking for some time. They report that it is very difficult to detect a significant positive effect of migration on income within a five-year period. Within the first few years after a move, their results reveal a strong *negative* impact of migration on earnings levels. Two to five years after a migration decision, the payoff still seems to be extremely small. This finding is all the more surprising as it applies to persons who moved only once (ie., excludes "trouble cases" such as return migrants). Thus, as the authors admit, results of their micro-study contradict findings in their previous work.

In addition to the above, Grant and Vanderkamp report that migration payoffs decline as the pre-income levels of the migrants increase. While individuals with low initial incomes receive the highest migration payoffs, even this result which seems encouraging from a social viewpoint, is cast into doubt. The reason, as the authors point out, stems from the fact that their analysis is limited to the experience of stayers and migrants who made only one move; if low-income persons are more likely to have a disappointing income experience after a move and are therefore more likely to make another move, then they are more likely to be excluded from their particular sample. Thus, low-income migrants may be in their sample *precisely because* they had a successful income experience.

The overall conclusion reached by Grant and Vanderkamp is that their empirical results provide, at best, weak support for the human capital model. How might this very important conclusion be explained? One possibility, in keeping with our 'core hypothesis', is that non-monetary motives for short-term migration (eg., less than five years), may be much more important in a relatively "rich" country such as Canada than "human capitalists" realize. In relatively rich contexts more people may be undertaking migration simply as a consumption item.

They may be financing their migration out of considerable savings largely for the "experience" or "joy of it" rather than as a direct response to anticipated or required income gains. If such individuals originate from a relatively prosperous "launching pad" (eg., well-to-do families, good health and education), their accumulated physical and human capital assets might also pre-dispose them to tolerate equivalence of post- and pre-migration incomes for longer periods of time.

In addition to the above, if such individuals are "buffered by wealth" they could probably afford to take more risks more often, than were they truly insecure (financially or in terms of health or social security). They could also probably afford to be wrong more often without disastrous effects. Possibly, such conditions permit large numbers of individuals to migrate without taking expected wage gains too seriously. This need not imply, however, that such individuals would not select places where wage levels are relatively high – as implied in the aggregate place-to-place migration models. High wages may simply go hand-in-hand with high growth areas which may be attractive to the relatively wealthy for their amenities, dynamism, etc.

With respect to Grant and Vanderkamp's (1980) finding that negative income gains to migration are experienced by individuals with relatively high pre-migration incomes, the authors offer an explanation not out of keeping with the view above. They suggest that persons with higher incomes can afford to indulge in special job or location preferences, thus perhaps sacrificing some potential income gains which could be derived from migrating. In addition, they point out that the higher a person's income, the greater the probability that moving costs are likely to be paid by the employer at the destination point (thus reducing the migration investment), and that high-income migrants are more likely to experience intra-firm transfers (where such transfers are often part of the training process within multi-establishment firms). Needless to say, such considerations are more likely to be relevant to internal migration in a developed country like Canada than, say, a poor third world country.

Appendix 1 to Chapter 3: Variables, Definitions and Details on Data Sources

Variables	Definitions	Data sources
CL	Regional cost of living differential; covers eight regions in Canada; covers four commodity groupings; represents approximately 75% of the urban consumer's budget; does not cover housing.	**Canada Year Book**, Statistics Canada and **Consumer Prices and Price Indexes**, Statistics Canada, Catalogue 62-010.
CPI	Consumer price index.	Historical series for 1914-81 provided by Sandra Shadlock, Prices Division, Statistics Canada.
CRIME	Number of violent crimes per 1,000 population in "Police Metropolitan Areas"; crimes of violence include murder, homicide, sexual offences, assaults which are not indecent, and robberies; crimes are reported by police according to their metropolitan area of jurisdiction.	**Crime Statistics**, and **Crime and Traffic Enforcement Statistics**, Statistics Canada, Catalogue 85-205; and unpublished data for the metropolitan areas of St. John's (Nfld.), Saint John (N.B.), Sudbury, Waterloo and Victoria; provided by Robert Allen, Justice Statistics Division, Statistics Canada.
$DIST_{ij}$	Distance in road miles between Census Metropolitan Areas, in 1970.	Geography Division, Statistics Canada.
DS	Number of residential dwelling starts in Census Metropolitan Areas per 1,000 CMA population.	**National Housing Statistics**, Canada Mortgage and Housing Corporation; data published on an annual basis.
EDUC	Number of persons with "some university, university degree or university degree plus" in Census Metropolitan Areas per 1,000 CMA population.	**Census of Population**, 1961, 1971, 1976, 1981, Statistics Canada.
FEM	Number of females in the labour force in Census Metropolitan Areas per 1,000 females in CMA's; this rate of female labour force activity is a "refined rate" as both numerator and denominator pertain to females aged 15 years and over.	For the earlier years (eg., 1956), data from the 1961 Census of Population were used; as 1951 data are not available, 1951 and 1961 data could not be averaged to produce a mid-decade figure.

Variables	Definitions	Data sources
FEM		For the middle years (1966), **Census of Population** data for 1961 and 1971 were averaged to produce a mid-decade figure. For the later years (1971-76), averages were not required and 1971 and 1976 Census of Population data were used accordingly. All data provided by Pat Grainger, Economic Characteristics Division, Statistics Canada.
GRANT	Amount of unconditional or general purpose federal grants to the provinces divided by the population of each province; deflated by the consumer price index (1971 = 100):	**Provincial Economic Accounts, 1962-77**, Statistics Canada, Catalogue 13-213; data for earlier years supplied as unpublished tables by Barbara Clift, National Product Division, Statistics Canada.
HOUSE	Average estimated total cost of new housing units in Census Metropolitan Areas financed under the National Housing Act; deflated by the consumer price index (1971 = 100).	**National Housing Statistics**, Canada Mortgage and Housing Corporation; data published on an annual basis.
IMMIG	Number of immigrants per 1,000 Census Metropolitan Area population that located in the CMA during each "migration period" (eg., 1956-61, 1976-81).	**Census of Population**, 1961, 1971, 1976, 1981, Statistics Canada.
JOBS	Employment growth per 1,000 employed in Census Metropolitan Areas; an industrial composite.	Labour Division, Statistics Canada; derived from unpublished figures on growth of employment.

Variables, Definitions and Details on Data Sources – Continued

Variables	Definitions	Data sources
JOBS	data based on monthly records of employment collected from larger business establishments; fishing, trapping, education, health and welfare services, religious organizations, public administration and defence.	
$LANG_{ij}$	Commonality of language between pairs of Census Metropolitan Areas.	A value of '1' is assigned if *both* cities in the CMA pair have 50% or more of their population of common French or English ethnicity. For example, $L_{ij} = 0$ for Montréal/Toronto or Québec City/Vancouver; $L_{ij} = 1$ for Montréal/Québec City or Montréal/Ottawa; $L_{ij} = 1$ for Toronto/Vancouver or Toronto/Ottawa.
M_{ij}	The ratio of the probability of moving (P_{ij}) between place 'i' and 'j' and the probability of staying at 'i'. (See the Appendix to Chapter 4 "Linear versus Logarithmic Functions" for the appropriate formula.) In the derivation of 'P_{ij}/P_{ii}', migrants are defined as persons who moved from city 'i' to city 'j' over the five-year census interval, *or*, residents of 'j' in census year (eg., t = 1981) who were residents of another city 'i' five years previously (ie., t − 5 = 1976).	Data have been derived from migration flow matrices for Census Metropolitan Areas as follows: 1956-61 matrix – unpublished table supplied by L.O. Stone, Statistics Canada. 1966-71 migration matrix obtained from unpublished table, Demography Division, Statistics Canada. 1971-76 migration matrix obtained from Statistics Canada Catalogue 92-828. 1976-81 migration matrix derived from a special unpublished tabulation from the 1981 Census, Statistics Canada.
NRR	Natural resource revenues per capita; sum of provincial indirect taxes from the resource sector, and net profits of resource-related provincially owned Crown corporations. deflated by the consumer price index (1971 = 100).	Consolidated Government Finance, Statistics Canada, Catalogue 68-202; Provincial Government Enterprise Finance, Statistics Canada Catalogue 61-204.
OWN	Home owners aged 25-34 years per 1,000 Census Metropolitan Area population aged 25-34 years.	Census of Population, 1951, 1961, 1966, 1971, 1976, 1981.

Variables	Definitions	Data sources
P	Total population of Census Metropolitan Areas; 1956 population according to 1961 CMA boundaries. 1966 population according to 1966 CMA boundaries. 1971 population according to 1971 CMA boundaries. 1976 population according to 1976 CMA boundaries.	**Canada Year Book**, annual, Statistics Canada, and 1981 Census of Population, Catalogues 95-901 to 95-903.
SNOW	Average centimetres of snowfall at weather stations in closest proximity to Census Metropolitan Areas; average snowfall calculated over two points of time, 1965 and 1980.	**Canada Year Book**, Statistics Canada.
UI	Amount of federal government unemployment insurance transfer payments to persons in each province divided by the total wage and salary income of the province; deflated by the consumer price index (1971 = 100).	Unemployment insurance data for the early years (1956-61) supplied in unpublished tables by Barbara Clift, Gross National Product Division, Statistics Canada. Unemployment insurance data for the later years (1962-77) published in **Provincial Economic Accounts**, Statistics Canada, Catalogue 13-213, Annual. Provincial total wage, salary and supplemental income published in **National Income and Expenditure Accounts**, Statistics Canada, Catalogue 13-513.
UI*	Average total payment of unemployment insurance benefits per unemployed worker in each province; deflated by the consumer price index (1971 = 100).	Derived using $(1) \times (2)/(3)$, where; (1) data on "average unemployment insurance per week", by province, in **Statistical Report on the Operation of the Unemployment Insurance Act, 1977**, Statistics Canada, Catalogues 73-001 and 73-201. (2) data on "total weeks of unemployment insurance paid", by province, in Catalogues 73-001 and 73-201, as above.

Variables, Definitions and Details on Data Sources – Concluded

Variables	Definitions	Data sources
UI*		(3) data on "average number of unemployed" by province, in **Historical Labour Force Statistics**, Statistics Canada, Catalogue 71-201; see also data source on UIPROB.
UIGEN	Unemployment insurance generosity index (a ratio): numerator: the average weekly payment of UI* benefits in the province 'i'. denominator: the average weekly wage of each CMA within the province 'i'. in the derivation of UIGEN, our measures of UI* and wages need not be deflated by the consumer price index.	**Statistical Report on the Operation of the Unemployment Insurance Act**, Statistics Canada, Catalogue 73-001. Wages: see WAGE.
UIPROB	Probability of obtaining UI benefits if unemployed (a ratio): numerator: total weeks of paid UI benefits in province 'i'. denominator: total number of weeks of unemployed labour in province 'i'. total weeks of unemployment calculated by multiplying total number unemployed in province 'i' by 52 weeks.	**Statistical Report on the Operation of the Unemployment Insurance Act**, Statistics Canada, Catalogue 73-001. **Historical Labour Force Statistics**, Statistics Canada, Catalogue 71-201.
UNEMP	Number of unemployed per 1,000 labour force of Census Metropolitan Areas; our data on unemployment derive from different sources over the four migration periods studied; as these sources are known to produce somewhat different estimates, errors of an unknown magnitude are introduced.	For the mid-1950's historical labour force statistics are provided for Ontario, Québec, British Columbia and two regions; the Atlantic region and Prairie region. Provincial estimates were made for the latter regions by using census estimates of provincial unemployment to disaggregate the regional unemployment figures. For the earlier years (eg., 1956), data were derived by averaging CMA unemployment rates, published by the **Census of Population**, 1951 and 1961. For the middle period (1966-71), data were derived from unpublished tables supplied by Kay Cockburn, Labour Force Survey Group, Statistics Canada.

Variables	Definitions	Data sources
UNEMP		For the later period (1976), data are published on an annual basis by the **Labour Force Survey**, Statistics Canada, Catalogue 71-001.
WAGE	Average weekly wages and salaries of Census Metropolitan Areas; an industrial composite. deflated by the consumer price index (1971 = 100).	Labour Division, Statistics Canada; data published on a regular basis in the **Canada Year Book**.

Appendix 2 to Chapter 3

Unemployment Insurance, the Budget Constraint and Labour Supply

Our purpose here is to convey how UI might alter labour supply. Following Rea, Jr. (1977) we employ a standard income-leisure diagram to illustrate the effects of UI on the worker's budget constraint before and after 1971.

To sharpen the pre- versus post-1971 contrast, let us compare parameters of the "seasonal benefits program" which existed previous to 1971 with parameters of the "regular program" following the sweeping revisions to the UI Act in 1971.

Parameters of the UI system	General values	
	Pre-1971	Post-1971
Number of weeks of employment required for eligibility	15	8
Weeks of waiting period before receiving first benefits	1	2
Number of weeks that benefits can be claimed:		
Minimum	13	26
Maximum	23	30
Fraction of weekly earnings paid to claimant	.50	.66

The pre-1971 figures pertain to workers covered under the "seasonal benefits program" which was established in 1955. Under this program, 13 weeks of benefits were payable in the winter months for those employed for a *minimum* of 15 weeks during the same year. Each additional week of employment increased the worker's eligibility for UI by 5/6 of a week. Thus, a maximum of 23 weeks of benefits could be received following a total of 28 weeks of employment (ie., 28 weeks of employment + 23 weeks of benefits + 1 week waiting period = 1 year). If weekly earnings were, say, $100 then the claimant would receive (.50) ($100) = $50 per week of UI benefits.

In contrast, the post-1971 figures pertain to a greatly expanded program with almost universal coverage. Under the new UI program, 26 weeks of benefits could be collected by workers who had been employed only eight weeks during the year. Additional weeks of work did not increase the benefit period until 15 weeks of employment had been surpassed. Then, each additional week of employment increased UI eligibility by one week. Thus, a maximum of 30 weeks of benefits could be received for 20 weeks of employment (ie., 20 weeks of employment + 30 weeks of benefits + 2 weeks waiting period = 1 year). If weekly earnings again average \$100, then the claimant would receive (.66) (\$100) = \$66 per week of UI benefits.

Several qualifications are in order concerning the parameters for the post-1971 period. First, they are most relevant to the period immediately following 1971. Since 1971, changes have been introduced almost yearly with major changes being introduced in 1979. Second, UI benefits have been taxable as of 1972. For our purposes, this will not be taken into consideration in the analysis to follow. Third, the average wage ceiling for entitlements was set at \$150. Fourth, the minimum benefit period is conditional on the level of national and regional unemployment. Our figure of 26 weeks of minimum benefits includes an adjustment for national unemployment rates which are assumed to exceed 5%. Were unemployment rates to fall below this level in any particular year, the minimum benefit period would fall by eight weeks to a total of 18 weeks. Finally, precise benefit entitlements are affected by several minor conditions such as presence of dependent children, etc. These will not be taken into consideration in the analysis to follow.

The effect of UI on the worker's budget constraint can be illustrated using the data above in the context of Figure A.3.1. For the pre-1971 period, the worker's budget constraint – in the absence of UI – is indicated by line ABEF. At point A the worker is employed 0 weeks and earns 0 income, whereas at point F the worker is employed full-time and earns \$5,200. The assumed weekly wage rate is \$100. In the presence of UI, the budget constraint of a typical seasonal worker becomes ABCDEF. With only 15 weeks of employment, the seasonal worker is entitled to 15 (\$100) + 13 (.50) (\$100) = \$2,150 rather than 15 (\$100) = \$1,500 in the absence of UI. Now, assume that the seasonal worker has 13 more weeks of employment. This would entitle him/her to 10 more weeks of benefits since each additional week of employment earns 5/6 of a week of benefits. At 28 weeks of employment, the worker's year is now potentially complete as he/she is entitled to 23 weeks of benefits with one week being reserved for the 'waiting period' (segment EF in Figure A.3.1).

Figure A.3.1: The Budget Constraint With and Without Unemployment Insurance

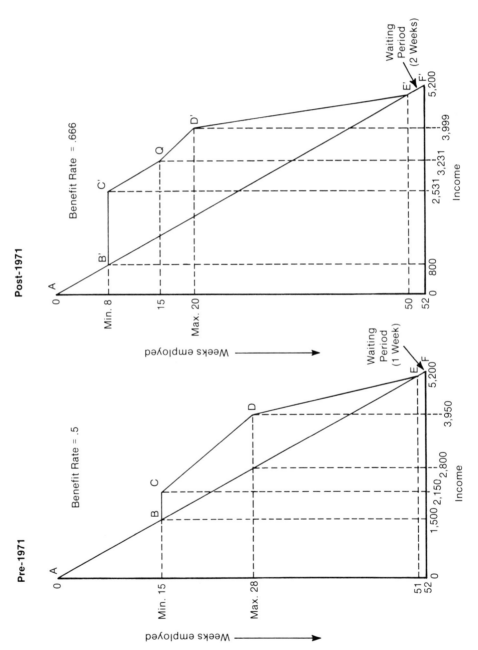

Under the system described above one can imagine workers with fewer than 15 weeks of employment being induced by UI benefits to increase their number of weeks of employment. It may also bid non-labour force individuals into the labour force just long enough to qualify for UI. For those working between 15 to 28 weeks, UI acts as a wage subsidy by boosting marginal returns to work. This is indicated by the slope of the CD segment on the new budget constraint. In contrast, for those on the DE segment, the UI program acts like a negative income tax since workers now experience a reduction in their marginal wage rate – relative to workers employed 15-28 weeks and drawing UI benefits. If leisure is a normal good, the declining marginal return to labour on the DE segment of the budget constraint could combine with the added income earned to motivate a cut-back in labour supply.

Turning to the post-1971 period, we observe that the budget constraint – in the presence of UI – shifts upward and to the right. In this case, only eight weeks of employment entitles the worker to 26 weeks of benefits. Point C' indicates that the worker would be entitled to $2,531 of income, or $1,731 more than he/she would receive in the absence of UI (C' – D'). For 15 weeks of employment, the worker would be entitled to 2.154 times what would be earned in the absence of UI (ie., $3,231 versus $1,500). In contrast, in the pre-1971 system the same worker with an average wage of $100 per week who was employed 15 weeks would be entitled to only 1.43 times what would be earned in the absence of UI (ie., $2,150 versus $1,500).

The incentive for those working less than eight weeks to increase their employment is clearly substantial in the post-1971 period. And if leisure is a normal good, we might imagine workers opting for eight and only eight weeks of employment. (Note that their marginal return to work would not increase until after 15 weeks of employment (segment QD'), implying no marginal gains to being employed eight to 15 weeks). Again, on segment D' E' we observe that the marginal return to work is less than on segment QD', implying that for workers on this segment the presence of UI behaves again like a negative income tax.

Appendix to Chapter 4:
Appropriate Model Specification and Data

Introduction

Consensus on appropriate "model specification" is only beginning to take shape in empirical studies of migration. For this reason, this appendix draws attention to key methodological issues in the process of specifying our empirical model. Our discussion is couched in a dependent:independent variable format whereas all statistical evaluations are performed using least squares multiple regression analysis. In addition to specifying our model, we also draw attention to strengths and weaknesses of our empirical data.

Appropriate Functional Form

Normalizing Migration

Should migration between place 'i' and 'j' be represented as a gross flow measuring one-way directionality (M_{ij}) or as a net flow (M_{ij} minus M_{ij})? Empirical work confirms that net flows obscure the fact that in-migration and out-migration respond to socio-economic characteristics differently. Vanderkamp (1971) illustrates this point when he disaggregates net flows into new migrants, return migrants and "autonomous" migrants. The latter include all moves not related to incomes such as armed forces transfers and students. Vanderkamp shows that while greater distance deters new migrants, it does not deter return migrants to the same extent. The reason is that return migrants are likely to be returning "home" to a known entity, possibly out of disillusionment with their initial move. Thus, a measure of net migration, which mixes two-way flows is likely to obscure the effects of socio-economic influences. For this and other reasons, determinants of migration can be best appreciated when migration is represented as a gross or uni-directional flow. This is the approach adopted here.

A decision must also be made on the appropriate population variable for standardizing or "normalizing" M_{ij}. Normalizing procedures have been the subject of debate for some time (Young:1975, Vanderkamp:1976). Migration might be normalized (ie., represented as a ratio), by using either of the following as a denominator; (i) the total population or labour force of the origin (a gross ratio of out-migration), (ii) the total population or labour force of the destination (a gross ratio of in-migration), or (iii) some combination or multiple of the two base populations. Most researchers prefer normalization M_{ij}/P_i since it is the city or province of departure in which decisions to leave are taken. And on the assumption that migration decisions of individuals are independent,

M_{ij}/P_i is commonly interpreted as the maximum likelihood estimator of the probability that an individual from 'i' will migrate to 'j'. Thus, we prefer normalization M_{ij}/P_i (see below however).

Linear Versus Logarithmic Functions

Should variables be entered linearly or in logarithmic form in least squares regression models? Many researchers have defended the use of logarithmic functions on the grounds that they provide a "better fit". Log transformations to base 'e' (log normal) are also attractive as they produce regression coefficients that can conveniently be interpreted as elasticities. Such, however, are not sufficient criteria for selecting logarithmic functions. Appropriate functional forms should be dictated by theory.

To illustrate, suppose the researcher expects migrants to respond positively to *relative* wage levels. In addition, suppose he/she predicts that the relationship between distance and migration will be negative but non-linear, under the assumption that fixed costs of relocation will taper off after a certain "distance threshold". The implied model in the absence of logarithmic transformation is;

1) $M_{ij}/P_i = \alpha_0 + \beta_1 W_j/W_i - \beta_2 D_{ij} + u$,

where; α_0 = intercept, W = wage level, D_{ij} = distance between place 'i' and 'j', u = error term with $E(u_i) = 0$, $E(u_i)^2 = \sigma^2$, i = 1, 2 ..n.

Now, applying properties of logs to the variable which is expressed above as a ratio (thus, no substantive theory is required) and transforming distance to satisfy the non-linearity hypothesis (thus, substantive theory is required), we obtain;

2) $M_{ij}/P_i = \alpha'_0 + \beta'_1 \ln W_j - \beta'_2 \ln W_i - \beta'_3 \ln D_{ij} + u$.

Equation (2) can be referred to as a semi-log transformation in that only those variables on the right-hand side are log transformed.

In contrast to equation (2), suppose the researcher now postulates that migration will respond to absolute differences in wages $(W_j - W_i)$. In this case, log transformation of the absolute difference between W_j and W_i is not appropriate unless the researcher explicitly assumes that marginal utility of income (its slope) will decrease (taper off) at higher-income levels.

A more recent approach to modelling migration, and the one adopted here, employs the polytomous logistic model. The polytomous model was developed in economics by McFadden (1973). Its advantages have been fully extolled in migration studies by Grant and Vanderkamp (1976), Gordon et al. (1982), Falaris (1982), Schultz (1982) and others. Accordingly, it will suffice to say the following. First, the polytomous model recognizes that migration decisions involve a choice between a finite number of mutually exclusive, discreet, alternative destinations. The utility of a particular destination, and the probability of its selection, is assumed to vary not only with its attributes but also with the characteristics of the individuals who make the choice. Second, the estimation of destination and personal characteristics makes use of a model that is linear in parameters but non-linear in empirical variables. Third, the dependent variable is represented as the ratio of the probability of moving (P_{ij}) between places 'i' and 'j' and the probability of staying in 'i' (P_{ii}). In the complete empirical formulation, both migration and its possible determinants are log transformed to produce a double-log function.

Use of probability measure P_{ij}/P_{ii} is preferable to M_{ij}/P_i as it embodies information on the frequency of non-migration as well as migration. This is;

$$3) \quad P_{ij}/P_{ii} = (M_{ij}/P_i) \Bigg/ \left[1 - \sum_{\substack{j=1 \\ j \neq i}}^{J} M_{ij} / P_i \right]$$

where; M_{ij} = number of migrants from origin 'i' to destination 'j', P_i = the population of place 'i'. In addition, since migration ratios are proportions whose values range from '0' to '1', the use of P_{ij}/P_{ii} in regression analysis has an advantage over M_{ij}/P_i. The summation of all P_{ij}/P_{ii} is constrained to equal '1', whereas the sum of M_{ij}/P_i may yield predicted total migration outside this range.

Some researchers have approximated $\ln(P_{ij}/P_{ii})$ by $\ln(M_{ij}/P_i)$ since the variation in P_{ij} is likely to be much greater than the variation in P_{ii}. That is, the summation of M_{ij} on the right side of equation (3) drops out and the P_i terms are rearranged to produce M_{ij}/P_i equivalent to P_{ij}/P_{ii}. However, coefficients deriving from equations which regress socio-economic variables against $1n(P_{ij}/P_{ii})$ are not directly comparable with those using $1n(M_{ij}/P_i)$. This fact is demonstrated by Grant and Vanderkamp (1976).

A *full* application of the polytomous logistic model requires that both P_{ij}/P_{ii} and origin and destination characteristics be calculated specific to individual migrants or migrant subgroups. Thus, if migrants are disaggregated into three groups by level of education, P_{ij}/P_{ii} should be calculated for each group. In addition, origin and destination characteristics relevant to each educational subgroup should be differentiated. The objective, of course, is to examine the migratory behaviour of, say, a high versus low education group in terms of, say, employment and income opportunities that are differentiated with respect to each level of education.

Our use of the polytomous model is to be construed as a partial application. Like all other applications currently in use, data *are* available to disaggregate migrants by socio-economic subgroup but they *are not* available on origin and destination opportunities, specific to each migrant subgroup. Until such time as micro or panel data are available on migration cohorts, a full application of the polytomous model must be ruled out.

Symmetrical Versus Asymmetrical Models

Just as net migration rates obscure important determinants of in-migration versus out-migration flows, symmetrical models obscure important differences in the impact of origin versus destination characteristics. To illustrate, suppose we hypothesize that P_{ij}/P_{ii} (as defined above), will increase as the ratio of wages (W) between place 'i' and 'j' increases. The symmetrical model represents the influence of wages as $1n(W_j/W_i)$, the asymmetrical model as $(1nW_j - 1nW_i)$. The latter form allows for the possibility that the expected positive effect of W_j and the expected negative effect of W_i will exert different magnitudes on P_{ij}/P_{ii}. In contrast, the symmetrical model obscures this possibility. Indeed, from an interpretive standpoint it restricts origin and destination characteristics to be of equal significance.

The symmetrical model rests on the assumption of perfect information between labour markets. Potential migrants are expected to be as receptive to changing labour market conditions in a faraway place as they would be to changes of the same magnitude in their present location.

However, as Fields (1982) observes, once we recognize that individuals know more about opportunities in their present location than in distant places, we are led to expect that changes in origin economic conditions will have a larger effect on migration than a like-sized change in destination conditions. Thus, we might expect a particular form of asymmetry in which origin conditions should dominate as determinants of place-to-place migration flows.

While the empirical literature confirms asymmetry in origin and destination characteristics, it is surprising that the form of the asymmetry is contrary to that proposed above. That is, economic conditions at destination are found to consistently "outperform" those at the origin in terms of consistency of sign, statistical significance and their contribution to R^2 values. Several explanations for this unexpected consensus have been proposed. Gary Fields (1982, p.541-42) notes three and it is worthwhile to paraphrase his insightful interpretation at length.

First, capital market imperfections may strongly impede migration. By this argument, superior economic conditions at the origin may increase the ability of potential migrants to finance profitable moves. Thus, better origin conditions may be positively, rather than negatively correlated with migration.

Second, migration itself may be desirable as a consumption good. By this argument, the income effect in high-income origins leads to greater consumption of most goods, including migration. Again, relatively favourable origin economic conditions may result in more out-migration.

A third possible explanation offered by Fields concerns "aggregation bias". He distinguishes between currently employed workers, and those who are currently unemployed or out of the labour market. Since currently employed persons are working in particular jobs with particular wages, fringe benefits, etc., they are more likely to face job opportunities which are proxied only imperfectly by average conditions in the origin. And since a large number of potential migrants are currently employed, we might expect this group to respond weakly to the effects of "average" origin conditions. In contrast, the unemployed are necessarily searching for jobs, so average labour market conditions in the origin may be a very good proxy for the job opportunities that they face in their present location. This group might be expected to respond strongly to the effects of origin conditions. The aggregation problem arises when the two groups are lumped together. The currently employed group, by virtue of its much larger size, would tend to "drown out" the response of the smaller, unemployed group to origin conditions.

Several additional *ad hoc* explanations could be invoked for the observed asymmetry in origin and destination characteristics. As Fields points out, what these explanations have in common is that favourable economic conditions at origin may increase the means of moving but reduce the incentives. Although the relative strength of these effects cannot be predicted *a priori*, they combine to produce a weak correlation between origin economic conditions and the rate of out-migration. In contrast, destination effects tend not to be obscured because changes in destination conditions affect incentives only.

More on Aggregation Bias

To some extent, all studies of place-to-place migration suffer from "aggregation bias". Whether aggregation bias can be tested for, let alone purged, depends on whether available data permit the disaggregation of migration rates, origin and destination characteristics, or geographical units of analysis.[1]

One way of testing for aggregation bias is to group migration flows according to different geographical areas. This approach allows the researcher to evaluate whether explanatory variables are more important to migration in some regions than for the country as a whole. It is adopted in Chapter 5 (following Winer and Gauthier:1983), to evaluate whether government transfer programs are more relevant to migration in eastern Canada.

Another approach is to disaggregate migration flows into smaller geographical units. Analysis of smaller, homogeneous units allows more rigorous evaluation of the response of migrants to place-specific conditions (eg., crime rates averaged across a city versus across an entire province). This point has been effectively illustrated by Morgan (1975/76), who re-evaluates an economic model of migration which was estimated by Miller (1973) using interstate migration data. Morgan uses the same model and explanatory variables as Miller but examines intermetropolitan rather than interstate migration. She argues that states are not sufficiently economically integrated to serve as proxies for classic labour markets, whereas metropolitan areas are.[2] That is, the various labour markets within a state rarely exhibit any real homogeneity of economic conditions.

Morgan shows that Miller's model, which purports to explain 88% of the variance in interstate migration is much less successful when metropolitan areas are used as the units of analysis. In fact, the explanatory power of the model drops to $R^2 = .496$. This type of debate marries well with our intended use of CMA's rather than provinces, as in past studies. (See, however, footnote 11, Chapter 1.)

A more refined approach to disaggregation would classify migrants according to personal characteristics (eg., by level of education). This approach, adopted in Chapter 5, allows the researcher to query whether conditions at place 'i' and 'j' exert the same effect on migrants when their personal characteristics are more tightly controlled. It proceeds on the assumption that migration flows may not be homogeneous but may be comprised of heterogeneous subgroups that do not fit the "typical" migrant mold. Finally, as noted previously, the most highly refined disaggregations require panel data to simultaneously disaggregate migrants by personal characteristics (eg., occupation), and to evaluate their behaviour in terms of group-specific opportunities at place 'i' or 'j' (eg., occupation-specific wage rates).

When aggregation bias cannot be "adjusted for", it is important to interpret results with much greater caution. This point has been amply illustrated in criticism of early studies on intermetropolitan migration in the United States which failed to disaggregate migrants by race. Blacks and whites were assumed to behave identically to place 'i' and 'j' characteristics. Subsequent studies, however, have shown that blacks and whites respond differently to origin and destination characteristics.[3] Such problems are serious when researchers are pressed for policy recommendations on the basis of their empirical findings. Regressions may show that wages and employment opportunities influence migration, but this need not imply that higher wages and employment opportunities will benefit all "target" groups equally.[4]

Unlike migration data for the United States, migration data for Canada need not be disaggregated by race – though French/English ethnicity must be taken into consideration. Also "autonomous" moves are not as problematic in Canada as in the United States.[5] For example, in certain areas of the United States, migrants consist largely of military transfers. When such transfers are "nested" in general migration rates, they obscure the true effects of economic variables on, say, labour force migration. Put differently, the rate of general migration is not a good proxy for the rate of labour force migration when autonomous moves are heavily represented.

Return Migration

Several researchers, following Vanderkamp (1971; 1972), have shown that "return" or "repeat" migrants may represent anywhere from 20-40% of all migrants.[6] Such migrants are hypothesized to respond differently to place 'i' and 'j' opportunities than "new" or "first-time" migrants. Lumping all migrants together is likely to result in yet another form of aggregation bias.

Fortunately, migration data from census sources are much more immune to such problems than data deriving from *yearly* income tax or family allowance "administrative files" (as used by Vanderkamp and others). One reason is that the census classifies individuals as migrants only if they change their *usual place of residence*. Thus, a census migrant is more akin to a "permanent" migrant. In contrast, administrative files impose no such qualification, with the result that many moves, intended to be temporary, are included.

In addition to the above, much return migration occurs only a year or so after an initial move. Such moves tend not to be enumerated by the census, though they are picked up by administrative data files. This problem has been quantified in a rare study by Henry Puderer (1982) who examines the prevalence of return and repeat migration in census versus administrative files. Puderer finds that return or repeat moves constitute approximately 30% of all moves reported by yearly tax filer data over a five-year period. This compares with about 5-10% for census data.

The problem noted above is likely to subtract from the analysis by, say, Winer and Gauthier (1983) which relies on yearly family allowance and tax filer data. At the same time, however, if one is more interested in the dynamics of the labour market per se, then problems with census data must also be acknowledged. For example, the total resource costs of the dynamic process of migration will tend to be underestimated by census data precisely because they ignore most repeat migration. Also, the dating of migration is much less precise for census data. This makes it more difficult to construct precisely timed variables and lag structures to explain migration decisions.

Simultaneity Bias

Simultaneity bias arises when models are specified in such a way that the relationship between the dependent variable (migration) and the independent variables (eg., wages), cannot be assumed to be one-way. Most studies of place-to-place migration suffer from simultaneity bias to some extent, though problems can be minimized.

To take an example, suppose we observe a strong positive correlation between high rates of migration at place 'j' at time 't' and high wage levels at place 'j' at time 't'. We would like to infer that the high wages attract the migrants, but to do so we must assume that the high wages are not, in turn, attributable to the migrants (eg., high-income migrants). In other terms, unless the assumption of independence applies, both migration and wages will exert simultaneous effects on each other and we will not know which came first – the high rates of migration or the high wages.

One way of minimizing simultaneity bias is to measure the relevant explanatory variables at the beginning of the migration period. Thus, if the migration rate pertains to a 1976-81 average, then the influence of, say, unemployment at potential destination might be measured as an average rate for the years 1975-77. This is the approach adopted here.

Another means of minimizing simultaneity bias is to estimate a system of simultaneous equations. This procedure involves the application of two- or three-stage least squares regression which aims to purge empirical measures of their joint interdependence. It is considerably more demanding of data. It also adds to technical complexity. For these and related reasons, most studies of migration steer clear of its use.[7]

Multicollinearity

Multicollinearity arises when empirical variables representing different explanatory constructs overlap. To illustrate, several authors recognize the important effect that friends and relatives have on the direction of migration, and have sought to capture this effect by a measure of "migrant stock". Migrant stock (MS) is usually represented as people born in place 'i' that were residing in place 'j' *previous to* the period in which migration between place 'i' and 'j' is being examined. Regression studies which include MS usually find that it makes a sizeable contribution to R^2.

As important as friends and relatives may be, measures of migrant stock per se (MS) are likely to be biased and theoretically inept. I have argued elsewhere that MS at time 't-n' is likely to be highly correlated with migration at time 't' not so much because it captures the "friends and relatives effect" but because migrants at time 't' are going to place 'j' for the *same reasons* that migrants at time 't-n' did.[8] Inclusion of MS in regression analysis artificially boosts the R^2 value while confounding the significance of socio-economic influences which are in fact determining migration. A similar point has been made with respect to the inclusion of population at destination or origin as an explanatory variable along with incomes, etc. (See Chapter 2, "Relative Importance of Variables".)

Multicollinearity may also arise when public and private sector variables are estimated in the same empirical model. Recall that we plan to evaluate measures of "federal government transfers to provinces" and "provincial natural resource revenues" along with measures of employment, wages and salaries, crime rates, etc. To some extent, fiscal variables will be intercorrelated with the private sector variables. One way of checking for multicollinearity is to examine zero-order correlation coefficients (see Appendix 5). If the degree of relationship between two explanatory variables exceeds, say $R^2 = .40$, it may be wise to drop one of the variables. Another way of checking for multicollinearity is to examine significance levels of regression coefficients as additional, possibly intercorrelated variables are added to estimating functions. If multicollinearity is detected, importance should not be attached to the *magnitude* of the affected regression coefficients. These procedures have been adopted in Chapters 4 and 5.

Age and Spatial Structure

Changing age and spatial structure can be problematic when estimating determinants of intermetropolitan migration over long periods of time. If a population ages, thereby producing more elderly who are not in the labour force, then fewer of its members would likely migrate for work-related reasons (eg., an increase in retirement migration). Were this to apply to Canada, the age structure would have to be controlled when determining if and why work-related reasons were declining as influences in intermetropolitan migration. On the other hand, if youthful components of the population grow over time (eg., lagged effects of a "baby boom"), rapid additions to the labour force might alter employment opportunities and risks of unemployment at different metropolitan areas (Wilson:1983). This might discourage migration for work-related reasons.

In this case, it would be necessary to introduce specific measures to control for employment and unemployment. In this study, we have already argued that a control for the elderly is not necessary (see Chapter 3, "Selectivity Considerations"), whereas specific measures to control for labour market conditions have been introduced.

Effects of changing spatial structure on migration over time can be illustrated with respect to distance. Suppose that one-half of all migratory flows in Canada at time 't' consist of moves between hard-to-travel places (eg., in the Canadian north) and one-half between relatively easy-to-travel places (eg., between cities along the Canada/U.S. border). In a statistical analysis which pooled these migration flows, the estimated coefficient on distance (eg., miles between places) would capture effects of both types of travel network. In contrast, suppose that at time 't + 30' years, 90% of all migratory moves in Canada were among relatively easy-to-travel places (eg., between cities along the Canada/U.S. border). In this case, the estimated coefficient on distance would probably decline reflecting not so much improvements in travel but a spatial shift in migration fields to places where travel was relatively easier and less costly.

In our study, growing shares of all migrants have moved westward (ie., more long-distance moves), but the share of all inter-CMA moves occurring in the west or in the east has not altered drastically. With respect to more long-distance moves, this should not affect the coefficient on distance unless, of course, roads and telecommunications are worse (or better) for travel *between* eastern and western CMA's than *among* CMA's in the east or in the west. We have no reason to believe they are. With respect to shares of all inter-CMA moves represented by CMA's in the west versus CMA's in the east, over time, these have changed but not to the extent that a control variable for spatial structure seems warranted. Between 1956-61, for example, approximately 24% of all inter-CMA migration flows in Canada occurred between CMA's in the west. Between 1976-81, the same western CMA's accounted for approximately 20% of all inter-CMA flows. Furthermore, we have attempted to control for changing spatial structure among CMA's by examining the same cohort of CMA's over four periods of time (17 CMA's achieving CMA status in 1961). More recent CMA's, possibly with different spatial networks, have been excluded.

It is also true that few economic studies of migration have acknowledged the potential importance of changing spatial structure in migration fields. Further research on this issue seems warranted. Simmons (1980, Table 6) has moved in this direction by examining the influence of various geographical barriers on migration between "urban-centred" regions in Canada. We have moved in this direction by disaggregating migration flows into those originating from CMA's in eastern Canada versus western Canada.

Data Caveats

Migration Data

Information on intermetropolitan migration in Canada has been processed from the 1961, 1971, 1976 and 1981 Censuses of Canada. Census data are attractive insofar as they have been subjected to a vast array of field and methodological checks during enumeration and computer tabulation. For example, we know that rates of "no response" to census migration questions were less than 1% in 1961. At that time, the census was administered by enumerators at the household level on a "handout, hand-back" basis. In 1971, rates of "no response" jumped to 5.6%. This was attributable to census enumeration for the first time on a "handout, mail-back" basis. In 1976, improvements in the mail-back system resulted in a drop of "no response" to 3.7%. By 1981, rates of "no response" had remained in and around 5%. Such rates of "no response" are acceptable from the standpoint of tolerable levels of sampling error.

Unfortunately, tolerable levels of sampling error do not tell the whole story about "no response" rates. "No response" is distributed unevenly among the Census Metropolitan Areas (CMA's) analyzed in this study. Rates of "no response" are, on average, one and one-half times higher for CMA's of predominantly French-speaking inhabitants than predominantly English-speaking inhabitants. Thus, the standard assumption in regression analysis that "disturbances" or errors associated with data are evenly distributed among geographic units, and thus cancel out, is violated. As the data cannot be corrected, the "error term" in our regression estimates will not be normally distributed and our estimates will be biased to a small, unknown extent.

Turning to census questions on migration, intermetropolitan migrants are defined as those living in a metropolitan area that is different from the one they were living in five years previous to "census day".

The census does not ask whether the individual moved more than once during the five years. Nor does the census establish whether the move is a new or "first-time" move, a repeat move, or return migration. As noted previously, absence of this type of information poses far less problems for migration data deriving from census records than for family allowance or tax filer records. Nevertheless, the incidence of return or repeat migration, in the order of 5-10%, will introduce an "aggregation bias" of a small, unknown magnitude in our regression estimates.

For each migration period, 17 Census Metropolitan Areas (CMA's) have been selected for evaluation. This results in a migration flow matrix for each period of 17 origin CMA's and 16 destination CMA's or, 17 $\times$ 16 = 272 uni-directional migration flows. Thus, grouping data into pre-1971 and post-1971 migration produces 2 $\times$ 272 = 544 observations for each group. This number is certainly sufficient for the kind of statistical analysis to be undertaken here. In addition, migration data for the 1976-81 period have been disaggregated by migrant's level of education. For our purposes, three levels of education have been identified; those with less than grade 12 education, those with grade 12 diploma or more (but less than a university degree), and those with a university degree or more.

The 17 CMA's examined in this study are the same for each migration period (see Appendix Table A.1.5). They correspond to the 17 CMA's first identified by the 1961 Census with populations in excess of 100,000. By 1981, seven more urban centres had qualified as CMA's, raising the total number to 24. As noted in Chapter 1, the more recent CMA's have not been included in our sample for two reasons. First, data on socio-economic or explanatory variables have not always been available for the new CMA's. Also, data on the new CMA's are at times, suspect, in the sense that they have not been systematically collected and published over long periods of time (as in the case of the older CMA's). Second, analysis of an identical group of CMA's fits nicely with the idea of examining the behaviour of a cohort, undergoing change, as Canadian society evolves over time.

Changing CMA Boundaries

Between 1956-81, Census Metropolitan Areas (CMA's) have undergone changes in their geographical boundaries. In most cases, this happens when growing fringe areas are incorporated into the CMA. In other cases, boundary changes have been initiated by political mandate at the provincial or local government level. The effect of such changes on the comparability of CMA data over time is extremely difficult to determine.

The standard approach to "changing boundaries" is to avoid use of absolute numbers and to transform all migration and related data into rates. Rates convey the incidence of particular behaviours or characteristics per 100 population *at risk*. As long as CMA boundary changes do not alter the "homogeneity" of the population at risk over time, then rates can be assumed to be generally comparable over time periods. If, however, the nature and population make-up of a CMA undergoes a distinct change due to boundary revision (eg., inclusion of a large rural area), then errors of an unknown magnitude will enter pooled "time series" census data.

Our approach has been to examine CMA boundary changes which may have disturbed population homogeneity. Changes are observable but not to the extent that specific adjustments or exclusion of CMA's are warranted. In other terms, this study assumes that errors attributable to boundary changes are more or less evenly distributed among CMA's. In our regression estimates, they are treated as random components of the "error term".

Data on Explanatory Variables

Most of our data on CMA characteristics derive from census or Statistics Canada sources. Thus, they are subject to the same kinds of assumptions or qualifications reviewed above. Some of our data, however, do not represent CMA's as closely as others. For example, crime rates are calculated on the basis of "Police Metropolitan Areas", not CMA's per se. Snowfall is measured at weather stations in closest proximity to CMA's, some of which are situated outside CMA boundaries. Still other data pertain to regions within which a CMA falls. Thus, geographical units upon which our migration rates and our explanatory variables are constructed do not always correspond one-to-one.

Lack of correspondence between dependent and independent variables – in terms of geographical base – plagues all studies of migration to one extent or another. In this study, it is likely to be most serious when data limitations require that CMA's be assigned values according to the province or region they lie in. This procedure has been adopted to represent the effects of (i) regional cost of living differences, (ii) un-conditional or general purpose transfers to provinces, (iii) provincial natural resource revenues, and (iv) provincial measures of unemployment insurance benefits. To illustrate, the regional cost of living index for Alberta was assigned equally to both Calgary and Edmonton.

With respect to federal government transfers to provinces (Chapter 3, Hypotheses 13 and 14), we would have preferred information on provincial government allocations of such funds to each of its CMA's. Such data are not available, however. Yet, were we to represent the possible effects of provincial government transfers on migration in this way, we would undoubtedly confront a problem of a different sort. That is, provincial governments receive such transfers to bolster the prosperity of their *entire* province. If a CMA is prospering relative to the rest of its home province, its provincial government might allocate all or most of its transfer money to, say, development of amenities and services in outlying areas. Under the assumption that migrants are cognizant of province-wide amenities or prosperity, this in turn, may affect the probability of leaving a CMA in one province for a CMA in another. All this is to say that our procedure of assigning a province-wide value to CMA's cannot be readily discredited, though an error of unknown magnitude is likely to be introduced.

Summing Up

The empirical model to be estimated in Chapters 4 and 5 takes on the following characteristics. First, in keeping with the polytomous logistic model, migration rates are normalized by the population at place of origin 'i' that are "stayers". Second, in keeping with most applications of the polytomous model, it disaggregates probabilities of migrating by personal characteristics of migrants (eg., levels of education). Third, in keeping with most evaluations of the polytomous model, it adopts a double-log specification and employs ordinary least squares regression analysis. Fourth, explanatory variables are evaluated separately to allow for possible asymmetries in the effects of origin and destination characteristics.

In addition to the above, various steps or precautions are taken to test for, or to minimize "aggregation" and "simultaneity" bias. With respect to aggregation bias, migration flows are to be grouped into different geographical areas (eastern versus western Canada), disaggregated into smaller geographical units than in past studies (CMA's versus provinces), and disaggregated by personal characteristics of migrants (education). With respect to simultaneity bias, explanatory variables are to be measured at the beginning of the migration period to reduce joint interaction between migration and its possible causes. This procedure is not possible when yearly migration data are derived from administrative tax or family allowance files (as in Winer and Gauthier:1983). Moreover, vague "explanatory" variables which run the risk of being intercorrelated with more precise "explanatory" variables are excluded (eg., population size, migrant stock).

Attention has also been drawn to potential weaknesses in our data or measurement procedures. The reader is further advised to consult the Appendix to Chapter 3 for further detail on our independent variables.

Appendix 5

APPENDIX TABLE A.5.1 Means and Standard Deviations of Variables in the Regression Analysis, Selected Time Frames[1]

Variables	Number of observations	Mean	Standard deviation	Minimum	Maximum
	(1)	(2)	(3)	(4)	(5)
1956-81 pooled data					
GRANT	1,088	45.26	73.12	.70	314.10
M_{ij}	1,088	3.30	5.41	.01	42.43
$LANG_{ij}$	1,088	.79	.40	.00	1.00
DIST	1,088	1,556.42	1,132.76	36.00	4,787.00
JOBS	1,088	42.97	62.80	.10	400.90
UNEMP	1,088	49.81	18.61	17.00	101.00
DS	1,088	11.36	4.53	3.30	25.70
HOUSE	1,088	24,635.22	5,363.47	18,014.00	42,497.00
IMMIG	1,088	39.12	22.52	6.00	114.00
SNOW	1,088	149.88	70.80	31.00	296.00
WAGE1	1,088	120.20	26.13	68.60	174.50
FEM	1,088	403.42	62.29	271.00	520.00
CRIME	1,088	5.05	2.74	1.10	11.50
EDUC	1,088	108.91	46.21	34.00	248.00
UIGEN	1,088	.34	.07	.22	.48
UIPROB	1,088	1.03	.22	.50	1.60
OWN	1,088	452.96	95.23	164.00	608.00
Pre-1971 data					
GRANT	544	22.27	31.90	.80	168.10
M_{ij}	544	2.98	5.09	.01	33.62
$LANG_{ij}$	544	.79	.41	.00	1.00
$DIST_{ij}$	544	1,563.22	1,157.44	36.00	4,787.00
JOBS	544	36.21	34.95	.10	153.20
UNEMP	544	38.03	10.45	17.00	69.00
DS	544	9.02	3.15	3.30	17.10
HOUSE	544	21,417.00	1,630.59	18,819.00	26,990.00
IMMIG	544	39.09	20.02	6.00	87.00
SNOW	544	151.69	69.95	31.00	296.00
WAGE1	544	99.68	12.00	68.60	133.70
FEM	544	361.14	39.00	271.00	444.00
CRIME	544	4.16	2.27	1.10	9.30
EDUC	544	150.17	17.57	34.00	128.00
UIGEN	544	.30	.04	.22	.44
UIPROB	544	1.01	.14	.73	1.36
OWN	544	437.30	110.60	164.00	587.00

[1] These data are not log transformed.

APPENDIX TABLE A.5.1 Means and Standard Deviations of Variables in the Regression Analysis, Selected Time Frames[1] – Concluded

Variables	Number of observations	Mean	Standard deviation	Minimum	Maximum
	(1)	(2)	(3)	(4)	(5)
Post-1971 data					
GRANT	544	68.25	87.89	.70	314.10
M_{ij}	544	3.63	5.60	.01	42.43
$LANG_{ij}$	544	.79	.40	.00	1.00
$DIST_{ij}$	544	1,556.42	1,132.76	36.00	4,787.00
JOBS	544	49.73	73.39	.10	400.90
UNEMP	544	61.59	12.27	38.00	101.00
DS	544	13.69	4.41	7.50	25.70
HOUSE	544	27,852.84	5,101.75	18,014.00	42,497.00
IMMIG	544	39.15	21.60	6.00	114.00
SNOW	544	149.88	70.80	31.00	296.00
WAGE1	544	142.03	14.97	110.80	174.50
FEM	544	445.39	43.95	363.00	520.00
CRIME	544	5.94	2.86	1.40	11.50
EDUC	544	142.73	29.30	83.00	248.00
UIGEN	544	.39	.03	.28	.48
UIPROB	544	1.05	.21	.50	1.60
OWN	544	469.23	70.91	265.00	608.00
NRR	544	88.80	151.16	1.00	813.00
1976-81 data					
GRANT	272	85.70	98.55	18.60	314.10
M_{ij}	272	4.12	6.24	.01	42.43
$LANG_{ij}$	272	.79	.40	.00	1.00
$DIST_{ij}$	272	1,556.42	1,132.76	36.00	4,787.00
JOBS	272	32.42	49.08	.10	161.90
UNEMP	272	69.23	13.57	41.00	101.00
DS	272	13.34	5.11	6.90	25.70
HOUSE	272	30,182.88	6,578.50	21,233.00	42,497.00
IMMIG	272	27.71	17.45	6.00	64.00
SNOW	272	149.88	70.80	31.00	296.00
WAGE1	272	147.26	14.12	126.90	174.50
FEM	272	462.06	43.60	399.00	520.00
CRIME	272	6.31	2.73	2.50	11.50
EDUC	272	166.82	33.14	111.00	248.00
UIGEN	272	.43	.04	.36	.48
UIPROB	272	.90	.28	.50	1.60
OWN	272	485.64	68.37	321.00	608.00
NRR	272	121.18	253.96	1.00	813.00

[1] These data are not log transformed.

APPENDIX TABLE A.5.2 Correlation Coefficient Matrix, 1956-81 Pooled Data[1]

	GRANT$_i$	GRANT$_j$	M$_{ij}$	LANG$_{ij}$	DIST$_{ij}$	JOBS$_i$	JOBS$_j$
			number of observations = 1,088				
GRANT$_i$	1.000	.084	.008	−.082	.108	−.105	.015
GRANT$_j$	.084	1.000	−.164	−.082	.053	.016	−.106
M$_{ij}$	.008	−.164	1.000	.188	−.295	.027	.029
LANG$_{ij}$	−.082	−.082	.188	1.000	.103	.104	.105
DIST$_{ij}$	.108	.053	−.295	.103	1.000	.003	−.011
JOBS$_i$	−.106	.016	.027	.104	.003	1.000	−.004
JOBS$_j$	.016	−.106	.029	.104	−.011	−.004	1.000
UNEMP$_i$	.454	.277	.030	−.089	.083	−.112	.048
UNEMP$_j$	.277	.455	−.005	−.089	.057	.048	−.112
DS$_i$	−.020	.158	.065	.055	.077	.205	.048
DS$_j$	.159	−.021	.174	.055	.100	.053	.205
HOUSE$_i$	−.121	.272	.072	.194	.027	.004	.053
HOUSE$_j$	.272	−.121	.278	.194	.051	.010	.004
IMMIG$_i$	−.513	−.033	−.016	.164	−.011	.224	.010
IMMIG$_j$	−.033	−.513	.425	.164	.026	.060	.224
SNOW$_i$	.509	−.038	−.064	−.314	−.084	.086	−.008
SNOW$_j$	−.038	.509	−.180	−.314	−.163	−.008	.087
WAGE$_i$	.020	.325	.061	.038	−.068	.034	.073
WAGE$_j$	.325	.020	.153	.038	−.054	.073	.034
FEM$_i$	.060	.284	.112	.138	−.041	.226	.043
FEM$_j$	.284	.060	.275	.138	−.043	.043	.226
CRIME$_i$	−.129	.133	.027	.071	−.014	−.052	.020
CRIME$_j$	.133	−.129	.123	.071	.007	.020	−.052
EDUC$_i$	.238	.321	.105	.026	.057	.064	.021
UIGEN$_i$	.429	.247	.068	−.027	.086	.017	−.042
UIGEN$_j$	.247	.429	−.002	−.027	.083	−.042	.017
UIPROB$_i$	.384	−.111	−.055	.074	.038	−.042	.086
UIPROB$_j$	−.114	.384	−.165	.074	−.005	.086	−.042
OWN$_i$	.039	.073	.064	.371	.137	.008	−.010

	UNEMP$_i$	UNEMP$_j$	DS$_i$	DS$_j$	HOUSE$_i$	HOUSE$_j$	IMMIG$_i$	IMMIG$_j$
				number of observations = 1,088				
GRANT$_i$	.455	.277	−.020	.159	−.121	.272	−.513	−.033
GRANT$_j$	.277	.455	.158	−.020	.272	−.121	−.033	−.513
M$_{ij}$	.030	−.005	.065	.174	.072	.278	−.016	.425
LANG$_{ij}$	−.089	−.089	.055	.055	.194	.194	.165	.164
DIST$_{ij}$	.083	.057	.078	.100	.027	.051	−.011	.026
JOBS$_i$	−.112	.048	.205	.053	.004	.010	.224	.060
JOBS$_j$	.048	−.112	.054	.205	.010	.004	.060	.224
UNEMP$_i$	1.000	.597	.140	.303	.349	.506	−.331	−.092
UNEMP$_j$	.597	1.000	.303	.140	.506	.349	−.093	−.331
DS$_i$	.140	.303	1.000	.226	.433	.280	.397	−.003
DS$_j$	.303	.140	.226	1.000	.280	.434	−.002	.397
HOUSE$_i$	.349	.506	.433	.279	1.000	.426	.247	−.132
HOUSE$_j$	.505	.349	.280	.434	.426	1.000	−.133	.247
IMMIG$_i$	−.331	−.093	.397	−.002	.247	−.133	1.000	.074
IMMIG$_j$	−.092	−.331	−.002	.398	−.133	.247	.075	1.000
SNOW$_i$	.109	−.022	−.182	.005	−.363	.013	−.487	.031
SNOW$_j$	−.022	.109	.005	−.183	.013	−.364	.031	−.487
WAGE$_i$	.653	.654	.396	.381	.660	.540	.104	−.076
WAGE$_j$	.654	.654	.380	.396	.540	.660	−.075	.103
FEM$_i$	.342	.591	.526	.314	.656	.471	.350	−.096
FEM$_j$	.591	.343	.313	.526	.471	.656	−.096	.350
CRIME$_i$	.112	.240	.256	.154	.346	.216	.212	−.049
CRIME$_j$	.240	.112	.155	.259	.216	.346	−.049	.212
EDUC$_i$	.599	.657	.452	.340	.666	.563	.053	−.145
UIGEN$_i$	.458	.456	.336	.326	.490	.521	−.287	−.156
UIGEN$_j$	.456	.458	.327	.334	.522	.490	−.156	−.287
UIPROB$_i$	−.053	−.199	.042	.092	−.323	−.097	−.002	.182
UIPROB$_j$	−.199	−.053	.090	.043	−.097	−.323	.182	−.002
OWN$_i$	.141	.133	.184	.074	.289	.128	.153	−.057

[1] Correlations are based on actual data, not log transformed.

APPENDIX TABLE A.5.2 Correlation Coefficient Matrix, 1956-81 Pooled Data[1] – Concluded

	$SNOW_i$	$SNOW_j$	$WAGE_i$	$WAGE_j$	FEM_i	FEM_J	$CRIME_i$	$CRIME_j$
				number of observations = 1,088				
$GRANT_i$	.510	−.038	.020	.325	.060	.284	−.129	.133
$GRANT_j$	−.038	.509	.325	.020	.284	.060	.133	−.129
M_{ij}	−.065	−.180	.061	.153	.112	.275	.027	.123
$LANG_{ij}$	−.314	−.314	.039	.038	.139	.139	.071	.071
$DIST_{ij}$	−.084	−.163	−.069	−.054	−.041	−.043	−.014	.007
$JOBS_i$	.087	−.008	.035	.073	.226	.043	−.052	.020
$JOBS_j$	−.008	.087	.073	.034	.043	.226	.020	−.052
$UNEMP_i$	.109	−.022	.653	.652	.343	.591	.113	.240
$UNEMP_j$	−.022	.109	.654	.653	.591	.343	.240	.112
DS_i	−.182	.005	.396	.381	.526	.313	.256	.155
DS_j	.005	−.183	.381	.397	.314	.526	.154	.258
$HOUSE_i$	−.364	.013	.660	.540	.656	.471	.346	.216
$HOUSE_j$	.013	−.364	.540	.660	.471	.656	.216	.346
$IMMIG_i$	−.487	.031	.104	−.075	.350	−.096	.211	−.049
$IMMIG_j$	.031	−.487	−.076	.103	−.096	.350	−.049	.212
$SNOW_i$	1.000	−.062	−.285	.001	−.151	−.004	−.309	.015
$SNOW_j$	−.062	1.000	.002	−.285	−.004	−.151	−.015	−.309
$WAGE_i$	−.285	.002	1.000	.713	.573	.640	.438	.260
$WAGE_j$	.001	−.285	.714	1.000	.641	.573	.260	.438
FEM_i	−.151	−.005	.573	.641	1.000	.528	.339	.229
FEM_j	−.004	−.151	.640	.573	.528	1.000	.229	.339
$CRIME_i$	−.309	.015	.438	.260	.339	.229	1.000	.058
$CRIME_j$	.015	−.309	.260	.438	.229	.339	.058	1.000
$EDUC_i$	−.113	−.007	.649	.708	.790	.611	.266	.272
$UIGEN_i$	.215	−.017	.280	.540	.535	.461	.109	.267
$UIGEN_j$	−.017	.214	.541	.281	.461	.535	.267	.110
$UIPROB_i$	.120	−.002	−.159	−.094	−.217	−.097	−.161	−.005
$UIPROB_j$	−.003	.120	−.094	−.159	−.098	−.217	−.005	−.161
OWN_i	.399	.022	.265	.138	.167	.127	.236	.055

	$EDUC_i$	$UIGEN_i$	$UIGEN_j$	$UIPROB_i$	$UIPROB_j$	OWN_i
			number of observations = 1,088			
$GRANT_i$	.237	.429	.247	.384	−.111	.039
$GRANT_j$	.321	.247	.429	−.114	.384	.073
M_{ij}	.105	.068	−.002	−.055	−.164	.064
$LANG_{ij}$	.026	−.027	−.027	.074	.074	.371
$DIST_{ij}$	.057	.086	.083	.038	−.005	.137
$JOBS_i$	.064	.168	−.042	−.042	.086	.008
$JOBS_j$	.021	−.042	.017	.086	−.042	−.010
$UNEMP_i$	.599	.458	.455	−.053	−.199	.141
$UNEMP_j$	.657	.456	.458	−.198	−.053	.131
DS_i	.452	.336	.327	.042	.090	.184
DS_j	.340	.326	.334	.092	.043	.074
$HOUSE_i$	.666	.490	.522	−.323	−.096	.289
$HOUSE_j$	.563	.521	.490	−.097	−.322	.128
$IMMIG_i$	.053	−.287	−.156	−.002	.182	.152
$IMMIG_j$	−.145	−.156	−.287	.181	−.002	−.056
$SNOW_i$	−.113	.215	.017	.120	−.003	−.399
$SNOW_j$	−.007	−.017	.214	−.003	.120	.022
$WAGE_i$	.649	.280	.541	−.158	−.094	.265
$WAGE_j$	.708	.540	.281	−.094	−.159	.140
FEM_i	.789	.535	.461	−.217	−.097	.167
FEM_j	.611	.461	.538	−.098	−.217	.127
$CRIME_i$	.266	.109	.267	−.161	−.005	.236
$CRIME_j$	.272	.267	.109	−.005	−.161	.055
$EDUC_i$	1.000	.665	.591	−.256	−.168	.037
$UIGEN_i$	.665	1.000	.704	−.134	−.069	.056
$UIGEN_j$	.591	.704	1.000	−.070	−.134	.183
$UIPROB_i$	−.256	−.134	−.070	1.000	.280	.124
$UIPROB_j$	−.168	−.069	−.134	.280	1.000	−.043
OWN_i	−.037	.056	.183	.124	−.043	1.000

[1] Correlations are based on actual data, not log transformed.

Footnotes

1. The process of aggregation reduces the total amount of variation that remains in any variable, unless all observations in each class are actually at the class mean.

2. Theoretically, the relevant spatial unit is one which could be considered as a single spatial labour market. The preferred observed spatial unit is one which approximates Kerr's job market, an area defined occupationally, industrially, and geographically within which workers are willing to move comparatively freely from one job to another. See Kerr (1950).

3. See Navratil et al. (1976/77).

4. See Greenwood (1975, p.401).

5. Schlottmann et al. (1982) found that 39% of all interstate moves were either military personnel or students.

6. Courchene (1974) shows that multiple and return moves are most prevalent among young migrants. For an excellent analysis of return and repeat movers in the U.S., see Long et al. (1977).

7. Problems with estimating simultaneous equations, however, are that (i) detailed data requirements may not allow the estimation of even a small simultaneous equation system, (ii) systems of simultaneous equations frequently lack enough observations to allow degrees of freedom necessary, and (iii) more complex models must be constructed.

8. See Shaw (1975, p. 83).

References

Addison, J.T. and W.S. Siebert, 1979, **The Market for Labor: An Analytical Treatment**, (Santa Monica, CA: Goodyear Publishing Co. Inc.).

Alperovich, G., J. Bersaman and C. Ehemann, 1977, "An Econometric Model of Migration Between United States Metropolitan Areas", **Urban Studies**, Vol. 14, p. 135-45.

Anderson, I.B., 1966, **Internal Migration in Canada 1921-61**, (Ottawa: Economic Council of Canada).

Bartel, A., 1979, "The Migration Decision: What Role Does Job Mobility Play", **American Economic Review**, Vol. 69, p. 775-86.

Beach, C.M. and S.F. Kaliski, 1983, "The Impact of the 1979 Unemployment Insurance Amendments", **Canadian Public Policy**, Vol. 9, p. 164-73.

Bernard, R., 1971, **Profils Migratoires, Comtés et Régions, Province de Québec, 1961-66**, (Québec: Bureau de la Statistique du Québec).

Bernard, R., 1972, **Évolutions démographiques régionales et migrations intérieures de population, Province de Québec, 1941-66**, (Québec: Bureau de la Statistique du Québec).

Betcherman, G., 1980, **Skills and Shortages**, (Ottawa: Economic Council of Canada).

Boadway, R.W. and A.G. Green, 1981, "The Economic Implications of Migration to Newfoundland" (Ottawa: Economic Council of Canada, Discussion Paper No. 189, Mimeo).

Boadway, R.W. and F. Flatters, 1982, "Efficiency and Equalization Payments in a Federal System of Government: A Synthesis and Extension of Recent Results", **Canadian Journal of Economics**, Vol. 15, p. 612-33.

Borooah, V.K., 1979, "Starts and Completions of Private Dwellings: Four Models of Distributed Lag Behavior", **Journal of Economic Studies**, Vol. 6, p. 204-15.

Borukhov, E. and E. Werczberger, 1981, "Factors Affecting the Development of New Towns in Israel", **Environment and Planning**, Vol. 13, p. 421-35.

Bourne, L.S., 1982, "Regional Policy in Canada: An Urban System Perspective", **Canadian Journal of Regional Science**, Vol. 5, p. 283-90.

Brown, C., C. Gilroy and A. Kohen, 1982, "The Effect of the Minimum Wage on Employment and Unemployment", **Journal of Economic Literature**, Vol. 20, p. 487-528.

Brown, D.L. and J.M. Wardwell, 1980, **New Directions in Urban-Rural Migration**, (New York: Academic Press).

Browning, H.L. and W. Feindt, 1969, "Selectivity of Migrants to a Metropolis in a Developing Country: A Mexican Case Study", **Demography**, Vol. 6, p. 347-57.

Cain, G.C., 1976, "The Challenge of Segmented Labour Market Theories to Orthodox Theory: A Survey", **Journal of Economic Literature**, Vol. 14, p. 1215-57.

Caldwell, J.C., 1970, **African Rural-Urban Migration**, (New York: Columbia University Press).

Carynnyk-Sinclair, N., 1974, "Rural to Urban Migration in Developing Countries, 1950-70: A Survey of the Literature", (Geneva: International Labour Office, **World Employment Research Paper**, Mimeo).

Cebula, R.J., 1979, "A Survey of the Literature on the Migration Impact of State and Local Government Policies", **Public Finance**, Vol. 34, p. 69-83.

Cebula, R.J., 1980, "Geographic Mobility and the Cost of Living: An Exploratory Note", **Urban Studies**, Vol. 17, p. 353-55.

Chang, J.H., 1976, **Cyclical Instability in Residential Construction** (Ottawa: Economic Council of Canada).

Clark, G.L., 1983, **Interregional Migration, National Policy and Social Justice**, (Totowa, New Jersey: Rowman and Allan Ltd.).

Clark, G.L. and K.P. Ballard, 1980, "Modelling Out-Migration from Depressed Regions: The Significance of Origin and Destination Characteristics", **Environment and Planning**, Vol. 12, p. 799-813.

Clemhout, S. and S.N. Neftci, 1981, "Policy Evaluation of Housing Cyclicality: A Spectral Analysis", **Review of Economics and Statistics**, Vol. LXII, p. 385-94.

Clodman, J. and A.H. Richmond, 1982, **Immigration and Unemployment**, (Ottawa: Submitted to the Multiculturalism Directorate, Department of the Secretary of State).

Collins, A.F., 1980, "The AH STF: An Overview of the Issues", **Canadian Public Policy**, Vol. 6, p. 158-65.

Copithorne, L.W., 1979, "Natural Resources and Regional Disparities: A Skeptical View", **Canadian Public Policy**, Vol. 2, p. 181-94.

Cornwall, J., 1981, "Do We Need Separate Theories of Inflation and Unemployment", **Canadian Public Policy**, Vol. 7, p. 165-78.

Courchene, T.J., 1970, "Inter-provincial Migration and Economic Adjustment", **Canadian Journal of Economics**, Vol. 3, p. 551-76.

Courchene, T.J., 1974, **Migration, Income and Employment: Canada, 1965-68**, (Toronto: C.D. Howe Research Institute).

Courchene, T.J., 1978a, "Economics and Federalism", **Royal Society of Canada, Transactions**, (Fourth Series), 16, p. 71-87.

Courchene, T.J., 1978b, "The Transfer System and Regional Disparities: A Critique of the Status Quo", in M. Walker (ed.), **Canadian Federation at the Crossroads: The Search for a Federal-Provincial Balance**, (Vancouver: The Fraser Institute), p. 145-86.

Courchene, T.J., 1981, "A Market Perspective on Regional Disparities", **Canadian Public Policy**, Vol. 7, p. 506-18.

Courchene, T.J., 1983, "Canada's New Equalization Program: Description and Evaluation", **Canadian Public Policy**, Vol. 9, p. 458-75.

Cousineau, J.M., 1979, "La mobilité interprovinciale de la main-d'œuvre au Canada: le cas de l'Ontario, de la Nouvelle-Écosse et du Nouveau-Brunswick", **L'actualité économique**, Vol. 55, p. 1-15.

Curtis, D.C., 1969, "Some Economic Aspects of Canadian Rural Farm Migration, 1956-61", in L.O. Stone, **Migration in Canada**, (Ottawa: Queen's Printer), p. 203-45.

Dabestani, A., 1975, "A Model of Interprovincial Migration Between British Columbia and Other Canadian Provinces", (Vancouver: B.C. Telephone Co., Mimeo).

DaVanzo, J., 1981, "Micro-economic Approaches to Studying Migration Decisions", in G.F. De Jong and R.W. Gardner, **Migration Decision Making**, (New York: Pergamon Press).

De Jong, G.F. and R.W. Gardner, 1981, **Migration Decision Making**, (New York: Pergamon Press).

Drummond, W.M. and W. MacKenzie, 1957, **Progress and Prospects of Canadian Agriculture**, (Ottawa: Queen's Printer).

Economic Council of Canada, 1982, **Financing Confederation**, (Ottawa: Ministry of Supply and Services Canada).

Elizaga, J.C., 1966, "A Study of Migration to Greater Santiago, Chile", **Demography**, Vol. 3, p. 352-78.

Evans, M., 1969, **Macro-economic Activity: Theory, Forecasting and Control**, (New York: Harper and Row).

Falaris, E.M., 1982, "Migration and Regional Wages", **Southern Economic Journal**, Vol. 48, p. 670-85.

Farber, S.C., 1983, "Post-Migration Earnings Profiles: An Application of Human Capital and Job Search Models", **Southern Economic Journal**, Vol. 49, p. 693-705.

Fielding, A.J., 1966, "Internal Migration and Regional Economic Growth: A Case Study of France", **Urban Studies**, Vol. 3, p. 200-14.

Fields, G.S., 1976, "Labor Force Migration, Unemployment and Job Turnover", **Review of Economics and Statistics**, Vol. 58, p. 407-15.

Fields, G.S., 1979, "Place-to-Place Migration: Some New Evidence", **Review of Economics and Statistics**, Vol. 60, p. 21-32.

Fields, G.S., 1982, "Place-to-Place Migration in Columbia", **Economic Development and Cultural Change**, Vol. 30, p. 539-58.

Fortin, P. and K. Newton, 1982, "Labor Market Tightness and Wage Inflation in Canada", in M.N. Baily (ed.), **Workers, Jobs and Inflation**, (Washington D.C.: Brookings Institution), p. 243-78.

Gauthier, D., 1980, "Some Economic Aspects of Internal Migration: Newfoundland's Case", (Ottawa: Economic Council of Canada, Discussion Paper, No. 178).

George, M.V., 1970, **Internal Migration in Canada: Demographic Analysis**, (Ottawa: Queen's Printer).

George, M.V., 1971, "Estimation of Interprovincial Migration for Canada from Place of Birth by Residence Data, 1951-61", **Demography**, Vol. 8, p. 123-39.

Gertler, L. and R. Crowley, 1977, **Changing Canadian Cities: The Next 25 Years**, (Toronto: McClelland and Stewart Ltd.).

Glantz, F.B., 1973, **The Determinants of Interregional Migration of the Economically Disadvantaged**, (Boston: Federal Reserve Bank of Boston, Research Report).

Gordon, I., 1982, "The Analysis of Motivation – Specific Migration Streams", **Environment and Planning A**, Vol. 14, p. 5-20.

Gordon, I. and R. Vickerman, 1982, "Opportunity, Preference and Constraint: An Approach to the Analysis of Metropolitan Migration", **Urban Studies**, Vol. 19, p. 247-61.

Grant, E.K. and J. Vanderkamp, 1976, **Economic Causes and Effects of Migration: Canada, 1965-71**, (Ottawa: Economic Council of Canada).

Grant, E.K. and J. Vanderkamp, 1980, "The Effects of Migration on Income: A Micro Study with Canadian Data 1965-71", **Canadian Journal of Economics**, Vol. 13, p. 381-406.

Grant, E.K. and J. Vanderkamp, 1982, "Repeat Migration and Disappointment", (Guelph: University of Guelph, Department of Economics Discussion Paper, No. 1982-4).

Graves, P.E., 1980, "Migration and Climate", **Journal of Regional Science**, Vol. 20, p. 227-38.

Green, C. and J.M. Cousineau, 1976, **Unemployment in Canada: The Impact of Unemployment Insurance**, (Ottawa: Economic Council of Canada).

Greenwood, M.J., 1968, "An Analysis of the Determinants of Geographical Labor Mobility in the United States", **Review of Economics and Statistics**, Vol. 51, p. 189-204.

Greenwood, M.J., 1971, "An Analysis of the Determinants of Internal Labour Mobility in India", **Annals of Regional Science**, Vol. 1, p. 137-51.

Greenwood, M.J., 1975, "Research on Internal Migration in the United States: A Survey", **Journal of Economic Literature**, Vol. 8, p. 397-433.

Greenwood, M.J., 1981, **Migration and Economic Growth in the United States**, (New York: Academic Press Inc.).

Greenwood, M.J. and D.S. Sweetland, 1972, "The Determinants of Migration Between Standard Metropolitan Statistical Areas", **Demography**, Vol. 9, p. 665-82.

Gustavus, S.O. and L.A. Brown, 1977, "Place Attributes in a Migration Decision Context", **Environment and Planning**, Vol. 9, p. 529-48.

Heeren, H.J., 1955, **The Urbanization of Djakarta**, (Djakarta: Djakarta School of Economics, University of Indonesia).

Hicks, J., 1932, **The Theory of Wages**, (London: MacMillan).

Hill, F.I., 1976, **Canadian Urban Trends: Metropolitan Perspective**, Vol. 2, (Toronto: Copp Publishing in association with the Ministry of State for Urban Affairs).

Jaffee, D.M., and K.T. Rosen, 1979, "Mortgage Credit Availability and Residential Construction", Brookings Papers on Economic Activity, p. 333-76.

Jenness, R.A., 1975, **Manpower in Construction**, (Ottawa: Economic Council of Canada).

Kantor, B., 1979, "Rational Expectations and Economic Thought, **Journal of Economic Literature**, Vol. 18, p. 1422-41.

Katz, D.A., 1982, **Econometric Theory and Applications**, (New Jersey: Prentice – Hall Inc.).

Kau, J.B. and C.F. Sirmans, 1977/78, "The Influence of Information Costs and Uncertainty on Migration: A Comparison of Migrant Types", **Journal of Regional Science**, Vol. 17, p. 89-96.

Kerr, C., 1950, "Labor Markets: Their Character and Consequences", **American Economic Review**, Vol. 40, p. 278-95.

Kerr, C., 1954, "The Balkanization of Labour Markets", in E. Bakke et al., **Labour Mobility and Economic Opportunity**, (Cambridge Technology Press of MIT).

Laber, G. and R.X. Chase, 1971, "Interprovincial Migration in Canada as a Human Capital Decision", **Journal of Political Economy**, Vol. 79, p. 795-804.

Lansing, J.B. and E. Mueller, 1967, **The Geographical Mobility of Labor**, (Ann Arbor: Survey Research Center, University of Michigan).

Leffler, K. and C.M. Lindsay, 1979, "How do Human Capital Investors Form Earnings Expectations", **Southern Economic Journal**, Vol. 46, p. 591-602.

Levy, M. and W. Wadycki, 1972, "A Comparison of Young and Middle-Aged Migration in Venezuela", **Annals of Regional Science**, Vol. 2, p. 73-85.

Lithwick, N.H., 1970, **Urban Canada: Problems and Prospects**, (Ottawa: Canada Mortgage and Housing).

Liu, B., 1975, "Differential Net Migration Rates and the Quality of Life", **Review of Economics and Statistics**, Vol. 57, p. 329-37.

Liu, B., 1980, "Differential Net Migration Rates and the Quality of Life: A Reply with Additional Evidence", **Review of Economics and Statistics**, Vol. 62, p. 160-62.

Long, L.H. and C.G. Boertlein, 1979, **The Geographical Mobility of Americans: An International Comparison**, (Washington D.C.: Bureau of the Census, Current Population Reports, No. 64).

Long, L.H. and D. Deare, 1980, **Migration to Nonmetropolitan Areas: Appraising the Trend and Reasons for Moving**, (Washington D.C.: Bureau of the Census, CDS-80-2).

Long, L.H. and K.A. Hansen, 1977, "Models of Return, Repeat, and Primary Migration by Age and Race", (Paper Presented at the Annual Meeting of the Population Association of America, Mimeo).

Long, L.H. and K.A. Hansen, 1979, **Reasons for Interstate Migration: Jobs, Retirement, Climate and Other Influences**, (Washington D.C.: U.S., Government Printing Office, Current Population Reports, No. 81).

Lucas, R.E., 1981, **Studies in Business – Cycle Theory**, (Cambridge Mass: MIT Press).

Lurie, M. and E. Rayack, 1966, "Racial Differences in Migration and Job Search: A Case Study", **Southern Economic Journal**, Vol. 32, p. 81-95.

Lycan, R., 1969, Interprovincial Migration in Canada: The Role of Spatial and Economic Factors, **Canadian Geographer**, Vol. 13, p. 237-54.

MacDonald, L.D. and J. MacDonald, 1968, "Motives and Objectives of Migrants: Selective Migration Practices and Preferences Towards Rural to Urban Life", **Social and Economic Studies**, Vol. 17.

Mandal, R.B., 1981, **Frontiers in Migration Analysis**, (New Delhi: Concept Publishing Co.).

Manpower and Immigration, 1974, **Three Years in Canada**, (Ottawa: Information Canada).

Maki, D.R., 1979, "The Effect of Changes in Minimum Wage Rates on Provincial Unemployment Rates, 1970-77", **Industrial Relations**, Vol. 34, p. 418-29.

Mar, J.M., 1961, "Migration and Urbanization", P.M. Hauser (ed.), **Urbanization in Latin America**, (Paris: UNESCO).

Marr, W.D., D. McCready and F. Millerd, 1978, "Canadian Resource Reallocation: Interprovincial Labour Migration: 1966-71", **Canadian Studies in Population**, Vol. 4, p. 17-32.

Marr, W.L. and F.W. Millerd, 1980, "Employment Income Levels of Inter-provincial Migrants versus Non-Migrants, Canada, 1971", in J.L. Simon and J. DaVanzo, (eds.), **Research in Population Economics**, Vol. 2 (Greenwich, Conn: JAI Press).

Martin, J.K. and D.T. Lichter, 1983, "Geographic Mobility and Satisfaction with Life and Work", **Social Science Quarterly**, Vol. 64, p. 524-35.

McFadden, D., 1973, "Conditional Logit Analysis of Qualitative Choice Behavior", in P. Zarembka, **Frontiers in Econometrics**, (New York: Academic Press).

McInnis, R.M., 1969, "Provincial Migration and Differential Economic Opportunity", in L.O. Stone, **Migration in Canada**, (Ottawa: Queen's Printer), p. 131-202.

McInnis, M., 1971, "Age, Education and Occupational Differentials in Interregional Migration: Some Evidence for Canada", **Demography**, Vol. 8, p. 195-204.

Miller, E., 1973, "Is Out-Migration Affected by Economic Conditions?", **Southern Economic Journal**, Vol. 39, p. 396-405.

Mills, K.E., M.B. Percy and L.S. Wilson, 1983, "The Influence of Fiscal Incentives on Interregional Migration: Canada 1961-78", **Canadian Journal of Regional Science**, Vol. 6, p. 207-30.

Mincer, J., 1978, "Family Migration Decisions", **Journal of Political Economy**, Vol. 86, p. 749-73.

Monu, E.D., 1982, "Migration Patterns of Manitoba Rural Youth: A Follow-up Study", **Canadian Review of Sociology and Anthropology**, Vol. 19, p. 237-44.

Morgan, C., 1975/76, "Is Out-Migration Affected by Economic Conditions? Comment", **Southern Economic Journal**, Vol. 42, p. 752-58.

Myrdal, G., 1975, **Economic Theory and Underdeveloped Regions**, (London: Methuen).

Navratil, F.J. and J.J. Doyle, 1976/77, "The Socio-Economic Determinants of Migration and the Level of Aggregation", **Southern Economic Journal**, Vol. 43, p. 1547-59.

Nechemias, C., 1981, "The Impact of Soviet Housing Policy on Housing Conditions in Soviet Cities: The Uneven Push from Moscow", **Urban Studies**, Vol. 18, p. 1-9.

Nelson, R.R. and S.G. Winter, 1983, **An Evolutionary Theory of Economic Change**, (Boston: Harvard University Press).

Nickels, J.B., 1976, "Studies of Expected and Effected Mobility in Selected Resource Frontier Communities", (Winnipeg: Centre for Settlement Studies, University of Manitoba, Mimeo).

Nickson, M., 1967, **Geographic Mobility of Labour in Canada, October 1964 – October 1965**, (Ottawa: Queen's Printer, Special Labour Force Studies No. 4).

Norrie, K.H., M.B. Percy and L.S. Wilson, 1982, "Financing Confederation: Principles and Practices of Equalization", **Canadian Public Policy**, Vol. 8, p. 290-93.

OECD, 1982, **The Challenge of Unemployment**, (Paris: Organization for Economic Co-operation and Development).

Perreault, J. and R. Raby, 1980, "Recent Developments in Interprovincial Migration in Canada and Possible Scenarios for the 1980's", **Demographic Trends and Their Impact on the Canadian Labour Market**, (Ottawa: Immigration Canada).

Piore, M.J., 1979, "Conceptualization of Labour Market Reality", in G. Swanson and J. Michaelson (eds.), **Manpower Research and Labor Economics**, (Beverly Hills, CA: Sage Publications).

Piore, M.J., 1979, **Birds of Passage: Migrant Labour in Industrial Society**, (Cambridge University Press).

Piore, M.J., 1983, "Labor Market Segmentation: To what Paradigm Does it Belong?", **American Economic Review** (Papers and Proceedings), Vol. 73, p. 249-59.

Plant, R., 1981, **Industries in Trouble**, (Geneva: International Labour Office).

Polèse, M., 1978, "The Impact of International Migration on the Regional Labour Market: A Quebec Case Study", **Papers of the Regional Science Association**, Vol. 41.

Polèse, M., 1981, "Regional Disparity, Migration and Economic Adjustment: A Reappraisal", **Canadian Public Policy**, Vol. 7, p. 519-25.

Porell, F.W., 1982, "Intermetropolitan Migration and Quality of Life", **Journal of Regional Science**, Vol. 22, p. 137-58.

Pryor, R.J. (ed.), 1979, **Migration and Development in Southeast Asia**, (Kuala Lumpur: Oxford University Press).

Puderer, H.A., 1982, "Comparison of the 1980 Current Population Profile (Labour Force Survey) Estimates of In-Migration to the Provinces of Alberta and British Columbia with Preliminary 1981 Census Data for the Population 15 Years of Age and Older", (Ottawa: Statistics Canada, Mimeo).

Rabianski, J.S., 1971, "Real Earnings and Human Migration", **Journal of Human Resources**, Vol. 13, p. 249-60.

Ralston, H., 1981, "Education and Migration Among Nova Scotia Youth: Some Sex Differences", **Canadian Studies in Population**, Vol. 8, p. 57-80.

Rea Jr., S., 1977, "Unemployment Insurance and Labour Supply: A Simulation of the 1971 Unemployment Insurance Act", **Canadian Journal of Economics**, Vol. 10, p. 263-78.

Renas, S.M. and R. Kuman, 1978, "Cost of Living, Labour Market Opportunities, and the Migration Decision: A Case of Misspecification?", **Annals of Regional Science**, Vol. 12, p. 95-104.

Renas, S.M. and R. Kuman, 1983, "Climatic Conditions and Migration: An Econometric Inquiry", **Annals of Regional Science**, Vol. 17, p. 69-78.

Ritchey, P.N., 1976, "Explanations of Migration", **Annual Review of Sociology**, Vol. 2, p. 363-404.

Robinson, C. and N. Tomes, 1982, "Self-Selection and Interprovincial Migration in Canada", **Canadian Journal of Economics**, Vol. 15, p. 474-501.

Rogerson, P. and R.D. MacKinnon, 1981, "A Geographical Model of Job Search, Migration and Unemployment", **Papers of the Regional Science Association**, Vol. 48, p. 89-102.

Roseman, C.C., 1983, "Labor Force Migration, Non-Labor Force Migration, and Non-Employment Reasons for Migration", **Socio-Economic Planning Sciences**, Vol. 17, p. 303-12.

Roseman, C.C. and J.D. Williams, 1980, "Metropolitan to Non-Metropolitan Migration: A Decision-Making Perspective", **Urban Geography**, Vol. 1, p. 283-94.

Rossi, P.H., 1980, **Why Families Move**, (Beverly Hills, CA.: Sage Publications, Second Edition).

Schlottmann, A.M. and H.W. Herzog Jr., 1981, "Employment Status and the Decision to Migrate", **Review of Economics and Statistics**, Vol. 63, p. 590-98.

Schlottmann, A.M. and H.W. Herzog Jr., 1982, "Home Economic Conditions and the Decision to Migrate: New Evidence for the U.S. Labor Force", **Southern Economic Journal**, Vol. 48, p. 950-61.

Schultz, T.P., 1977, "A Conditional Logit Model of Internal Migration: Venezuelan Lifetime Migration Within Educational Strata", (New Haven: Yale University, Economic Growth Center, Discussion Paper No. 266, Mimeo).

Schultz, T.P., 1982, "Lifetime Migration within Educational Strata in Venezuela: Estimates of a Logistic Model", **Economic Development and Cultural Change**, Vol. 30, p. 559-593.

Schwartz, A., 1976, "Migration, Age and Education", **Journal of Political Economy**, Vol. 60, p. 534-38.

Scott, A., 1952, "Federal Grants and Resource Allocation", **Journal of Political Economy**, Vol. 60, p. 534-38.

Scott, A., 1964, "The Economic Goals of Federal Finance", **Public Finance**, Vol. 19, p. 241-88.

Scott, A., 1982, "Financing Confederation: Introduction", **Canadian Public Policy**, Vol. 7, p. 282-86.

Shaw, R.P., 1974a, "Modelling Metropolitan Population Growth and Change: The IIPS Simulator", **International Journal of Socio-Economic Planning Sciences**, Vol. 8, p. 169-80.

Shaw, R.P., 1974b, "A Note on the Costs-Returns Framework and Decisions to Migrate", **Population Studies**, Vol. 28, p. 167-69.

Shaw, R.P., 1975, **Migration Theory and Fact**, (Philadelphia: Regional Science Research Institute).

Shaw, R.P., 1978, "On Modifying Metropolitan Migration", **Economic Development and Cultural Change**, Vol. 26, p. 677-92.

Shaw, R.P., 1979, **Canada's Farm Population: An Analysis of Incomes and Related Characteristics**, (Ottawa: Queen's Printer).

Shaw, R.P., 1980, "Bending the Urban Flow: A Construction – Migration Strategy", **International Labour Review**, Vol. 119, p. 467-80.

Shaw, R.P., 1983, **Mobilizing Human Resources in the Arab World**, (London/Boston: Routledge and Kegan Paul Ltd.).

Shaw, R.P., 1985, "The Burden of Unemployment in Canada", **Canadian Public Policy**, Vol. 10, (Forthcoming, March).

Simmons, J.W., 1977, **The Canadian Urban System**, (Toronto: University of Toronto Press).

Simmons, J.W., 1980, "Changing Migration Patterns in Canada: 1966-71 to 1971-76", **Canadian Journal of Regional Science**, Vol. 3, p. 139-62.

Sjaastad, L.A., 1962, "The Costs and Returns of Human Migration", **Journal of Political Economy**, Vol. 70, p. S80-S93.

Smith, L.B., 1983, "The Crisis in Rental Housing: A Canadian Perspective", **Annals of the American Academy of Political and Social Science**, Vol. 465, p. 58-74.

Speare Jr., A., F. Kobrin and W. Kingkade, 1982, "The Influence of Socio-Economic Bonds and Satisfaction on Interstate Migration", **Social Forces**, Vol. 61, p. 551-74.

Statistics Canada, 1977, **International and Interprovincial Migration in Canada, 1961-76**, (Ottawa: Statistics Canada, Catalogue 91-208).

Statistics Canada, 1982, "Characteristics of Migrants to Alberta and British Columbia: 1976-80", (Ottawa: Ministry of Supply and Services, Labour Force Survey Research Paper No. 28, 8-3100-503).

Stillwell, J.C., 1978, "Interzonal Migration: Some Historical Tests of Spatial Interaction Models", **Environment and Planning**, Vol. 10, p. 1187-1200.

Stone, L.O., 1967, **Urban Canada**, (Ottawa: Queen's Printer).

Stone, L.O., 1969, **Migration in Canada: Some Regional Aspects**, (Ottawa: Queen's Printer).

Stone, L.O., 1971a, **On the Analysis of the Structure of Metropolitan Areas Migration Streams: A Theoretical Framework with Empirical Glimpses from Canadian and American Census Data**, (Toronto: Ontario Institute for Studies in Education).

Stone, L.O., 1971b, "On the Correlation Between In and Out Migration by Occupation", **Journal of the American Statistical Association**, Vol. 66, p. 693-701.

Stone, L.O., 1974, "What We Know About Migration Within Canada: A Selective Review and Agenda for Future Research", **International Migration Review**, Vol. 8, p. 267-81.

Stone, L.O., 1978, **The Frequency of Geographic Mobility in the Population of Canada**, (Ottawa: Statistics Canada).

Stone, L.O., 1979, **Occupational Composition of Canadian Migration**, (Ottawa: Statistics Canada).

Stone, L.O. and S. Fletcher, 1976, **Migration in Canada: 1971 Census Profile Study**, (Ottawa: Statistics Canada).

Termote, M.G., 1980, "Migration and Settlement: Canada", (Vienna: International Institute for Applied Systems Analysis, Mimeo).

Termote, M.G. and R. Frechette, 1979, "Les Variations du Courant Migratoire Inter-provincial", (Montréal: Report prepared for the Ministry of State for Urban Affairs, Institut National de la Recherche Scientifique).

Todaro, M.P., 1969, "A Model of Labor Migration and Urban Unemployment in Less Developed Countries", **American Economic Review**, Vol. 59, p. 138-48.

Todaro, M.P., 1976, **Internal Migration in Developing Countries: A Review of Theory, Evidence, Methodology and Research Priorities**, (Geneva: International Labour Office).

Todaro, M.P., 1980, "Internal Migration in Developing Countries: A Survey", in R.A. Easterlin (ed.), **Population and Economic Change in Developing Countries**, (Chicago: University of Chicago Press), p. 361-402.

Todd, D., 1981, "Rural Out-Migration in Southern Manitoba: A Simple Path Analysis of 'Push' Factors", **The Canadian Geographer**, Vol. 25, p. 252-66.

United Nations, 1974, **Population Policies and Programmes**, (New York: United Nations, E/CONF. 60/BP/10).

United Nations, 1981, **Population Distribution Policies in Development Planning**, (New York: United Nations).

United States, 1981, **Geographical Mobility: March 1975 to March 1980**, (Washington: U.S. Department of the Census, Current Population Reports, Series P-20, No. 368).

Usher, D., 1980, "How Should the Redistributive Power of the State be Divided Between Federal and Provincial Governments", **Canadian Public Policy**, Vol. 6, p. 3-15.

Vanderkamp, J., 1968, "Inter-Regional Mobility in Canada: A Study of the Time Pattern of Migration", **Canadian Journal of Economics**, Vol. 1, p. 595-608.

Vanderkamp, J., 1970, "The Effects of Out-Migration on Regional Employment", **The Canadian Journal of Economics**, Vol. 3, p. 541-49.

Vanderkamp, J., 1971, "Migration Flows, Their Determinants and the Effects of Return Migration", **Journal of Political Economy**, Vol. 79, p. 1012-32.

Vanderkamp, J., 1972, "Return Migration: Its Significance and Behavior", **Western Economic Journal**, Vol. 10, p. 460-65.

Vanderkamp, J., 1973, **Mobility Behavior in the Canadian Labour Force**, (Ottawa: Economic Council of Canada).

Vanderkamp, J., 1976, "The Role of Population Size in Migration Studies", **Canadian Journal of Economics**, Vol. 9, p. 508-17.

Vanderkamp, J., 1977, "The Gravity Model and Migration Behavior: An Economic Interpretation", **Journal of Economic Studies**, Vol. 4, p. 89-102.

Vanderkamp, J., 1982, "Financing Confederation: Transfers and Migration", **Canadian Public Policy**, Vol. 8, p. 293-97.

Vanderkamp, J., 1984, "The Efficiency of the Interregional Adjustment Process", (Guelph: Background Paper prepared for the Royal Commission on the Economic Union and Development Prospects for Canada, Mimeo).

Vining Jr., D.R., 1982, "Migration between the Core and the Periphery", **Scientific American**, Vol. 247, p. 45-53.

Weinstein, P.A., 1981, "The United States Construction Industry: The Economic, Demographic and Industrial Relations Environment", **Labour and Society**, Vol. 6, p. 243-61.

Weller, B., 1982, "Urban Impact Assessment in Public Policy Processes: The Canadian Record, 1968-82, **Canadian Journal of Regional Science**, Vol. 5, p. 39-66.

West, E.G. and M. Mckee, 1980, **Minimum Wages: The New Issues in Theory, Evidence, Policy and Politics**, (Ottawa: Economic Council of Canada and the Institute for Research on Public Policy, Canadian Government Printing Centre).

Wachter, M.L., 1974, "Primary and Secondary Labor Markets: A Critique of the Dual Approach", **Brookings Papers on Economic Activity**, Vol. 3, p. 637-93.

Wilkinson, R.K. and C. Archer, 1976, "Uncertainty Prices and the Supply of Housing", **Policy and Politics**, Vol. 5, p. 63-74.

Wilson, F.D., 1983, "Cohort Size Effects and Migration", **International Migration Review**, Vol. 17, p. 485-504.

Winer, S.L. and D. Gauthier, 1983, **Internal Migration and Fiscal Structure**, (Ottawa: Economic Council of Canada).

Wrage, P., 1981, "The Effects of Internal Migration on Regional Wage and Unemployment Disparities in Canada", **Journal of Regional Science**, Vol. 21, p. 51-63.

Yap, L.S., 1977, "The Attraction of Cities: A Review of the Migration Literature", **Journal of Development Economics**, Vol. 4, p. 239-64.

Yezer, A. and L. Thurston, 1976, "Migration Patterns and Income Change: Implications for the Human Capital Approach to Migration", **Southern Economic Journal**, Vol. 42, p. 693-702.

Young, G., 1975, "The Choice of Dependent Variable for Cross-Section Studies of Migration", **Canadian Journal of Economics**, Vol. 8, p. 93-100.

Index